IMAGE

The Revelation Of God Himself

By Paul Tubach, Jr.

IMAGE

"IMAGE" by Paul B. Tubach, Jr. is licensed under a Creative Commons Attribution-NonCommercial-NoDerivatives 4.0 International License

You are free to copy, share and redistribute the material in any medium, format or language as long as the text and content is not altered or misconstrued. Freely it was received… freely it is given. The licensor cannot revoke these freedoms as long as you follow these license terms:

- **Attribution** — You must give appropriate credit, provide a link to the website, and indicate if any changes were made. You may do so in any reasonable manner, but not in any way that suggests the author endorses you or your use. "Attribute this work" as: Paul Tubach, Jr., www.newearthministries.org.
- **NonCommercial** — You may not use the material for commercial purposes, i.e. not for any private, corporate, nonprofit or otherwise financial gain.
- **NoDerivatives** — If you remix, transform or build upon the material, you may not distribute the modified material. The creation or development of any derivatives, secondary workbooks or manuals from this book is reserved solely by the author.
- **No additional restrictions** — You may not apply legal terms or technological measures that legally restrict others from doing anything the license permits.

Paperback ISBN 978-1-949892-10-9
Library of Congress Control Number - pending
Produced in the United States of America
New Earth Ministries

Scriptures taken from the New King James Version. Copyright © 1982 by Thomas Nelson. Used by permission. All rights reserved.

Books and other materials are available online through www.newearthministries.org.

March 2018

Table of Contents

Introduction	xiii
The Mystery of God Revealed	1
Jesus Our Creator	5
God Our Father	10
Theophanies	13
The Lord God	23
The Lord Your God	28
Jesus – Lord of Israel	37
Jesus Knew His Identity	41
If – You Are the Son of God	47
He, Him, His – as Himself	49
Only Three Things	50
Have You Ever Wondered	52
The Spirit of Man Revealed	55
Almighty God	59
Jesus is Lord Jehovah	63
I Am Who I Am	69
Trinity Prelude	79
The Father of the Son	82
In The Beginning	84
Origin and Source	87
Thoughts Beget Words	97
The Trinity	99
Father and Son Oneness	103
Father IN the Son	104
Father WITH the Son	107
Father SEEN as the Son	112
The Express Image	114
If Jesus Did It – So Can We	122

Once Upon A Cross	125
Three More Scriptures	128
The Blood Price	131
I Am With You	140
The Message	143
Love is the Message	146
Lord of Heaven and Earth	148
The Lord Is With You	158
Christ In Us	161
Elohim in Us	163
God is Spirit	166
The Forgetful Prince	170
Grasshoppers and Ants	172
Expression and Manifestation	173
The Spirit of Jesus Christ	177
Spirit with the One	182
The Un-Jung Archetype	191
The Pattern Made Known	196
In The Spirit, Jesus Lived	198
Manifested Spirit-Filled Life	211
Atmosphere of Heaven	215
Making The Father Known	219
Jesus, The Way	219
No Ordinary Man	224
Christ Is The Mystery	230
Who Has Known Him	232
More Than Just A Man	232
I'll Show You How To Live	233
Now You Do It	233
What Would You Do?	237
The House of God	241
Men Are Houses	241
A Little Lower Than Angels	243
Brethren and Friends of Jesus	248
Who Is Jesus (In Summary)	253
The Final Word	261

The Image Bearer Series

2. Listen – How To Hear God's Voice – better
3. Image – The Revelation Of God Himself
4. Dominion – Our Heavenly Mandate To Occupy Earth
5. Understand – What Jesus Wants You To Know – and Why
6. Commission – Created On Purpose For A Purpose
7. Gateways – Manifesting Heaven In The Midst Of Chaos
8. Here – The Kingdom Of Heaven Is

The Image Bearer Series is based upon Genesis 1:26-28: "Let us make man in Our image, according to Our likeness… and grant them dominion."

"Image" explains 'who' the Lord of Heaven and Earth is, "Understand" explains 'why' we are here, "Commission" explains 'what' man is and 'how' we were created by the Lord, "Dominion" explains 'what' we are supposed to be doing, "Gateways" explains 'how' we are to accomplish our earthly mission, and "Here" explains our eternal destination is actually – Earth.

Many tools were given to mankind that enables us to accomplish our mission objective to have dominion over the kingdom of darkness – and we need to comprehend this truth: earth is our 'Here' – and our 'when' is now! How God created us – and why – is directly related to our sanctification and accomplishing our multifaceted mission for being on earth.

Why are you here – and what's your purpose in life? These books will answer those questions.

When I began writing in August 2012, four drafts were completed within a year, then on Sept. 27, 2013, the Lord spoke to me and said: "You are My writer. Now write!" and then the Spirit directed me to finish draft #4 which became the initial book, "*Regenesis*: *A Sojourn To Remember Who We Are*," released in August 2014. Next, the Spirit directed me to work on draft #3 (in reverse order) and then, on October 24, the Spirit told me, "That is not one book with seven chapters – those are seven books." Thus, I have been writing the Image Bearer series under His anointing by hearing His voice and writing what I am directed to write.

Regenesis helped us discover man's true identity, as spiritual beings that are having a human experience, who were created good and upright by God "in His Own image according to His likeness" (Gen. 1:26-27), whereby we have been blessed with many wonderful grace attributes by the Lord to accomplish all that He purposed for man… since the beginning.

Yet for most of us, we've forgotten who we are… and we've forgotten what we are supposed to be doing. Regenesis reminds us who we are, and now, the Image Bearer series is reminding us what we are supposed to do, how we should do it – and more importantly "why" we are doing it.

The Image Bearer series builds upon that knowledge of truth that mankind was created good so as to become what we were created for: to bear His image and imitate Jesus in every respect according to His earthly example – and operate as His heavenly ambassadors for earth.

The heavenly pattern for mankind is: imitate Jesus.
The earthly pattern for this world is: become like heaven.

Who you are is not based upon what you do; "what you do" is based upon "who you are." We get our identity from Jesus. This realigned perspective regarding "who" we are … is to reorient the applecart of faith pointing in the right direction, to focus on Jesus, and to accomplish our primary mission: have dominion on earth – in the name of Jesus.

The numeric order in which the Spirit directed these books: 1,2,8,3,5,4,6,7 was not linear in the least. Let the Spirit guide you in the order He wants you to read them; however, learning how to "Hear God's Voice" is always mission critical to get started on His path for anyone.

On October 24, 2015, the Lord told me to put these books on the internet for free. This was unexpected, and then the Lord whispered to me, "Can you make money on My words? Freely you have received... freely give."

When the Lord tells you what to do, He will also give you His authority, with power and provision, to do all that He commands. We need to embrace this perspective regarding our life on earth in order to understand and comprehend who we are and what we are supposed to be doing. There is much joy and peace living in this manner, and yet... we all make this choice daily to live according to His purpose for His glory – or to live according to our best laid plans. If I can do it – so can you.

Jesus did it, and therefore – "As He is, so are we in this world" (1 John 4:17). I hope you enjoy the Image Bearer series. Grace and peace be yours in abundance.

It's all about Jesus – and God gets the glory!

Glossary of Terms and Definitions

These are some keys to help navigate and understand the scriptures.

Heaven – God's throne, God's home and the permanent place where God's glory dwells
heaven – the spiritual reality of God's kingdom and Christ's presence upon earth
Glory – the fullness of God's presence; the fullness of all God is
Shekinah Glory – the manifest presence of God's Spirit
Christ – the manifest expression of God in Jesus, and regenerate (born anew) men
Jesus – the manifested Living God; Lord of heaven and earth; Lord of Glory; Lord of Hosts
Host – army (a very important term omitted in the NIV and some other versions)
Host of heaven – angels; sons of God and our heavenly brethren (Rev. 19:10)
Host of earth – sons of men, becoming sons of God in the regeneration
Man – the generic term for male and female to connote mankind, humanity, etc.
Earth – the planet; one of three permanent places within the kingdom of God
Hell – the absence of God; one of three permanent places within the kingdom of God; the pit
World – temporary realm on earth under the dominion and operational control of Satan
Satan – Prince of "this world" (formerly known as Lucifer before he rebelled and fell to earth)
Sin – the operating system of this world in opposition to God's sovereignty; separation from God; things done that cause separation
Spirit – the operating system on earth under the Lord's dominion; the Holy Spirit; God's Spirit
Grace – attributes of God's character that are freely given to man

Light – a metaphor implying God's truth
Darkness – a metaphor implying evil – and sinful lies of "this world"
Wickedness – taking credit for what God has done
Evil – using God's glory and power to accomplish your personal agenda
Paradigm – the operating systems of sin or "by the Spirit" on earth
Paradise – the earthly realm in oneness with God apart from sin
Dwelling – a temporary place to live
Abode – a permanent place to live (of existence)
Rest – the permanent state of being where God's presence abides (in your heart and in heaven)
Kingdom of God – all places under the authority of Jesus
Kingdom of heaven – a term used exclusively in the gospel of
    Matthew to describe the kingdom of God as it pertains to earth under the Lordship of Jesus Christ

- Life – the source from which all creation exists, and is made alive, as coming from God through Christ Jesus, who is "the Life" and the "author and finisher" of faith (John 14:6; Heb. 12:2)
- Living – those persons spiritually alive with life, who no longer operate in the shadow of Death while sojourning in earthen vessels that will eventually perish for lack of life
- Alive – the spiritual state of being in existence from God's perspective, even apart from the body, and abiding eternally in communion with God's Presence and Spirit
- Dead – the spiritual state of being in existence from God's perspective, but temporarily separated from Him; the eventual disposition of the earthen body without life
- Death – the spiritual state of being permanently and eternally separated from God; the temporary holding place of unregenerate dead that wait there until the judgment

Introduction

Jesus is the most enigmatic figure in human history! Jesus wants us to seek Him, find Him, know Him and imitate His example, but "who" is Jesus? The knowledge of this truth is the cornerstone to understand the Image Bearer series.

"Image" is a scripture-based book about the identity of Jesus that explains why He does what He does. How was He able to perform all those miracles and walk on water? This insightful book reveals the answers to those mysteries.

Jesus is Lord. This benchmark of Christian theology is the keystone of our salvation, yet our comprehension of who Jesus is has been minimized by man-centric and mystical doctrines which have forgotten the greater aspects of who He is, was, and always will be. Jesus was not promoted from a junior lieutenant position to govern all creation as the reward for living a sinless life and being raised to life again; Jesus has always been Lord of all.

There are 111 names for Jesus in the Bible. Jesus is the Alpha and the Omega, the Beginning and the End, the First and the Last, and the always Eternal One who proceeds from the Father since before the beginning of anything. Jesus is Lord over all. Jesus created everything and He is the Image of the invisible God (Col. 1:15-18). Jesus is the Manifested One. Once we come to the knowledge of this truth, that Jesus is King of kings and Lord over everything in heaven and on earth, we will then be able to fully grasp His identity as is found in all books of the Bible, we will be able to comprehend the larger picture of our faith in Christ, and we will more fully understand *our true identity* in Christ as well.

Jesus is the Message and the Messenger. Jesus came to earth as the Son of Man for one primary reason: to teach us about the Father and show us how to live as sons and daughters of our heavenly Father. We get our identity from Jesus. Our true identity is found – in Christ!

In all our deliberations to know Christ, we must endeavor not to add any man-made doctrines to the reality of who we think Jesus is, or add anything to the knowledge of Christ Jesus, or take anything away from this understanding, nor put any additional teaching, theology, doctrine, philosophy or psychology between our understanding of Jesus and the reality of who Christ is. Since Jesus is Lord of all, then He is Supremely Lord of everything, from beginning to end. Anything less than this full profession minimizes our faith in the Divinity of Jesus Christ – and the gospel Jesus taught us.

For this reason, no secondary sources, commentaries or theological opinions were consulted; only the words of Jesus Christ as found in the Bible (NKJV) and the guidance of the Holy Spirit were used to compose this book. Strong's Concordance was used to help explain certain Greek and Hebrew words. And after all is said and done in the earth, we will soon fully comprehend…

It's all about Jesus – and God gets the glory…forever and ever!
Amen.

"For unto us **a Child is born**,
Unto us **a Son is given**;
And the government will be upon His shoulder.
And His name will be called
Wonderful, Counselor, Mighty God,
Everlasting Father, Prince of Peace" (Isa. 9:6)

The Mystery of God Revealed in Christ

> "But we speak the wisdom of God in a mystery, the hidden wisdom which God ordained before the ages for our glory" – "and to make all see what is the fellowship of the mystery, which from the beginning of the ages has been hidden in God who created all things *through* Jesus Christ" (1 Cor. 2:7; Eph. 3:9).

If I were to ask you "who" you are, most people would begin to describe themselves according to "what" they do. You might say, I am a plumber or carpenter, a husband and father – or wife and mother, a member of such-and-such organization, where you live, what church you attend, and begin listing sports, hobbies and other personal information; however, these are "what" you do... these are not "who" you are. Oftentimes, we approach God in the same manner and begin describing Him based upon what He does, but if we want to know "who" He is, then we need to quietly ask Him and allow the Spirit to guide us through the scriptures to discover who Jesus is.

"I am the way, the truth and the life!
No one comes to the Father except through Me" (John 14:6)

Christianity's most celebrated and controversial claim is that Jesus is the only way to get to heaven. We will take a new look at who Jesus really is – and comprehend the veritable truth of this claim with fresh understanding.

When people are asked about the reason Jesus came to earth, their thoughts quickly turn to baby Jesus in the Christmas manger and then say, "To save the world," but this remembrance of Jesus is an idealized, memorialized perspective that is celebrated without truly understanding who Jesus really is, was and always will be: Jesus is Lord of all. And Jesus has been Lord of heaven and earth *before* He ever came to earth... and before He even created the earth!

For thousands of years, we have been taught to perceive the reality of Jesus from a mystical perspective, as a theoretical or theological construct that man cannot fully spiritually comprehend. Some have subscribed to the irreverent teachings of gnostics in an effort to know Christ and to understand Him as God apart from His incarnation in the flesh, but these teachings created a schism between truth (spiritual reality) and myth (cultural perception).

The knowledge of Christ can be learned intellectually and experientially in one of two ways, as Spirit-anointed reasoning or as human-based rationality. Yet man continues to put two things together in order to make sense of spiritual things without coming to a firm conclusion (Eccl. 7:27), but the Spirit freely reveals truth to those whose hearts and minds are completely surrendered (yielded) to God's will and, therefore, willingly choose to focus the entirety of their attention and affection on Him, that is, Jesus Christ.

Once again, the Spirit is bringing revelation (words from God with understanding to men) that they might comprehend with their '*dianoia*' thoroughly open mind and see with their heart the truth regarding the King of heaven and earth, Jesus Christ. Jesus taught the mysteries of the kingdom to His disciples, whose hearts and minds were being opened to the truth; their minds were being completely opened so that they could operate within the mindset of a *thoroughly open 'dianoigo'* heaven – continuously, with full uninterrupted access to spiritual things from above, and we are yet another generation that is being prepared as well. Let me explain…

… but first, a quick digression regarding a TV show I saw recently. A female religious cleric was describing the life of Christ in a manner that is quite typical of many traditional denominations and doctrines. She was pontificating about who Jesus was, when did Jesus realize who He was, when did He learn what His earthly ministry was, and how did He come to know when this ministry would begin. She was describing the "mystical Jesus" who entered into a time period of His life when He encountered John the Baptist, whereby "He became the prophetic arm of God's mysterious plan who would soon become the Messiah – and save us." When did Jesus know who He really was? Little did this cleric know, but Jesus always knew; however, we will never understand this aspect of Jesus if we continue to perceive the reality of Jesus from an earthly perspective. Jesus always knew who He was, even at the age of twelve:

> "Did you not know that I must be about My Father's business?" (Luke 2:49).

Jesus did not have an epiphany one day and come to the realization that He was the Christ. Jesus never had an epiphany – ***Jesus is the epiphany!*** Jesus knew who He was all along – "And the Child grew and became strong in spirit, filled with wisdom; and the grace of God was upon Him" (Luke 2:40). And "Jesus increased in wisdom and stature, and in favor with God and men" (v.52). Jesus spent 33 years listening and living in oneness with His heavenly Father.

Jesus was begotten, not made, one in being with the Father, through Whom all things were made (Apostles Creed). Jesus existed in Oneness with the Father before the beginning of anything, even before God spoke light into existence. Jesus created the heavens and the earth (Col. 1:15-17), and ***all things that exist were created by Him, through Him and for Him***. Think about this for a moment: all things were created by Jesus, and *through* Him they came into being, because they are *for* Him. Jesus of Nazareth was not just an ordinary man whom God chose among all other prophets to save mankind from sin. Jesus is the Predetermination of God Himself, to restore the kingdom of heaven in righteousness, truth, justice and peace.

Jesus was born as a person, like the rest of us, but He was not like the rest of us. Jesus came to earth as the God-Man, who is God eternal and was then born in the usual way – as a Man. In this regard, the Christ-child did not transition into a "divine reality" such that He entered into a Messiah-role while upon the earth, but rather, He always had His Divine nature, His glory and His

Lordship from the moment He was conceived by the Holy Spirit to a virgin named Mary.

Why Jesus would do this still remains a mystery to some of us, such that He Himself created history, wrote Himself into history, and then was sent to us by the Father in this manner – as our Immanuel: God with us. Comprehending this mystery is a work of grace which only comes as a gift of understanding from the Holy Spirit… because this divine mystery is just too fantastic to be spiritually comprehended with the natural mind of man alone; we need the Spirit to guide us into all truth to comprehend such a great mystery.

Jesus knew exactly who He was. Jesus is God who came in the manner and likeness of all men, as soul and spirit, clothed with human flesh, to be the Way, the Truth and the Life, our Immanuel: God with us. This was God's plan all along; there were no accidents or mistakes. Everything happened for a reason and everything happened according to schedules, times and seasons.

Jesus knew exactly who He was. And Jesus also knows exactly who you are because our soul resided *in Him* before time began (Prov. 8:22, 23) "just as He chose us *in Him* before the foundation of the world" (Eph. 1:4). Jesus knew us before we were born (Psa. 139:13-16), Jesus knows who you are at this very moment, and Jesus knows who you will be – because Jesus carried us then… and He continues to carry us now (Isa. 46:3, 4). The reason this does not make sense to us is because we have been taught that man has a soul rather than he "*is*" a soul, and to perceive man as a human being in search of a spiritual experience, when in fact, he is a spiritual being that is having a human experience. This body of flesh is just a temporary "garment" during this phase of our eternal journey that does not end when our body dies.

You are not an accident of happenstance resulting from an element of chance when two people came together in union; yet there is only one way of knowing who you will ever be, so let go, trust God – and believe in Jesus as Lord of all – to discover who you were destined to be. Your earthly reality according to the flesh will never be able to comprehend the spiritual reality of *who* you have been destined to be in Christ – *if* you continue to play the mystic games of unregenerate men. You must be born *anew* (*anothen* – from above), according to the Spirit, if you are ever going to know, understand and perceive this truth – and comprehend "who" you really are.

We need to remember who we are – and for this reason I was called to write – that we might remember, know, understand, believe... and perceive the spiritual reality of God's kingdom that surrounds us. But we must first thoroughly comprehend who Jesus is, from His perspective, and why He came to earth with three missions: as the Way, Truth and Life.

Jesus Our Creator

Let's start with a basic question: who created the heavens and the earth? Most people will say God, and most people can quote Genesis 1:1, "In the beginning, God created the heavens and the earth," but if your understanding *only* envisions our heavenly Father, then you would be wrong. Everything originates from the Father and comes from Him – except for Jesus, who has always been eternal and in Oneness with the Father since before "the beginning" ever happened. Jesus and our Father operate in spiritual Oneness, and in regard to all Creation, both Father and Son participated in the plan, but only one of them created it "by Himself."

> "Thus says the Lord, your Redeemer, and He who formed you from the womb: "I am the Lord, who makes all things, Who stretches out the heavens all alone, Who spreads abroad the earth ***by Myself***" (Isa. 44:24).

Our heavenly Father and Jesus, united in glory and Oneness, made and created man – as well as everything around us. As we read the following scriptures and come to understand Jesus as *'our'* Creator, I would like you to take notice of a significant name introduction that God in Oneness uses to describe *Himself* in Gen. 2:4 as "LORD *God.*"   But first...

About a year ago, as I was reading the Apostle's Creed to my son, I commented to him that I had a problem with the first sentence: "I believe in One God, Father Almighty, maker of heaven and earth." I told him that it was through Jesus that all things were created and I proceeded to show him, beginning in the book of Colossians, how Jesus created all things by Him, through Him and for Him. A little while later, as I was driving my car, the Holy Spirit brought understanding to me – in the form of a correction. He said the Creed was correct, but I was not. The Creed clearly says Father Almighty *made* heaven and earth; indeed, God *made* everything, and it was Jesus who *created* all things visible and invisible (Col. 1:15-17; Eph. 3:9: Heb. 1:2). Look closely, now, at the subtle personal pronoun change in the Genesis creation account from "Our image" to "His own image."

> "Then God said, "Let Us *make* man in **Our image**, according to Our likeness; let them have dominion over the fish of the sea, over the birds of the air, and over the cattle, over all the earth and over every creeping thing that creeps on the earth." [27] So God *created* man in **His own image**; in the image of God He created him; male and female He created them" (Gen. 1:26, 27; verse 26 *Our* image, is plural, but v. 27 *His* image, is singular)).

Verily, the Creed was accurate down to the very word because these men were guided by the Holy Spirit to exact a level of accuracy *before* the New Covenant scriptures were canonized. Since the Holy Spirit inspired those men as He also does men today, perhaps we should spend more time listening to Him rather than rearranging our prejudices in support of *our* kingdom preferences and doctrinal predispositions based upon the Bible translation *we* prefer.

So now, let's take a moment to consider many other scriptures to see Jesus as our Creator:

IMAGE

- "So God created man in **His own** image; in the image of God He created him; male and female He created them" (Gen. 1:27)
- "That they may *see and know, and consider and understand* together, that the hand of the Lord has done this, and the Holy One of Israel has created it" (Isa. 41:20)
- "Everyone who is called by My name, Whom I have created for My glory; I have formed him, yes, I have made him" (Isa. 43:7)
- "In the beginning was the Word, and the Word was with God, and the Word was God. He was in the beginning with God. *All things were made through Him, and without Him nothing was made that was made.* In Him was life, and the life was the light of men. And the light shines in the darkness, and the darkness did not comprehend it" (John 1:1-5)
- "And to make all see what is the fellowship of the mystery, which from the beginning of the ages has been hidden in God who created all things through Jesus Christ" (Eph. 3:9)
- "He is the image of the invisible God, the firstborn over all creation. For by Him all things were created that are in heaven and that are on earth, visible and invisible, whether thrones or dominions or principalities or powers. *All things were created through Him and for Him.* And He is before all things, and in Him all things consist" (Col. 1:15-17)
- "And have put on the new man who is renewed in knowledge according to the image of Him who created him" (Col. 3:10)
- "God, who at various times and in various ways spoke in time past to the fathers by the prophets, [2] has in these last days spoken to us by His Son, whom He has appointed heir of all things, *through whom also He made the worlds*; [3] who being the brightness of *His* glory and the express image of His person, and upholding all things by the word of His power" (Heb. 1:1-3)

- "You, LORD, in the beginning laid the foundation of the earth, and the heavens are the work of Your hands" (Heb. 1:10)
- "You are worthy, O Lord, to receive glory and honor and power; for You created all things, and by Your will they exist and were created" (Rev. 4:1)

Other scriptures include: 2 Cor. 4:4; John 1:18; 17:5; Phil. 2:5-7; Heb. 2:10. Jesus Christ is the One who created all things, visible and invisible, material and immaterial. His hands created us! He created every single human being on this planet, in the beginning, and He knew us before the world was ever created.

Jesus is our Lord and Redeemer, and Jesus is the Creator of all things, "Who spreads abroad the earth *by Myself*." Jesus is the Lord of Glory, and Jesus is both God and Christ! And He made you! We were sent to earth in the likeness of men in human flesh exactly the same as He was, and in this, Jesus knows you more than you can imagine. He came to show us the way – and what better way than to come as Incarnate Logos, Living Word, and The Way – as the Archetype of the better way.

Now that we know who our Creator is, I want to key in on several things in Genesis 2:4. If you have yet to understand the entirety of Jesus' identity in the scriptures... as Lord God, then keep reading. The very first mention of "*Lord God*" can be found as He expresses Himself after He (Jesus) created all things, including "*the host of heaven and the host of earth*" (i.e. heavenly angels and earthly sons of men; Gen. 2:1):

> "This *is* the history of the heavens and the earth when they were *created*, in the day that the **LORD God** made the earth and the heavens" (Gen. 2:4).

This is the first time Jesus revealed Himself as Lord God in the scriptures. Up until this point, God (*YHWH*) is often perceived as being objective, obtuse, obscure, impersonal and lofty, who created everything and then stepped away to seemingly watch what happens from a distance, yet now we know Jesus as Lord God who has now manifested Himself in His word to become very personal and intimately involved with His creation whereby He desires to reveal Himself in more friendly ways – as the living God who desires to dwell among us. We will look at the term Lord God in relation to Jesus in more detail a little later on.

Let me state this as simply as possible: it is ALL about JESUS! Nothing else matters, nor does it even come close. Our entire physical reality was created by Christ Himself! Any time we minimize the character or identity of Jesus Christ to perceive Him from a theological or man-centric perspective *without* asking Him to teach us *who He is* from His perspective, sadly, then, we will certainly find everything that we are looking for, but it may not be true to His identity.

Jesus is Preeminent in all creation. We need to let the Holy Spirit show us who Jesus is, and in this manner, we will then be able to more clearly know Jesus, our heavenly Father, and also the person of the Holy Spirit – operating in Triune Oneness. One God, revealed as three persons, being manifested in one person: Jesus Christ

I try not to use the term God anymore, because I see it as a vague, ambiguous, ubiquitous and all-inclusive word to describe the Divine in a broad-brush impersonal manner. "We believe in one God," and yet, we should focus all of our Spirit-anointed reasoning to completely know, understand and thoroughly comprehend the person and identity of Jesus until an epiphany happens in our mind: Jesus is *LORD God*! On earth, it is all about Jesus, and you will soon discover in the following pages that everything which happens upon the earth pertains to Jesus. Jesus created the heavens and the earth, and all things visible and invisible; everything exists for Him; by Him, through Him and with Him, all things exist – and in Him all things consist and are held together (Col. 1:17). Jesus created everything for Himself, for this was God's good pleasure according to the Father's plan, and we need to move beyond the mystical Jesus in order to comprehend the fullness of the spiritual reality of God manifested by one person: Jesus of Nazareth, the Christ of God.

Jesus is God – before anything ever was. Jesus created the world and everything in it – and then He came to dwell in the earth He created... and He desires to dwell *within* you as well.

God Our Father

God our heavenly Father is invisible, but so we may come to intimately know the Father, Jesus revealed the Father to us – in word, in deed and in physical form.

> Jesus said, "And the Father **Himself**, who sent Me, has testified of Me. You have neither heard His voice at any time, nor seen His form" (John 5:37).

We often think of Jesus in a priestly manner, as the Son of God, as a mighty Prophet and High Priest sent by God to save the world, and for many of us, He still hangs upon a cross above an altar. We can read about His life and His three years of public ministry upon the earth, and we are more than capable to describe the attributes of Jesus, but if we were asked to describe God's nature and who God is, even theologians stammer through the answer. And it is precisely for this reason the Son was sent from the Father: to show us once and for all Who the Father is. Jesus said, "He who has seen Me has seen the Father" (John 14:9) because Father and Son abide in Oneness; They are One. So, if you want to know who God is, as your heavenly Father, then study Jesus in the synoptic gospels Matthew, Mark, Luke and John... especially John.

Consider all these scriptures that confirm the invisible reality of the Father, whom Jesus revealed in His *parousia*:[1]

---

[1] ***Parousia*** – (παρουσία-3592) is an ancient Greek word ***meaning*** presence, arrival, royal visit, official visit or advent, especially of the second coming of Christ. (Definition compiled from various sources).

IMAGE

- The Father is Spirit (John 4:23, 24)
- The Father is invisible, His attributes are invisible (Rom. 1:20)
- "No one has seen the Father at any time" (John 1:18)
- "No one has seen God at any time" (1 John 4:12)
- "Not that anyone has seen the Father, except He who is from God" (John 6:46)
- Jesus is the "image" of God (2 Cor. 4:4)
- "He is the image of the invisible God, the firstborn over all creation" (Col. 1:15), "who being the brightness of *His* glory and the ***express*** image of His person, and upholding all things by the word of His power" (Heb. 1:3)
- "Now to the King eternal, immortal, *invisible*, to God who alone is wise, be honor and glory forever and ever. Amen" (1 Tim. 1:17).

"God is spirit and incorporeal, invisible, without material substance, without physical parts or passions and therefore free from all temporal limitations."[2]

Jesus came to reveal the image of our invisible Father so that, when we enter into faith through the Door called Jesus, He will lead us along His Way into the Father's presence. Jesus is the only way whereby we can come into the glorious presence of our Father – who is wrapped in Glory and light. There are many traditions and various new age teachings that claim to have a personal encounter with the Father as a bright light, being enlightened by ascended thinking, but unless you are guided by the Holy Spirit, who is the Doorkeeper for the Door of the sheepfold, and come into the presence of Jesus, who is the only way and "the Door" to the Father, then the brilliance of that light cannot be the Father. This statement will be proven in later chapters.

Jesus created you and me – He knows the Father intimately – and He knows you better than you know yourself. All power and

---

[2] Willmington's Guide To The Bible, p.594, IV.A; (Elemental Theory, p. 23).

authority has been given to Jesus by the Father, and in His hand is the kingdom, the power, the glory and the dominion. Jesus is Lord of all, and all power and authority has been delegated to Him, *and we need to begin to see this reality of Jesus as "God personified" whenever we say "Lord" or read the word "Lord" or "God" in the scriptures*.

> "And beginning at Moses and all the Prophets, He [*Jesus*] expounded to them in all the Scriptures the things concerning Himself" (Luke 24:27), "And He opened their understanding, that they might comprehend the Scriptures" (v.45) that all scripture points to the reality of Jesus as Lord of all (John 5:39).

Jesus is Lord of All, and He is the center of it all; Jesus is the center of the universe – and for this reason we celebrate Jesus as Lord God and as *Almighty God (El Shaddai)* ... as King of kings and Lord of lords. God became manifest – and we know Him as Jesus Christ. For this reason, Jesus was begotten of the Father that we may know – and understand – and comprehend such a great mystery.

Through Christ Jesus, the mystery of God was made known and revealed to men so that we may thoroughly know and reverently believe that the Father loves *every one of us* more than we will ever know. *And for this reason Jesus came to earth – to reveal the Father's love toward us.*

It is all about Jesus – and God gets the glory!

When we pray, can we continue to pray using the generic term "God"? Dear God this, dear God that, yada yada, and we ask all this, in the name of Jesus… as if the name Jesus is just the punctuation or authorized footnote attached to our prayers? Or do we now see Jesus for who He really is – as Lord! Lord of heaven, Lord of earth, King of all creation, Lord of all things created, Lord of all things material, Lord of all things visible and invisible, Lord over our prayers and Lord of our soul? Indeed, Jesus created you as soul and spirit, and knew you before you were formed in your mother's womb, so that, one day, you may come to the knowledge of the truth and worship God in spirit and in truth.

So now, when I pray, I pray to the Lord, knowing that I am praying to Jesus who lives in Oneness with the Father in unity with the Holy Spirit, and I give all thanks and glory to the Father, as I am guided by the Holy Spirit. As you begin to fathom this revelation, I hope you are able to see this truth – and to understand "Who" the scriptures refer to as "the Lord God."

If this teaching is too difficult to comprehend, then keep reading... because your "God box" concerning the knowledge of Jesus is about to get larger... much larger!

Theophanies

God is Spirit, and is invisible, so any time there is a *physical* manifestation of God in the Old Testament in which He appears to men, these are called Theophanies; they are pre-incarnate biblical appearances of Jesus manifesting Himself in the flesh before He was born to Mary. His second and third appearance to Abraham gives us a *very* clear indication of the names He uses to identify Himself:

> "When Abram was ninety-nine years old, *the LORD [YHWH] appeared* to Abram and said to him, "*I am Almighty God [El Shaddai]*; walk before Me and be blameless. ² And I will make My covenant between Me and you, and will multiply you exceedingly" (Gen. 17:1).

> "Then *the LORD [YHWH] appeared* to him by the terebinth trees of Mamre, as he was sitting in the tent door in the heat of the day. ² So he lifted his eyes and looked, and behold, *three men were standing by him*; and when he saw them, he ~~ran~~ [*leapt*] from the tent door to meet them, and bowed

himself to the ground, [3] and said, "***My Lord***, if I have now found favor in Your sight, do not pass on by Your servant" (Gen. 18:1-3).

Jesus operated then – and still does today – outside of physics, time and space; He operates in the spiritual dimension and these appearances were written down to help us understand and believe that Jesus is who He claims to be: Son of God, Lord God, Creator, Redeemer, Teacher, Savior, the Firstborn (meaning: Preeminence) over all creation, King of kings and Lord of lords, Master (*Adonai*), Almighty God (*El Shaddai*), God Most High (*El Elyon*) and especially… *YHWH*-Jehovah: Lord over all.

1. Abram saw Him (Gen. 12:7)
2. The Lord Jesus appeared again to Abram and made a *covenant* with Abraham (Gen. 17:1)
3. Abraham saw Him again and leaped to bow down (in '*shachah*' worship) to Him (Gen. 18:1-3; 16-22) and the Lord told him that Sarah would have a son (v.10)
4. Jesus comforted Hagar in the wilderness (Gen. 16:7-13)
5. He spoke to Abraham from heaven as "the Angel of the Lord" (Gen. 22:11)
6. He appeared to Isaac *twice* (Gen. 26:2, 24; Ex. 6:3)
8. Jesus spoke to Jacob as "Lord God" in a dream (Gen. 28:13) and "redeems" him (v.16)
9. The Angel of the Lord (the God of Bethel) appeared to Jacob in a dream (Gen. 31:11, 13)
10. Jesus wrestled with Jacob (Gen. 32:24-30) [3]
11. He appeared to Moses as an Angel in "a flame of fire" in the burning bush (Exodus 3:2)
12. He manifests as "an Angel of the Lord" in the pillar of cloud and fire (Ex. 14:19, 20, 24; Num. 20:16; note: a similar event happened to Abraham, in Gen. 15:17)
13. The Lord came down upon Mount Sinai to speak the commandments to Moses (Ex. 19:20; Deut. 33:2)

---

[3] "So Jacob called the name of the place Peniel: "For I have seen God [*Elohim*] face to face, and my life is preserved" (Gen 32:30), which repudiates the Jehovah's Witnesses claim that "No one can see God and live."

14. Moses, Aaron, Nadab and Abihu, and seventy of the elders "saw the God of Israel"… "and as it were the body of Heaven in His clearness" (Ex. 24:10 - KJV)
15. He appeared to Moses as a pillar of cloud a second time (Ex. 33:9), He gave Moses a glimpse of Himself, face to face, on Mount Sinai (Ex. 33:11) and then put him in the cleft of the rock as His glory passed by (v.22) without revealing what His face looked like
16. He appeared to Aaron and Miriam as a pillar of cloud and stood before them (Num. 12:5)
17. He appeared to Moses and Joshua as a pillar of cloud to inaugurate Joshua (Deut. 31:15)
18. He appeared to Joshua and identified himself as "the Commander of the Army of the LORD " (Joshua 5:13-15; He received Joshua's worship, which heavenly angels reject)
19. He opened Balaam's eyes (as a type and shadow of Saul's Damascus experience), and caused his donkey to speak (Num. 22:22-35)
20. He revealed Himself to Israel as the Angel of the Lord when He speaks of "My covenant" (Judges 2:1-5; and yet He came to His own people, but they did not comprehend Him and they rejected Him)
21. Gideon saw the Angel of the Lord face to face (Judges 6:11-22)
22. The Angel of the Lord announced the birth of Sampson (Judges 13:3-23)
23. "I have heard of You by the hearing of the ear, but now my eye sees You" (Job 42:5)
24. He joined Daniel's three friends in the Babylonian fiery furnace (Dan. 3:25)
25. Daniel saw a certain man clothed in linen, with resplendent features (Dan. 10:6; 12:6)
26. Zechariah referred to the Angel of the Lord as "the Lord" (Zech. 1:12; 20)
27. Isaiah said he saw His glory and spoke of Him (John 12:41)
28. He appeared to Jeremiah and His hand touched his lips (Jer. 1:9)

29. Some suggest that it was Jesus who "*walked*" with Adam and Eve in the cool of the Garden (and since God does not have a physical form, I subscribe to this opinion)
30. "Some theologians believe that when this title (the angel of the Lord) is found in the Old Testament, it is actually another name for the Lord Jesus Christ" [4] and is found also in:
    - The angel stayed the hand of Abraham from killing Isaac (Gen. 22:11)
    - The angel of the Lord guided Abraham's servant to find a bride for Isaac (Gen. 24:7)
    - The angel of the Lord prepares Israel for the promised land (Ex. 23:20-23; Psa. 34:7; Isa. 63:9; 1 Cor. 10:14)
    - The angel of the Lord ministers to Elijah (1 Kings 19:7)
    - The angel of the Lord saves Jerusalem (Isa. 37:36)
    - Jesus Himself says, "I, Jesus, have sent My angel" (Rev. 22:16); see also (Ex. 32:34)
31. In addition to these Theophanies, the Old Testament contains nearly 80 references to the Spirit of God and anticipates the arrival of God's Son, the Messiah.[5]

Some suggest Melchizedek, the priest-king of Salem who appeared to Abraham, is Jesus (Gen. 14:18-20); however, Abraham already knew what Jesus looked like (v.12:7) and would meet Him again soon after (v.17:1; 18:1). Jesus is Lord (*YHWH*) and He described Himself as *El Shaddai* (Almighty God–in Gen. 17:1) and Abraham referred to the Lord (*YHWH*) as "God Most High (*El Elyon*), the Possessor of heaven and earth" (Gen. 14:18, 22), so – in one sense – Melchizedek as a priest of God Most High appears to be a type and shadow of pre-incarnate Jesus as High Priest of God Most

---

[4] Willmington's Guide To The Bible, p.40; K.3. This may be one reason why Jehovah's Witnesses falsely believe that Jesus was an angel and not the Son of God; however, the "Person" that received '*shahcah*' worship (v.18:1) could not have been an angel; and secondly, to which of God's angels did He say, "You are My Son, Today I have begotten You" (Heb. 1:5; Psa. 2:7; Acts 13:33; Heb. 5:5). Conversely, has any angel referred to God as My Father? Furthermore, angels are not allowed to receive worship, yet Jesus received worship (Matt. 8:2; 9:18; 14:33; 15:25).

[5] Notes on "The Trinity in the Old Testament," NKJV Study Bible, p. 1424.

High: "You are a priest forever according to the order of Melchizedek" (Psa. 110:4; Heb. 5:6).

However, there is another very interesting explanation that merits consideration. Since no record of this "order" continued in existence, and since this term does not appear again except in regard to Jesus, is there another way to reconcile this matter? Yes! Consider this: Jesus could have appeared pre-incarnate to Abraham in one manner yet manifested Himself in a different manner that was unfamiliar to Abraham – first as a friend, and then as the King of Salem (meaning: King of Peace). After the Lord's resurrection, Jesus appeared to Mary who supposed Him to the gardener because His appearance was altered, and He appeared to two disciples on the road to Emmaus – yet they did not perceive it was Jesus who walked with them. Luke 9:29 describes the Lord's transfiguration as "the appearance of His face *was altered*" (*egeneto heteron*-1096, 2087) "became (*ginomai*) different (*heteros*)"[6] and thus, Jesus could have presented Himself to Abraham – as two different manifestations of the same expression – first as a Friend and then as a King. (Note: when we study Revelation a little later, section titled: "The Spirit and The One," we will see how Jesus manifested Himself to John... seven different ways).

Thus, there are thirty instances of Jesus in the Old Testament!!

> "What is man that You are mindful of him, **and the son of man that You visit him**?" (Psa. 8:4)

The Lord of Glory has visited... us... many times! And much like Melchizedek, the unanticipated appearance of Elihu in Job 32 in the crucible of Job's testing, appears as a wise young man as a type and shadow of Christ amongst three older friends, much like the story in Daniel who appears amidst three friends in the fiery furnace.

---

[6] Strong's Concordance, study on *metamorphoo*-3339.

In fact, the Bible records as many as 111 names for Jesus Christ [7] but His favorite name for Himself on earth was "Son of Man." This is most interesting, *since He made man in His image – and then He came to earth in the image of a man.* What an incredible mystery, indeed!

Likewise, there are as many as 17 physical appearances and manifestations of Jesus (Christophanies) that were reported and recorded after His death and resurrection.[8]

1. To Mary Magdalene (Mark 16:9; John 20:11-18)
2. To other women returning from the tomb (Matt. 28:5-15; Mark 16:2-8; Luke 24:1-11)
3. To two disciples on the road to Emmaus (Mark 16:12, 13; Luke 24:13-35)
4. To Peter in Jerusalem (Luke 24:34; 1 Cor. 15:5)
5. To ten apostles (Luke 24:36-43; John 20:19-25)
6. To eleven, including Thomas, in the upper room (John 20:24-29)
7. To seven disciples in Galilee, after the disciples fished all night (John 21:1-25)
8. He is worshipped by the eleven despite some remaining doubt (Matt. 28:16-20)
9. He appears in the upper room to the eleven and James, the half-brother of Jesus (Mark 16:14; Luke 24:44-49; 1 Cor. 15:6)
10. The Ascension at the Mount of Olives (Mark 16:19, 20; Luke 24:50-53; Acts 1:4-12)
11. To five hundred people (1 Cor. 15:6)
12. To Paul as a bright light on the road to Damascus (Acts 9:1-6; 22:1-10; 26:12-18; 1 Cor. 15:8)
13. And two more times to Paul (Acts 18:9; 23:11)
15. And perhaps two other times as well (Acts. 27:23; 2 Cor. 12:9)

---

[7] Willmington's, p.614-615. Some names for Jesus are: Branch, Door, Light, Rod, Rock, Seed, Almighty and Word.
[8] "The Appearances of the Risen Christ," NKJV Study Bible, p. 1633 and Willmington's Guide to the Bible, p.339.

17. To John in a vision (Rev. 1:12-18)

"In my view (and not only in my view) it was indeed our Lord Jesus Christ who appeared to Adam and Eve in the garden, for He has always been the Father's *manifest* representative on earth, appearing for Him and as Him." [9]

Jesus has always been Lord of heaven and earth... since before the universe ever was!

> Jesus said, "No one has ascended to heaven but He who came down from heaven, *that is,* the Son of Man who is in heaven" (John 3:13).

Jesus came down from heaven to earth, but the only way Jesus could say He ascended is if He had descended at least once before, and indeed, we have proof of at least 30 such instances.

> "*I came forth from the Father* and have come into the world. *Again*, I leave the world and go to the Father" (John 16:28).

Does this give you a greater sense about who Jesus really is? Jesus can come and go as He pleases, to appear to whomever He desires and manifest Himself in whatever form He chooses. He did it then – and He can do it now or whenever He wants – especially today. Jesus is not just the center of it all – Jesus is all in all! More than life itself, Jesus is the "I AM" origin of all life – because Jesus *is the Life*! Jesus is our Creator and Jesus invites you to partake of His divine nature so that you may dwell with Him as He abides in you (John 17:23; 2 Pet. 1:4). Jesus wants to have a personal encounter with everyone, and yes, even a face-to-face living encounter resulting in life eternal with you! And Jesus continues to speak to those who diligently seek Him so that they may enter into a personal relationship with Him...

---

[9] Conversation about Christology, by Robert (Bob) Luginbill; www.ichthys.com.

> "*God*, who at various times in many ways, *spoke…*"
> (Heb. 1:1)

Jesus did not just come to earth "once" as a little baby lying in a manger. Jesus came at various times and in many ways to be a Shepherd for those who acknowledge Him as Lord, God, Master and Savior… to teach us in ways everlasting. Truly, Jesus has been Lord of Heaven and Earth since before the beginning ever began, and Jesus wants to reveal Himself to you and me!

Jesus spoke *rhema* words and came at many times and in many ways – to speak to *all* people. He spoke through dreams, visions, signs, visitations, parables, miracles and supernatural events. *Jesus was not just the messenger,* **Jesus is the Message**! Every time you read the word "God" in the scriptures, envision Jesus in your mind when you read it. Jesus is God, in Oneness with the Father, and He manifested Himself as the Father's representative, as God incarnate (in the flesh) so that He might be a Teacher to all of us and show us how to live (Gen. 3:8; Ex. 4:15).

Jesus speaks to us today just as He did to the psalmist and to the prophets…

> "Then He said to them, "*These are the words which I spoke to you* while I was still with you, that all things must be fulfilled which were written in the Law of Moses and the Prophets and the Psalms *concerning Me*" (Luke 24:44).

And Jesus still has many things to say, so He speaks to us through the Holy Spirit…

> "I still have many things to say to you, but you cannot bear them now. [13] However, when He, the Spirit of truth, has come, He will guide you into all truth; for *He will not speak on His own authority*, but whatever He hears He will speak; and He will tell you things to come. [14] He will glorify Me, for **He will take of what is Mine** and declare it to you.

¹⁵ ***All things that the Father has are Mine***.
Therefore I said that He will take of Mine and
declare it to you" (John 16:12-15).

Jesus is the voice we hear, and when you hear the sound of His voice, true disciples follow.

"My sheep hear My voice, and I know them, and
they follow Me" (John 10:27).

If you truly comprehend that it is Jesus who speaks to you, then revelation truth has become manifest in you – because Jesus is the Truth. And truly, it is the Lord Jesus and/or the Holy Spirit who speaks to us, and for this reason, we should be very suspect by all claims to the contrary. Even angels are messengers sent to proclaim the will of God, so if an angel appears to you, be sure to test the spirits to determine if Jesus is their Lord – or not (1 John 4:1-3).

If your patriarchal or matriarchal traditions have taught you that only Father God speaks to us, then consider this: Jesus and the Father are One – and therefore thus, they are both speaking to you, if you will. However, because of the religious traditions that the Lord's Disciples were taught by teachers of Judaism, they also had a very hard time believing in Jesus – even after witnessing all the miracles and healings (Matt. 28:17). They wanted to believe, but their ears had grown heavy and their hearts too hardhearted from too much toxic theology, so they asked Jesus to show them the Father as one final proof of His Divine claim as Messiah. But they, as yet, did not know what they were asking, for no one had seen the Father... or had they? The Father is God and Jesus is God, so then, if you have seen one, then you have seen the other, and if you have known the One, then you have known the Other.

"If you had known Me, you would have known My
Father also; ***and from now on you know Him and
have seen Him***." ⁸ Philip said to Him, "Lord, show
us the Father, and it is sufficient for us." ⁹ Jesus said

> to him, "Have I been with you so long, and yet you have not known Me, Philip? ***He who has seen Me has seen the Father***; so how can you say, 'Show us the Father'? ¹⁰ Do you not believe that I am in the Father, and the Father in Me? The words that I speak to you I do not speak on My own authority; but the Father *who dwells in Me* does the works. ¹¹ Believe Me that *I am* in the Father and the Father in Me, or else believe Me for the sake of the works themselves" (John 14:7-11).

Show us the Father? It seems they heard the message, but still did not *'suniemi'* understand. The people of Jesus' generation had actually seen God Almighty – and talked with Him! They had actually seen the Father, being manifested in Oneness with Jesus, but this truth they could not comprehend… apart from the Spirit.

> "I and My Father are one" (John 10:30).

> "He who has seen Me has seen the Father" (John 14:9).

And now for the Trinity epiphany, Jesus spoke this truth to the prophet Jeremiah:

> "You shall call Me, "My Father," and not turn away from Me" (Jer. 3:19).

The Father and the Son are One. And by grace, through faith in Jesus Christ, we are united in Christ by the Spirit of Christ to become one with Christ who dwells in oneness *with* the Father. Through faith, Christ abides in our hearts, and if Christ abides in our hearts, then the Father also abides in us, and – we abide *with* Them. This is what I believe and this is what the scriptures teach, so, if this teaching is too difficult to comprehend, then keep reading… because your "God box" concerning Jesus is about to get even larger!

> "That they all may be one, as You, Father, are in
> Me, and I in You; *that they also may be one in Us*,
> that the world may believe that You sent Me" (John
> 17:21)

Jesus says, "that they also may be one *in Us*." Just take a moment (or a millennium) to ponder that! Through faith, with Christ in us (our hope of glory), we are united to the Father and we become one *with* God... just like Jesus! By faith *in Christ*, you and I can also boldly say the same words Jesus said: "I and My Father are One."

The Father is in you because Christ is in you, and therefore, "the kingdom of God is in you" (Luke 17:21) on account of faith in Christ and the Spirit of Christ in you (Rom. 8:9). You do not need to pray a special prayer to invite God into your life because God is everywhere and He is already within you, but He is waiting for you to "enter in" and find Him in your heart.

The Lord God

Jesus told us over and over, in a variety of ways and manners, that the God who continually manifests Himself in the scriptures is the Son of Man, Jesus Himself. He tried to explain this truth to the teachers and leaders of Israel in word and deed, but their institutionalized perception of God had hardened their hearts, and therefore, they failed to see God Himself when He spoke truth to them.

> Jesus said, "Your father Abraham rejoiced to see
> My day, and *he saw it* and was glad. Then the Jews
> said to Him, "You are not yet fifty years old, and
> have You seen Abraham?"[58] Jesus said to them,
> "Most assuredly, I say to you, before Abraham was,
> I AM" (John 8:56-58).

Jesus called Himself "I AM" and said Abraham saw Him, and indeed, this is recorded in (Gen.12:7) and Jesus also appeared at least twice more to Abraham (17:1; 18:1-3) because one of these three men that physically appeared before him was worthy to receive worship – and we know that angels cannot accept '*shachah*' worship. Abraham believed *upon the Lord* and his faith was accounted to him as righteousness (v.15:6); likewise, when any of us believe *upon the Lord Jesus* like Abraham did, in obedience, our faith is accounted to us as righteousness as well.

Abraham called Jesus "Lord" when He appeared to him – and likewise, so should we (v.12:8).

Who, then, is "the Lord God" that is mentioned in the Bible? There are some who can only see God the Father in this capacity because the spirit of institutionalized religion and much toxic theology has marginalized their understanding of who Jesus really is. Or perhaps "fatherology" in the church today may be a reactionary response to centuries of "maryology" whereby many perceived Father God as an idol in their heart to counter many false doctrines in Catholicism, but I shall endeavor to prove beyond any doubt that Jesus is Lord, and Lord God, and the Lord our God… who is our Redeemer, Savior, Lord Almighty and God Most High (*El Elyon*).

Jesus appeared to Abraham, who called Him "Lord," and Jesus also appeared to Abraham's grandson, Jacob, in a dream:

> "And behold, *the **Lord** stood above it* and said: "***I am the Lord God*** of Abraham your father and the God of Isaac; the land on which you lie I will give to you and your descendants" (Gen. 28:13).

The Lord God (Jesus) spoke the same message to Moses:

> "Moreover God said to Moses, "Thus you shall say to the children of Israel: 'The **Lord God** of your fathers, the God of Abraham, the God of Isaac, and the God of Jacob, has sent me to you. ***This is My name forever***, and this is *My* memorial to all generations" (Ex. 3:15).

"Then the LORD said to Moses, "Reach out your hand and take *it* by the tail" (and he reached out his hand and caught it, and it became a rod in his hand), ⁵ that they may believe that the ***Lord God*** of their fathers, the God of Abraham, the God of Isaac, and the God of Jacob, ***has appeared to you***" (Ex. 4:4, 5).

"And God spoke to Moses and said to him: "I *am* the LORD. ³ ***I appeared to Abraham, to Isaac, and to Jacob, as God Almighty***, but by My name *Lord* [*YHWH*] I was not known to them" (Ex. 6:2, 3).

"You shall observe My judgments and keep My ordinances, to walk in them: ***I am the Lord your God***" (Lev. 18:4; 20:8).

Jesus is Lord God of the Hebrews, who appeared to Abraham, Isaac and Jacob, and revealed Himself as "the Lord God" of *their* fathers, "the God of Abraham, the God of Isaac, and the God of Jacob," "but by My name ***Lord*** (*YHWH*)" Jesus was not known to them. This was a great mystery within Judaism, yet the mystery of God revealed in Jesus Christ as Lord God was clearly revealed and made manifest to them 'if' only they had just listened to His voice, observed His ordinances and walked according to His way!

Elijah spoke this same message regarding the Lord God:

"And it came to pass, at the time of the offering of the evening sacrifice, that Elijah the prophet came near and said, "***LORD God of Abraham, Isaac, and Israel***, let it be known this day that You are God in Israel and I am Your servant, and that I have done all these things at Your word. ³⁷ Hear me, O LORD, hear me, that this people may know that You are the LORD God, and that You have turned their hearts back to You again." ³⁸ Then the fire of the LORD fell and consumed the burnt sacrifice, and the wood and the stones and the dust, and it licked up the water that was in the trench. ³⁹ Now when all the people saw it, they fell on their faces; and they said, "***The LORD, He is God! The LORD, He is God***" (1 Kings 18:36-39)

The LORD Jesus… He is God!

The Lord God appeared to Gideon and spoke…

> "And it came to pass, when the children of Israel cried out to the LORD because of the Midianites, ⁸ that the LORD sent a prophet to the children of Israel, who said to them, "Thus says the ***LORD God*** of Israel: 'I brought you up from Egypt and brought you out of the house of bondage; ⁹ and I delivered you out of the hand of the Egyptians and out of the hand of all who oppressed you, and drove them out before you and gave you their land. ¹⁰ *Also I said to you*, "*I am the LORD your God*; do not fear the gods of the Amorites, in whose land you dwell." But you have not obeyed My voice.'" ¹¹ *Now the Angel of the LORD came and sat* under the terebinth tree which *was* in Ophrah, which belonged to Joash the Abiezrite, while his son Gideon threshed wheat in the winepress, in order to hide it from the Midianites. ¹² ***And the Angel of the LORD appeared to him***, and said to him, "The LORD is with you, you mighty man of valor!" (Judges 6:7-11; Theophany #18).

Hezekiah spoke to the Lord God …

> "Then Hezekiah prayed before the LORD, and said: "O ***LORD God*** of Israel, ***the One*** who dwells between the cherubim, You are God, You alone, of all the kingdoms of the earth. You have made heaven and earth" (2 Kings 19:15).

King David spoke of Him...

> "O **Lord God** of Abraham, Isaac, and Israel, our fathers, keep this forever in the intent of the thoughts of the heart of Your people, and fix their heart toward You" (1 Chron. 29:18).

Jeremiah also spoke of Him...

> "Ah, **Lord God**! Behold, You have made the heavens and the earth by Your great power and outstretched arm. There is nothing too hard for You" (Jer. 32:17).

Therefore, this Jesus is the One, True, Living God who reveals Himself as "the God of the living." To those who refuse to hear His voice and follow after Him, He speaks in parables (Ezek. 20:49; Psa. 78:2; Matt. 13:13), but to those who desire to hear His voice and follow after Him, He calls as disciples unto Himself and reveals secrets to them so that they may understand the mysteries of the kingdom of God, but to everyone else, Jesus says:

> "I will open My mouth in parables; I will utter things kept secret from the foundation of the world" (Matt. 13:34).

> "And the disciples came and said to Him, "Why do You speak to them in parables?" [11] He [*Jesus*] answered and said to them, "Because it has been given to you [disciples] to know the mysteries of the kingdom of heaven, but to them it has not been given. [12] For whoever has, to him more will be given, and he will have abundance; but whoever does not have, even what he has will be taken away from him. [13] Therefore I speak to them in parables, because seeing they do not see, and hearing they do not hear, ***nor do they understand***" (Matt. 13:10-13).

If you *are not* a true disciple of Jesus Christ, then don't expect to understand the mysteries of the kingdom either. Jesus never kept His identity hidden from anyone when they diligently seek Him with all their heart, soul, mind and strength. Perhaps the only difference between sheep and goats is that true disciples desire to hear His voice, to thoroughly understand "the Lord who calls them," and to comprehend the spiritual reality of the kingdom that surrounds them – and therefore, they desire to follow Him and live in obedient reverence and faithfulness to the Lord God who calls them into unity and Oneness with Himself.

The Lord Your God

The first time we see this term used in the scriptures is when Moses returns to Egypt and speaks to the elders about his divine encounter with the Lord and speaks a message of deliverance that he received from the Lord for "His" people; "So the people believed; and when they heard that *the* LORD had visited the children of Israel and that He had looked on their affliction, then they bowed their heads and worshiped" (Ex. 4:31). They worshipped Jesus!!!

Jesus revealed Himself to Moses whereby He established a personal relationship with Israel as "their God" and the nation Israel bowed their heads and worshipped Him. From this moment forward, Israel refers to Jesus as "the Lord our God" and Jesus refers to Himself as "the Lord your God;" however, "By My name Lord (*YHWH*) I was not known to them" (Ex. 6:3). Even though they had experienced Him, they did not know Him personally! And thus, the God in the Bible that Israel refers to as "the Lord our God" and "the God of our fathers" is none other than Jesus Christ Himself. When anyone in Judaism comes seeking God and believes "*in* Jesus" as "the Holy One of Israel" who will save them and restore them in Oneness to God, they shall be redeemed, and delivered from the darkness, and restored into the kingdom of God through faith in Christ Jesus! JESUS IS LORD!!!

This is the main message: Jesus is Lord God over all the earth – and over all people on earth.

Jesus, Who is God Almighty, is also the Messenger *and* the Message of the kingdom, who came as the Archetype to show us the only way back to the Father – through faith in Him.

Repent – and believe – for the kingdom of heaven is at hand!

True faith that results in salvation is not just acknowledging Jesus is Lord of your life as a one-time utterance from your lips, or the intellectual ascent of an idea that merits your approval; true faith understands and thoroughly comprehends that Jesus is God, Lord God and God Almighty, whereby you submit yourself completely and entirely under His Lordship as your Master and Sovereign Savior, such that the revelation of this truth which is planted deep within your soul and consciousness compels you to thoroughly convert and turn away from the things of this world and be sanctified as someone who has been set apart for service in the kingdom of God – and therefore, you have become a true disciple of Jesus Christ and will listen *only* to Him.

Somehow, it seems, that when the church professes Jesus is Lord, they are doing this without the full knowledge that JESUS IS GOD.

Jesus called His disciples, and they stopped everything they were doing to follow the Lord.

Likewise, Jesus has called everyone to faith in Him, "to repent – and believe," but this command by Jesus is treated more like an invitation at the end of a good sermon that we accept on our terms… whereby the church has become full of lukewarm Christians who appeal to good preaching but do not regard Jesus as God. Our prayers in church are spoken only to the Father and our only regard for Christ is the by-word footnote "in the name of Jesus." Anathema!

The Gentiles worshipped according to what they did not know, and Jews knew "what" they worshipped (according to their religious laws, traditions and ordinances of men; John 4:22), but the church today worships in the knowledge of the truth without understanding "WHO" it is that calls them unto Himself into union with Himself. We boldly proclaim Jesus as Lord, but this proclamation falls eternally short of calling Him the words He used for Himself: God Almighty!

> "*I am* the Lord, your Holy One, the Creator of Israel, your King" (Isa. 43:15).
>
> "Thus says the Lord, the King of Israel, and his Redeemer, the Lord of hosts: '*I am* the First and I am the Last; **besides Me there is no God**' (Isa. 44:6).
>
> "Thus says the Lord, your Redeemer, and He who formed you from the womb: "*I am the Lord*, who makes all *things,* Who stretches out the heavens all alone, Who spreads abroad the earth *by Myself*" (Isa. 44:24).
>
> Jesus said, "*I am* the Alpha and the Omega, the Beginning and the End," says the Lord, "who is and who was and who is to come, *the Almighty*" (Rev. 1:8).
>
> "They sing the song of Moses, the servant of God, and the song of the Lamb, saying: "Great and marvelous *are* Your works, **Lord God Almighty**! Just and true *are* Your ways, O King of the saints!" (Rev. 15:3)

Read it again! Jesus is referred to as "Lord" and "Almighty" and "Lord God Almighty"!!!

> ***"But let him who glories glory in this, that he understands and knows Me, that I am the Lord**, exercising lovingkindness, judgment, and righteousness in the earth. For in these I delight," says the Lord"* (Jer. 9:24; see John 16:8-10).
>
> "Behold, ***I am the Lord**, <u>the God of all flesh</u>*. Is there anything too hard for Me?" (Jer. 32:27; Jesus is Lord *and* Redeemer of all flesh *and* creation).
>
> "And I will establish My covenant with you. ***Then you shall know that I am the Lord***" (Ezek. 16:62).
>
> "I will put sinews on you and bring flesh upon you, cover you with skin and put breath in you; and you shall live. ***Then you shall know that I am the Lord***" (Ezek. 37:6; Gen. 2:7).
>
> "***Then you shall know that I am the Lord**, when I have opened your graves, O My people, and brought you up from your graves*" (Ezek. 37:13; John 11:25).

The message about the resurrection was not fully revealed in the scriptures by the prophets, yet when Jesus was questioned by the Sadducees about the resurrection (in order to test Him because they did not believe in it – or Him), Jesus taught as one having authority because He is "the Living God" who also says of Himself "*I am* the Resurrection and the Life" (John 11:25). And this same Jesus, who is "Lord God" and "the Resurrection" is the one true living God who continues to speak the same message of life and truth to you and me today:

> "Jesus answered and said to them, "The sons of this age marry and are given in marriage. [35] But those who are counted worthy to attain that age, and the resurrection from the dead, neither marry nor are given in marriage; [36] nor can they die anymore, for

they are equal to the angels and are sons of God, being sons of the resurrection. ³⁷ But even Moses showed in the burning bush passage that the dead are raised, when he called the Lord 'the God of Abraham, the God of Isaac, and the God of Jacob.' ³⁸ *For He is not the God of the dead but of the living, **for all live to Him***" (Luke 20:34-38).

The foundational truth that Jesus is Lord God cannot be any more plain in truth than this! Jesus is "Who" created all things, Who divided the seas, Who formed us in the womb, is the same one Who raises us to newness of life because He is also "the Resurrection" and will raise the dead from the grave by the power of the Spirit. The earth is the Lord's and all therein! This earth is the Lord's – it is His footstool and it all belongs to Jesus – and everything that dwells upon the earth is His inheritance. And we are partakers of this inheritance, having become "equal to the angels and are sons of God" through faith in Christ, so as "to have a share in" the glorious riches of His inheritance (Eph. 1:18).

The earth is His dominion – and His kingdom will never end. The Father put all things into His hands… and now Jesus is delighted to give all things to us, through faith in Christ (Rom. 8:32; 2 Pet. 1:3), and Jesus will put all things under our feet as we reign *with* Him (Psa. 8:6).

What greater testimony is this, than to know that this entire world belongs to Jesus; He created it!!! Having been thoroughly persuaded and convinced that Jesus is God and He desires to give us "all things," whereby He lives in our heart through faith (Eph. 3:17), "and He has put eternity in your heart" as well (Eccl. 3:11), so, let me ask you just one question: what more could a loving God do than die for you – so that God Himself (Jesus Christ) could live in you?

Well, that is exactly what God in Christ Jesus did! He died for you so that you could live in oneness with Him! And this is the mystery of grace: God in Christ Jesus did it all because we were unable to do any of it.

> "Likewise you also, reckon yourselves to be dead indeed to sin, but alive to God in Christ Jesus our Lord" (Rom. 6:11).

> "For we are not, as so many, peddling the word of God; but as of sincerity, but as from God, we speak in the sight of God in Christ" (2 Cor. 2:17).

Jesus is Lord; however, we speak this truth in church without any first century context of what "Lord, Master, Sovereign" means. Therefore, we need to see every act done by God in the Bible as Jesus doing it – in oneness with the Father. We need to understand and thoroughly comprehend the spiritual reality of who Jesus is: Jesus Christ is Lord, Messiah, the Holy One of Israel, Christ, the Anointed One, Lord God, Lord Almighty, God Almighty, the Alpha and the Omega, the Beginning and the End, the Creator of Israel, the King of Israel, the Lord of hosts, Creator, Redeemer, Deliverer, Son of God – and Savior who takes away the sin of the world.

If we had this frame of mind, Jesus would no longer be just a footnote to our prayers.

King of kings and Lord of lords – Jesus – the Name above all names!!!

And yet, the message we hear in church on Sunday sounds more like a desperate plea for sinners to please-please invite Jesus into your heart to be your Savior without any comprehension that Jesus is God Himself, who lives in Oneness with the Father, who laid down His life and picked it up again, and *not* merely the Son of God whom we treat like a second-class, less-than version of the Almighty Father, who yielded His life into the hands of unregenerate sinners to become a sacrificial offering unto God so we can go to 'sweet by-and-by' heaven on greasy-grace terms.

Jesus is God Most High, in Oneness with the Father... and there is no other God! And He is the only God anyone on this earth has ever known!

We are surrounded by such a great cloud of witnesses who know this truth and have walked in the Way, but to the church on earth, this truth seems to have become shrouded in mystery by the spirit of institutional religion that focuses on the Father or Mary while disrespecting Jesus as Lord God Almighty! How can you resist so great a love as His? He came to earth and allowed Himself to be tortured and murdered so that you might live in Oneness with Him! Does this point put it into better perspective? Can you begin to fathom so great a love as this... that He would come to earth and offer His life unto death so that you can have a personal relationship with Him and eternal salvation?

He is only your Savior if you also make Him Lord and Sovereign of your entire life!

Do you believe? I mean, do you really, really believe and thoroughly comprehend this teaching? Jesus didn't come to earth to die upon a cross to establish a new religion so that everyone in this spiritual fraternity gets to go to heaven on account of what we believe. Eternal life is not based upon "what" you believe... but upon "Who" is abiding within you as your Lord and Master.

Are you living wholly unto Jesus? Have you been consecrated and set apart, by grace through faith, with this same Jesus who is "Lord God" and "the Lord your God," who says of Himself:

> "Thus **I will magnify Myself and sanctify Myself**,
> and I will be known in the eyes of many nations.
> *Then they shall know that **I am the Lord**"* (Ezek.
> 38:23; 36:23; John 17:19; 10:36; who commands us
> "to make disciples of all nations")

Jesus will magnify Himself in the eyes of many nations, and *then* they shall know Him as "the Lord." Jesus is not just *YHWH* "the God who sees" (Gen. 6:5), but He is also "the God who is seen," and all nations *will* bow down and worship Him (Psa. 86:9; Rev. 15:4)

Now, consider this: the Father is holy and never needed to sanctify Himself. Jesus, the Son of God, is also holy, and He is the Holy One of Israel and the Righteous One, yet He was sanctified by the Father (John 10:36) and Jesus sanctified Himself (John 17:19) in fulfillment of the scriptures (Ezek. 38:23). Everything upon the earth must be sanctified regardless of sin or not – as "something" that must be called out from the darkness into the kingdom of light. So then, sanctification is not the process of salvation; it is the process whereby God's glory is being revealed in us and through us, as His "called out" consecrated and set-apart ones – for His glory. Therefore, sanctification is the reuniting of men into Oneness with the Father, through faith in the Son, by the workings of the Spirit in us and through us.

> "Speak also to the children of Israel, saying: 'Surely My Sabbaths you shall keep, for it is a sign between Me and you throughout your generations, that you may know that I am the Lord who *sanctifies* you" (Ex. 31:13; Lev. 11:44; Ezek. 20:12, 20; also see Lev. 19:30; 26:2; Mark 2:27).

> "And I will sanctify ***My*** great name, which has been profaned among the nations, which you have profaned in their midst; and the nations shall know that I *am* the LORD," says the Lord GOD, "when I am *hallowed* [*sanctified*] ***in you*** before their eyes" (Ezek. 36:23).

> "For both He who sanctifies and those who are being sanctified *are all of one*, for which reason He [*Jesus*] is not ashamed to call them brethren" (Heb. 2:11).

Thus, sanctification is not about us; it is happening in us and to us on account of Jesus Christ, who is Lord God *and* Lord Jehovah our

Sanctifier, who has called (and chosen) us so that He may sanctify us, abide within us – and be revealed to all nations through us.

Thus, the spiritual renewal process through (into) sanctification whereby we are being saved out of the kingdom of darkness into the kingdom of God's glory can be summarized as follows:

- We have been commanded to "believe," so we must believe, having been thoroughly persuaded and convinced that Jesus is God, Lord, Master, Christ and Savior (faith)
- We must repent from our rebellion and unbelief (sin), and turn toward God (salvation)
- We must become a new creation (born anew by the Holy Spirit) to live in spirit and in truth through faith in Jesus Christ in order *to understand* the spiritual reality of God's kingdom that surrounds us (John 3:3)
- We must be transformed and continuously changed (converted) by the Holy Spirit's renewing of our mind so that the Lord can dwell in us as a sign to all around us, including nations, regarding Whose we are (sanctification)
- We shall be become like Him and then become eternally one with Him (glorification)

Newness through truth, change and oneness is what our salvation in Jesus Christ is all about!

It's all about Jesus – and God gets the glory!!! Amen!

Believe and repent – Jesus is Lord God – and the kingdom of heaven is at hand! If there is any question in your mind thus far about the majestic divinity and power of Jesus because of much toxic theology you have been taught by institutionalized religion, then now is *your* time to "believe and repent" in Jesus Christ – and be "born anew from above" by the Spirit of Christ!

Do it now! Call upon Jesus to manifest Himself to you… or do you prefer darkness over light?

Jesus – Lord of Israel

> "As for our Redeemer, the LORD of hosts is His name, The Holy One of Israel" (Isa. 47:4).

> "It shall be, in regard to their inheritance, that *I am* their inheritance. You shall give them no possession in Israel, for *I am* their possession" (Ezek. 44:28).

Jesus is our Lord and Redeemer, and Jesus is the Holy One of Israel. Jesus created all things, and all people, and for this reason "the Lord of hosts is His name." Jesus calls Himself "the Lord of hosts" to signify His preeminence as Creator of the host of heaven (angels) and the host of earth (men) (see Gen. 2:1) which at least one Bible translation failed to properly translate 235 times (NIV), and in doing so, did much harm to an entire generation of believers who grew up in Christ without any understanding regarding this principal identify of Jesus, nor any understanding what or who "the host of heaven and earth" are! The sons of men *are* the host of earth, and there is an earthly dominion reason why we were created as the host of the earth and put on the earth for that purpose.[10] Now, back on point...

Jesus is Lord God and the Holy One of Israel! Oh, how my heart grieves for Israel, who did not recognize their Lord in the day of His visitation. He chose them, covenanted with them, tabernacled with them, dwelt among them, and even today, His promises to her are eternal – if only she would repent and believe that Jesus is Lord and Messiah – ***then*** He would fulfill all His promises according to the covenant which He made with them.

And oh, how my heart grieves for the institutional church; it talks a good talk and proclaims sacred assemblies, but it does not know that from beginning to end, that it is all about Jesus. Oh, how my heart grieves, that they do not even recognize their Savior anymore; they pray to Father God and declare all things in the

---

[10] Read "Dominion" the third book in the Image Bearer series by the author.

Father's name, only to put the three-word punctuation at the end of every prayer – "In Jesus' Name" – as if God will now supply all their needs according to His riches in glory through the Jesus buzz-word, yet somehow, completely ignoring their need for the divine relationship *by* abiding in His presence as disciples of Jesus! The riches and the inheritance and the glory of this world all belongs to Jesus Christ, for He alone is the glory, the honor, the majesty, Lord God, King of kings and Lord of lords – the Almighty!

> "*I am* the living bread which came down from heaven. If anyone eats of this bread, he will live forever; and the bread that I shall give is My flesh, which I shall give for the life of the world." (John 6:51; meditate on this profound verse).
>
> "*I* am the vine, you *are* the branches. He who abides in Me, and I in him, bears much fruit; ***for without Me you can do nothing***" (John 15:5).
>
> "*I* am the Alpha and the Omega, *the* Beginning and *the* End," says the Lord, "who is and who was and who is to come, ***the* Almighty**." (Rev. 1:8).

Jesus is Lord. Jesus is God. Jesus is Creator. Jesus is the Life. Jesus is Almighty! Jesus is the Center of it all – and in Him all things are held together! Jesus is the Living Bread which He gave for the life of the world. Jesus is the Bread which came down from heaven (manna) and the Spirit of Jesus is the fountain of living water. Jesus only – and now the church needs to return to this fundamental teaching in order for the truth to be made known to all nations. We are entering into a time in history when this truth will be attacked by the spirit of darkness in more vile, venomous and vitriolic ways never imagined. The days of evil are coming to an end, but before the end comes, evil will become more violent, hateful, vengeful and soul-consuming because evil exists for three purposes: to annihilate life, to obliterate truth, and to hinder the restoration of the kingdom of God upon the earth – and thus, violent men manifesting evil are taking it forcefully for themselves!

> "And from the days of John the Baptist *until now* the kingdom of heaven suffers violence, and the violent take it by force" (Matt. 11:12).

Jesus came proclaiming "the kingdom of heaven is at hand." Jesus came to establish the kingdom of heaven in the earth, as well as in the heart and soul of faithful followers – in the hearts of all who will hear the truth and believe. The revelation of this kingdom began with John the Baptist, who was the messenger sent ahead to prepare the way for the Messiah and to announce the eminent revelation of Jesus. Jesus came to establish His kingdom and to proclaim a kingdom that will never perish, as *the kingdom* that will never end. The kingdom of heaven is relationship-based, not place-based or time-based… because Jesus *represents the manifest* kingdom of heaven *as the manifest* King of heaven – and this can be discerned by reading the above verse again. Jesus created all things, including heaven; Jesus is the King and Jesus is the Kingdom. The Alpha and the Omega and the Beginning and the End – is all about Jesus! And all things were created by Him, through Him – and for Him.

This world may seem like it is coming apart at the seams, but faithful ones – know this, and believe this: Jesus is in control. Jesus is victorious! Trust in Him – believe – and do not doubt!

IMAGE

Jesus Knew His Identity

Jesus did not have to come to earth to learn who He was; He always knew. Jesus did not need to prove who He was: He already was and always is I AM. Jesus did not seem concerned with convincing anyone about His mission from the Father; He simply said, "I AM." Jesus knew all things, and in this capacity, He was able to be Who He was commissioned to be. And the same is true with you and me. It is vitally essential for us to know Who Jesus is – *in order for us to know who we are in Christ* – so that we can come to faith in Him and operate in oneness with the Father – and do what we were sent to accomplish on the earth.

Let's look at two scriptures to understand even more that Jesus knew all things – including His Lordship. Jesus *never* referred to His Father as Lord God, so this should be a great indication to authenticate who Jesus is... and who the scriptures refer to as "the Lord God;" however, He does mention His Father as "*Lord*" on one occasion – for a specific reason...

> "At that time Jesus answered and said, "I thank You, *Father, Lord of heaven and earth*, that You have hidden these things from the wise and prudent and have revealed them to babes. ²⁶ Even so, Father, for so it seemed good in Your sight. ²⁷ *All things have been delivered to Me* by My Father, and no one knows the Son except the Father. Nor does anyone know the Father except the Son, and the one to whom the Son wills to reveal Him." (Matt. 11:25-27; Luke 10:21, 22; John 3:35; 5:27:17:2)

In essence, Jesus said, 'My Father is Lord – and He has given heaven and earth, and all things, and all authority, to Me. Therefore, believe... *I am* Lord of heaven and earth.'

This is highly significant, since there are some who question the authenticity and authority of Jesus in this regard, so Jesus made it plain as peanut butter: The Lord of heaven and earth has delivered this Lordship "to Me" because *I am*, always, without beginning or end, and forever will be – Lord of heaven and earth.

> "For David himself said by the Holy Spirit: 'The Lord said to *my* Lord, "Sit at My right hand, Till I make Your enemies Your footstool"'" (Mark 12:36; Psa. 110:1; Matt. 22:44; Luke 20:42; Acts 2:34).

Jesus is telling us with tremendous emphasis encoded within this high octane declaration – I am Lord of All! And so it is, from Genesis to Revelation, Jesus is Lord of all – Lord of all people, Lord of the earth, Lord of all creation, and Jesus is the Lord of hosts of heaven and earth (Gen. 2:1; Acts 10:36; Rev. 4:11; 17:14; 19:16).

Jesus is telling us His Father is Lord of heaven and earth – *AND* – the Father delivered all things to Him, including the Lordship of heaven and earth. (God Most High delivered heaven and earth to His Son, Lord God Almighty).

So now, if you need wisdom in this area, then ask Jesus for wisdom and understanding, and He will liberally give wisdom to all without reproach, as long as you don't ask with predetermined doubt concerning Jesus as Lord, Christ and Messiah (James 1:5, 6). If you need wisdom, or desire to know *and* understand anything, or you need anything, then we are to ask Jesus – because Jesus is our Lord *and* Teacher, and then, in all things, give praise and thanksgiving to the Father.

> "And whatever you ask in My name, that I will do, ***that the Father may be glorified in the Son***. If you ask anything in My name, I will do it" (John 14:13, 14).

There was just one time in which it appears there is some confusion about the Lordship of Jesus, which is when He tells His disciples to pray "the Father" *even after* He told them to ask for all things in His name. However, when we examine closely the original Greek words, we clearly see why Jesus told His disciples to pray in this manner, but it was only for one specific point of time – which was during His death and burial when no one could talk with Him.

> "And in that day you will *ask* (*erotao*) Me *nothing* (*no question*). Most assuredly, I say to you, whatever you *ask* (*aiteo*) the Father in My name He will give you. [24] Until now you have *asked* (*aiteo*) nothing in My name. *Ask* (*aiteo*), and you will receive, that your joy may be full" (John 16:23, 24).

"Jesus was referring to a specific time during His death and burial as one moment in time when they (the disciples) would not be able to *ask* Him any question (*erotao* – to ask as a friend and companion on equal footing). At that specific time, during His absence, Jesus told them to *ask* the Father (*aiteo*– as suppliants on a lesser footing), but after the resurrection, they could *ask* (*aiteo*) Jesus anything, thereby acknowledging His supremacy, Divinity and Lordship. Jesus is our Lord, so ask Him and you will receive from HIM so that your joy may be full. Then in all things, give thanks and glory and praise to the Father." [11]

Jesus is our Teacher! Jesus is Lord of heaven and earth and we have been instructed by Christ Himself to approach the throne of grace to ask Him, Who is seated at the right hand of the Father, for Divine assistance whenever we have need. The earth is the dominion of the Lord Jesus, and it is time to recognize and honor the will of the Father in this regard as an expression of His delegated authority to His Son. All things have been delivered to Jesus, but it seems we keep running to Abba Daddy when Jesus tells us to do things we do not want to do. This must stop!!!

All authority in heaven and earth has been given to Jesus. Period! Now is the time to live accordingly, with Jesus as our Lord, Master *and* Teacher, that is, *if* you desire to be His disciple.

---

[11] Copied from Regenesis, p. 222.

"And Jesus came and spoke to them, saying, "All authority has been given to Me in heaven and on earth" (Matt. 28:18).

"But why do you call Me 'Lord, Lord,' and not do the things which I say?" (Luke 6:46).

"Not everyone who says to Me, 'Lord, Lord,' shall enter the kingdom of heaven, but he who does the will of My Father in heaven. [22] Many will say to Me in that day, 'Lord, Lord, have we not prophesied in Your name, cast out demons in Your name, and done many wonders in Your name?' [23] And then I will declare to them, 'I never knew you; depart from Me, you who practice lawlessness!'" (Matt. 7:21-23; other scriptures include Mal. 1:6; Nah. 1:7; Matt. 25:12; Luke 13:25-27; John 10:14; 1 Cor. 8:3; 13:12; 2 Cor. 5:12; Gal. 4:9; 2 Tim. 2:19).

"Then the King [Jesus] will say to those on His right hand, 'Come, you blessed of My Father, inherit the kingdom prepared for you from the foundation of the world" (Matt. 25:34).

If Jesus is your Lord, then take Him seriously and do what He says. "Take My yoke [of obedience and truth] upon you – and learn from Me." Jesus is our Teacher, Administrator and Intercessor of the New Covenant, He has all authority, and is able to act on His own accord – as Lord of heaven and earth (Isa. 44:24; Matt. 28:18; John 10:17, 18; 15:10; 17:2). Why, then, do we keep putting priests and pastors upon the teaching pedestal in the substitutionary place of Christ Himself? And again, I say, this must stop!

We have been living the past 2,000 years with a tepid halfway-house type Judeo-Christian theology... it is half Judaism that does not know Jesus is God – and half Christian that professes Jesus as Lord but focuses all attention on God the Father. Jesus is God Almighty and He came to earth to show us the way and the truth, and Jesus taught us (by example) how to live in reverent obedience and relationship to God, as someone living subordinately under the authority of God. Jesus referred to His Father as the One He was submitted to, and since there was no one greater than Himself to submit to,[12] He taught us by His example to "say and do" as someone subordinate to a Greater Authority. In order to properly teach us as by example as the Archetype of the better way, Jesus was placed in a subordinate role in submission to the Father, as a Son, so that we could live according to this template as disciples subordinate to Jesus Christ; but instead, the church seems to submit only to a Father God they cannot see, yet perceives Jesus only from His earthly example whereupon His life is celebrated and glorified by His reconciling death and shed blood upon the cross and, umm, oh yes, His subsequent resurrection.

Now therefore, we need to see ***Jesus as the God of the entire Bible***, not just the Author of a New Covenant but the Author and Mediator and Intercessor of all covenants and agreements with mankind. Jesus is the Lord and we also need to perceive Him as OUR God in manifest glory!

Let this truth sink way down within your Christian consciousness:

- There is only one mediator between God and man – and His name is Jesus Christ (1 Tim. 2:5); "Now a mediator does not mediate for one only, but *God is **one**"* (Gal. 3:20).
- There is only one covenant maker between God and man – and His name is Jesus Christ (Gen. 17:1-4; Judges 2:1-5 (Theophany 17); Luke 22:20; Rom. 11:27; Heb. 8:6,13; 10:6)
- There is only one way to come to the Father – so if you want to approach the Father, then this is only possible through Jesus Christ (John 14:6)
- Eternal life and salvation only comes through Jesus Christ (1 Thess. 5:9; 2 Tim. 3:15)

---

[12] To see this in greater clarity, refer to Abraham's encounter with Melchizedek.

- JESUS IS LORD!!!

This is the good news of the gospel regarding the kingdom of God: ***Jesus is Lord and God***!!!

Jesus was not promoted to become Lord because of the resurrection, Jesus has always been Lord and God since before He even created the heavens and the earth. But what gospel has the church adopted? The hybrid gospel message teaches all *followers* of Christ to "only say and do" what the Father says and does, thereby disregarding Christ all together by turning believers of Christ into *followers* of the Father. Our doctrines teach us to believe in Jesus whereby we become children of the Father, but we are rarely taught the most important and vital interim step: ***be a disciple of Jesus***. Why do we skip over this part? Jesus told us to follow Him and to imitate Him, not imitate Him imitating the Father! It seems the church is disregarding Christ except to acknowledge Him when two or more are gathered in His name and then boldly declare all our needs met with the authorized three-word footnote "in Jesus' name." Jesus is not only God, Jesus is Lord and God of the entire Bible; He is OUR GOD and OUR GOD REIGNS!!!

Jesus showed us that He did the Father's will in servant obedience as a yielded vessel in order to teach us how to live so that we could thoroughly comprehend how to live in friendship and servant obedience to our Lord and Master Jesus Christ. Jesus is our Example for us to imitate, so likewise, we are to submit unto Jesus, as yielded subordinate vessels to do God's will ***under*** the Lordship and Authority of Jesus Christ (John 5:30; 6:38; 1 Pet. 2:21).

Just as Jesus came, and only said and did according to the will of the Father, likewise we are to walk in obedience to Jesus Christ, and only say and do what Jesus tells us to say and do. This does not dishonor the Father when we operate in a "Jesus only" manner; on the contrary, when we say and do what Jesus commands us to do, then we are glorifying the Father by giving glory and honor to the Son. This is the will of the Father, so now it's time to stop thinking in patriarchal terms and to start thinking and doing obediently what Jesus commands us to do!

> "The centurion answered and said, "Lord, I am not worthy that You should come under my roof. But only speak a word, and my servant will be healed. [9] ***For I also am a man under authority***, having soldiers under me. And I say to this one, 'Go,' and he goes; and to another, 'Come,' and he comes; and to my servant, 'Do this,' and he does it." [10] When Jesus heard it, He marveled, and said to those who followed, "Assuredly, I say to you, I have not found ***such great faith***, not even in Israel!" (Matt. 8:8-10).

Go now – and do likewise. In the authority Jesus has given you – "do all that He tells you."

IF – You Are the Son of God

Many of us are familiar with the story when Jesus was led by the Holy Spirit into the wilderness to be tempted by Satan (Matt. 4:4). Why did the Spirit lead Jesus, who was filled with the Spirit, into the wilderness to be tempted? How do we know this happened since there were no disciples to witness it? And why did Satan only ask three questions during this forty-day period?

These are all good questions, which we will get to in subsequent sections, including the question that was raised in Regenesis: did Satan know who Jesus is? Satan did not know because the identity of the Messiah was kept hidden from everyone, and known only to the Father, so his questions "If you are the Son of God" are quite relevant. However, putting these questions aside for a moment, let's take another look at the answers that Jesus gives to Satan, and this time, let's look at it from the perspective of Jesus, *from His perspective*, as Lord of all, God – and Christ.

"*If* you are the Son of God, command that these stones become bread." But He [Jesus] answered and said, "*It is written*, "Man shall not live by bread alone, but by every [*rhema*] word that proceeds from the mouth of God.'" Jesus is telling us many things folded within His first response to Satan, but I want us to key in on one aspect: Jesus refers to Himself while in oneness with the Father – as God, who spoke the word (*rhema* utterance) that proceeds from Him, just as Jesus also tells us that He is the only begotten of the Father, who proceeds forth from Him (John 8:42; 17:8; Deut. 4:4) and this is why Jesus is called the "Logos" the Living Word and the incarnate Word of God. Jesus could say this because He knew who His Father is and because He knew who He is, as one who proceeded forth… as having come from the Oneness of God. Satan was tempting Jesus to do a miraculous work of God (turning stones onto bread) as an action independent from hearing God's voice and then doing it on His own initiative. This is what Satan successfully tempted Adam and Eve to do in the Garden, so as to do a good thing, but do it independently (apart from Oneness in Union with God) from the "hearing of rhema words that proceeds from the mouth of God." And furthermore, Jesus is the mouth of God.

"*If* you are the Son of God, throw yourself down." And Jesus said to him, "*It is written again*, 'You shall not tempt the Lord your God.'" Jesus knows that Satan knows the scriptures because he has just quoted Psalm 91 – twice, but he does not *understand* the scriptures, having been blinded in his ability to understand because of sin. Faithful ones, if we are blinded by sin, we will not understand the scriptures either, nor will we be able to see clearly the same thing that Jesus just told Satan: "You shall not tempt Me – I am the Lord your God!"

"Again, the devil took Him up on an exceedingly high mountain, and showed Him all the kingdoms of the world and their glory… All these things I will give You *if* You will fall down and worship me." Then Jesus said to him, "Away with you, Satan! For it is written, 'You shall worship **the Lord your God**, and Him only you shall serve.'" How incredibly powerful and sublimely magnificent are these words of Jesus! Jesus is "the Lord your God," so worship Jesus and "*Him* only you shall serve." Allow this deep truth to wash over your soul to transform you by the renewing of your mind according to power of the Holy Spirit at work within you.

He, Him, His – as *Himself*

Jesus referred to Himself as "He, Him, His" on many occasions: "God created man in ***His*** *own* image" (Gen. 1:27; the image of Jesus, since God is spirit only). "And I say to you, My friends, do not be afraid of those who kill the body, and after that have no more that they can do. ⁵ But I will show you whom you should fear: Fear **Him** who, after He has killed, has power to cast into hell; yes, I say to you, fear **Him**" (Luke 12:4, 5). And also… "Jesus answered and said to her, "If you knew the gift of God, and who it is who says to you, 'Give **Me** a drink,' you would have asked **Him**, and **He** would have given you living water'" (John 4:10).

> "Jesus said to him, "You shall love the Lord your God with all your heart, with all your soul, and with all your mind.'" (Matt. 22:37; please keep in mind that Jesus *is* the Lord your God).

The first thing we learn from Jesus is that He is who He says He is: the Christ of God, the Holy One, the only begotten Son of God, the Word made flesh, Lord God, the Lord your God, Creator, and the Son of Man (His title upon the earth). The second thing we learn is to worship Him – and Him *only* shall we serve. The third thing we learn is how to use our only offensive weapon against Satan, the Sword of Truth, which is the Word of God (Eph. 6:17): "It is written…"

If we do not know what the scriptures mean, then we are at an incredible disadvantage against our adversary, the devil, Satan, our principal enemy, who seeks to devour us with lies, deception and half-truth; however – *if* we understand and comprehend what the scriptures teach, then Satan is at an incredible disadvantage because he is not able to understand the scriptures, nor will he be able to withstand us when we come against him with Biblical truth.

If any scriptures or prophecy has been veiled from our understanding, then only those saints who have the Holy Spirit working within them will be able to understand and discern what is happening or what will happen, which puts the enemy at an incredible disadvantage, especially regarding the end times.

> "Resist the devil and he will flee from you" (James 4:7; and now, within the larger context…)

> "Therefore, submit to God. Resist the devil and he will flee from you. Draw near to God and He will draw near to you. Cleanse your hands, you sinners, and purify your hearts, you double-minded." (James 4:7-9).

The first thing we must do, in all things, is to submit to God by declaring Jesus "as Lord God" and draw near to Him. Then, we need to come against the enemy with 1) understanding in our mind, 2) the Word of God, 3) clean hands and a purified heart, and 4) single-mindedness in our God-given mission and commission. Most importantly, we must remove any double-mindedness regarding the identity of Christ Jesus our Lord!

Now, once again, let's get this revival thing moving – for it is time for us to have dominion!

Only Three Things – and A Fourth

There are only three things I desire: 1) to know Jesus – 2) *and* the power of His resurrection:

> "and be found in Him, not having my own righteousness, which is from the law, but that which is through faith in Christ, the righteousness which is from God by faith; [10] *that I may know Him and the power of His resurrection*, and the fellowship of His sufferings, being conformed to His death, [11] if, by any means, I may attain to the resurrection from the dead" (Phil. 3:9-11).

3) And the exceeding greatness and glory that resides in Him – as He dwells in me:

> "...that Christ may dwell in your hearts through faith; that you, being rooted and grounded in love, *^{18} may be able to comprehend with all the saints what is the width and length and depth and height— ^{19} to know the love of Christ* which passes knowledge; *that you may be filled with all the fullness of God*" (Eph. 3:17-19).

And fourthly... the fellowship of His suffering. This is not a popular topic, but it is extremely important and one which will be discussed within the context of having dominion in "Image Bearers: Commission."

It seems now, more than ever before in history, we need to fully comprehend the reality of Who Jesus is – and who we are in Christ. More than just our Savior and Redeemer... Jesus is the very breath we breathe. You were created by Jesus, He created the air that you breathe and He breathed His "breath of life" into you, and this is the Spirit of life in Christ Jesus that operates within us even now.

> "And *the LORD God [Jesus]* formed man of the dust of the ground, and breathed into his nostrils the breath of life; and man became a living soul" (Gen. 2:7).

Jesus created the air and the dust, and Jesus created man and breathed into him the breath of life through his nostrils. Man was already a soul with life – but at this moment, man became a living soul as a spiritual being inhabiting human form. Now, in order to stimulate an epiphany in your mind, let me remind you that the breath of life that is being breathed into every man – is Jesus Himself. Jesus said, "I am the Way, the Truth and the Life." Jesus created everything – and He is the Life of all living things. Jesus created everything for Himself and He created us for several reasons, but the main reason is this: to inhabit us as living tabernacles, to manifest His presence in us and through us, and to crown us with glory and honor as a testimony against the spirit of darkness on the earth.

Jesus is already in us on account of the life that is within us, but we must yield our lives to Him in order for Him to be Lord of our life. We must get off our throne and then exalt Him upon it.

This is really not that difficult to understand – unless you only see Jesus from a human perspective, as just a godly man. Jesus is God, who created the earth, then came to the earth He created and had a human experience with the very people He created.

Well, perhaps this is why you find life perplexing – because you perceive yourself as a human being rather than as a spiritual being having a human experience. The thorough understanding of "who" Jesus is or who you are – cannot be known or comprehended from a human perspective; it must be encountered and experienced from a spiritual perspective, with understanding given by way of the Spirit according to the birthing anew by the Spirit, as someone who is being guided and Spirit-led into all truth *and* understanding by the Spirit (John 3:3-8).

Jesus also came to establish the kingdom of heaven on the earth, and since that time, heaven has been completely open since the resurrection of Jesus. This word "open" is '*dianoigo*,' meaning: to be thoroughly open, not as a window or door can be opened and closed, but completely open – never to close again. A way between heaven and earth has been thoroughly open for the past 2,000 years and, now, Christ is being revealed according to the Spirit of truth so that we may completely know everything about Jesus – from Beginning to End!

Have You Ever Wondered

Have you ever stopped to wonder why the Lord Jesus created the heavens and earth, then came to earth as a man, to completely open heaven to us so that the inhabitants of earth could have an open and unrestricted access to Jesus in a thoroughly open heaven?

Jesus is not just a historical figure who dramatically changed the world more than any other person that ever lived. Jesus didn't just make history – He didn't just change history – Jesus is history – because history itself is all about Him and *HisStory* (sic). Jesus was inserted into human history at just the right time, in the fullness of time, because this was the Father's plan, ever since the beginning in the Garden. Nothing is out of place, time or sequence in the kingdom of God! Everything is as it should be.

He came, He died, and He arose – so that we may be united to the Father again.

One day, early on in my listening phase, as I was reading, John 10:17 leaped off the page at me. The inherent meaning was so profound that I thought a great mystery had been revealed only to me, so I did not share it right way, as if I was not to casually share this truth with just anyone unless the Lord directed me to do so (this is just how primitive my concept of Christ was).

> "Therefore My Father loves Me, because I lay down My life that I may take it again. [18] No one takes it from Me, but I lay it down of Myself. *I have power to lay it down, and I have power to take it again.* This command I have received from My Father" (John 10:17, 18)

How could Jesus have the power to lay down His life and pick it up again? I was still thinking and perceiving the truth about Jesus in earthly human terms, even though the Spirit of truth was within me, I only knew in part – and had not yet come to the full understanding of who Jesus is. Jesus is God, He knew what was going to happen and He already knows everything that is going to happen – from beginning to end. He knew He had to lay down His life and He had the power to pick it up again in order to accomplish His third mission parameter: take away the sin of the world.

He already knows you and who you are – from the inside out – and the Lord Jesus wants to abide in you, but He wants you to be you. He created you to be someone very unique, extraordinary and unlike anyone else, so, just be you… and let Him be Christ in you and through you.

The Lord God is already in you. He is your future and your past, your beginning and your end. He breathed the breath of life in you and you became a living soul – and all your days have been numbered (Psa. 139:16). Now, He is calling all men to this understanding so that you do not need to ask others about Him; His Spirit is already at work in us, but we must yield to the Holy Spirit and to the effects of sanctification, whereby the Spirit will guide you into all truth and reveal the truth that you need. Heaven is completely open and you are breathing His atmosphere and are walking on His earth and you are partaking of His creation. You do not need to strive to earn His love and affection, but only – abide in Him. Jesus is already in you… but you need to seek Him and find Him by opening the door of your heart to Him and make Him Lord and Sovereign of your life. He is not very far away, for indeed, the kingdom of heaven is at hand; the kingdom of God is in your midst; and if this kingdom of God is within you (Luke 17:21) – then all you need to do is open your heart to Jesus – and walk in it. The Holy Spirit will take care of the rest.

There is a predetermined (predestination) plan for all of us, but we must walk in (enter into) it. There have always been two paths along this pathway of life – yet this choice is yours alone:

- Plan A) "There is a way that seems right to a man, but its end is the way of death" (Psa. 14:12; 16:25), or
- Plan B) "Trust in the LORD with all your heart, and lean not on your own understanding; in all your ways acknowledge Him, and He shall direct your paths" (Prov. 3:5, 6).

> "Choose for yourselves this day whom you will
> serve... but as for me and my house, we will serve
> the LORD (Joshua 24:15).

Whichever path you take is your choice – and yours alone, for the Lord God will never deny you free will and your individual sovereignty to rule over your own life, but if you choose plan B, then it begins by totally surrendering your sovereign will over to Him so that He can reveal the fullness of His purpose and His plan for your life to you. There can only be one sovereign for your life, so if Jesus Christ is your Sovereign, then give your life completely into His trustworthy and lovingkindness hands, but know this – you cannot keep standing in between two ways; either Jesus is Lord God of your life, or He isn't. Luke-warm in-between is merely an illusion... and yet this choice is also yours.

Why Do You Think

So, why do you think this truth is being revealed at this time? Because these are the last days...

The Spirit of Man Revealed

The reason these things have been written and recorded is for you to believe Jesus is who He said He is (John 6:29), so that you thoroughly believe Jesus is Lord – *and* live accordingly. Jesus was more than just a good man who lived a sinless life; He is *the* perfect Man who became *our* example whereby we might imitate Him. Jesus is not restricted by the dimensions of time, space and place, but for the short time that He was on earth, He operated within these parameters just like you and me. He retained His Divine nature, as well as His glory, yet in all manner of things, He operated from *'his spirit'* to show us how to live – as men in the flesh and living this life through our spirit according to the Holy Spirit – in the hope that we might remember who we are – and live accordingly, as spiritual beings and sons and daughters of God.

We know that Jesus is Lord and we know that , but have you ever wondered why Jesus was led by the Spirit into the wilderness to be tempted by Satan? Or, why, after the temptation, Jesus returned in the power of the Spirit (v.14)? Why did Jesus, since He is God, need to be filled with the Holy Spirit (Luke 4:1)? Doesn't all this spirit-stuff seem redundant if Jesus is already fully God Himself "in whom the Godhead dwelt bodily"?

Yes, indeed, it does, because Jesus is living His life as an example – *for us*, as a manifest demonstration to show us how to live according to the way of the spirit within us. Jesus chose to live this earthen experience in the manner of all flesh, as a man, with soul and spirit, not as a powerful expression of Lord God Almighty, but as a meek and lowly expression of God being revealed in man through the spirit within him. Everything Jesus did was done as an ordinary man operating through His spirit-man partnered *with* the Holy Spirit, so that we can learn from this Way and also live exactly as Jesus lived. Like Jesus, as our example and our Archetype, we can live according to His example as spiritual people with the Holy Spirit dwelling with our spirit, so that when we are filled with the Holy Spirit, we can operate as well from our spirit-man – in the power and fullness of the Spirit – like Jesus.

This is the most important point of this book, so be sure to comprehend this concept thoroughly.

We are spiritual beings who are having a human experience, as the host of earth, and through our spirit that resides within us, we are able to live according to the way Jesus taught us and demonstrated to us – and likewise, we may be filled with the Holy Spirit and then live this life in the power of the Spirit, which Jesus referred to as "the way."

The reason why some people still have a hard time comprehending who Jesus really is stems from 2,000 years of religious teaching by religious institutions that have bowed to the spirit of religion and the spirit of control. If the deceiver can prevent us from knowing and understanding "Who" Jesus really is, as well as prevent us from knowing who we really are (that we are spiritual beings sent by the Lord as the host of earth to have dominion over the earth), and prevent us from comprehending why the Holy Spirit was sent so that we may do greater works through our spirit-man, then the spirit of religion (and Satan) is all too happy to tell us how to live like good little Christians that keeps us in bondage to rules, doctrines and ordinances created by men… without ever understanding WHY! And he is all too happy to let us pray to Mary and whomever as "any other way" to keep our focus off of Jesus – and doing the Father's will.

This has got to stop now!

Almighty God

We have already learned that no one has ever seen the Father and He does not have a physical form (John 1:18; 6:46; Rom. 1:20; Col. 1:15), so therefore, all the physical manifestations of God in the scriptures are Jesus, and now – we must come to terms with knowing Almighty Jesus. I always perceived Jesus and God as One, but up until only a short while ago, I thought of the Father as Lord Almighty – until I re-read the second appearance of Jesus to Abraham.

> "When Abram was ninety-nine years old, ***the LORD appeared*** to Abram and said to him, "***I am Almighty God*** (*El Shaddai*); walk before Me and be blameless. ² And I will make My covenant between *Me* and you, and will multiply you exceedingly" (Gen. 17:1, 2).

Jesus is Lord! Jesus is Almighty God. Jesus is Lord Almighty. And Jesus is *El Shaddai*. Jesus is operating in Oneness with the Father as Lord Almighty – **and Jesus is our covenant maker**. Isn't this incredible! All the covenants and agreements that God ordained with man were made between Jesus and man. Jesus is not just the maker of the new covenant – Jesus *IS* the Covenant Maker and Jesus is the mediator of all agreements and promises between God and man.

> "For there is one God and one Mediator between God and men, the Man Christ Jesus" (1 Tim. 2:5)

> "Now a mediator does not mediate for one only, but ***God is one***" (Gal. 3:20).

Jesus is the covenant maker and Overseer of the Old Covenant – as well as the Architect of the New Covenant, a covenant He made of Himself – in His blood (Matt. 16:28; Luke 22:20; 1 Pet. 2:25). This is the Everlasting Covenant made by the Everlasting God –

Jesus Christ (Gen. 21:33; Deut. 32:40; Isa. 45:5-7; Heb. 8:6, 13; 13:20).

> "Now see that *I, even I, am He*, and there is no God besides **Me**" (Deut. 32:39).

> "For the LORD *is* our Judge, the LORD *is* our Lawgiver, the LORD *is* our King; He will save us" (Isa. 33:22)

Jesus told us, truthfully, that *all* the scriptures point to Him and testify of Him (John 5:39); these are not just stories about Him, but messages communicated by the Messenger, the Incarnate Logos, the Living Word made flesh, so that we may believe – and be saved. Christ is revealed in every book of the Bible because Jesus Himself *is* the Revelation of God. "He is promised in Genesis, revealed in the Law, prefigured in its history (Theophanies), praised in poetry, proclaimed in its prophecy, provided in the Gospels, proved in the Acts, preeminent in the Epistles and prevailing in Revelation."[13]

> "Then He said to them, "These are the words which I spoke to you while I was still with you, that all things must be fulfilled which were written in the Law of Moses and the Prophets and the Psalms ***concerning Me***" (Luke 24:44).

Jesus has always been the Father's *manifest* representative on the earth – and Jesus has always been Lord over all creation!

The earth is His dominion. The earth is His footstool. And I say again, the earth is His dominion! Jesus is Lord of the earth… always has been… and always will be.

Everything that has ever been spoken about "the Lord" or spoken as "thus says the Lord" were spoken by Jesus or the Spirit of Christ to men – for and on His Father's behalf.

---

[13] Willmington's Guide To The Bible, p.338.

"And in Him all things *consist* (*stand together*)" (Col. 1:17).

In fact, have you ever wondered how Jesus was able to quote the scriptures so perfectly and interpret them with pinpoint spiritual accuracy even though He never knew letters (had formal training and teaching in the scriptures; John 7:15)? This is the truth: Jesus Himself spoke these words to the psalmist and the prophets which are now regarded as scripture. Jesus did not memorize the scriptures – *Jesus was repeating Himself*! He is the Person who originally spoke spiritual truth to the prophets and they recorded it as *rhema* words (spoken utterances) from God. We need to see "the Lord" of the scriptures for Who He really is: Jesus Christ, the Living Word, and the Son of God.

How many times does Jesus need to repeat Himself before we believe?

> "Listen to Me, O Jacob, and Israel, My called: *I am He, I am the First, I am also the Last.* [13] Indeed My hand has laid the foundation of the earth, and My right hand has stretched out the heavens; when I call to them, they *stand up together* [*consist*]" (Isa. 48: 12, 13; see also Col. 1:17; Rev. 1:11).

> "*I, even I*, have spoken" (Isa. 48:15).

> "*I, even I*, will chastise you seven times for your sins" (Lev. 26:28)

> "Now see that *I, even I, am He*, and there is no God besides Me; I kill and I make alive; I wound and I heal; nor is there any who can deliver from My hand" (Deut. 32:39; Isa. 45:6, 7)

> "*I, even I, am the Lord*, and besides Me there is no savior" (Isa. 43:11).

"*I, even* I, *am He* who blots out your transgressions for My own sake; and I will not remember your sins" (Isa. 43:25).

"*I, even I, am He* who comforts you. Who are you that you should be afraid of a man who will die, and of the son of a man who will be made like grass?" (Isa. 51:12).

"Has this house, which is called by My name, become a den of thieves in your eyes? Behold, *I, even I*, have seen it," says the Lord" (Jer. 7:11; see Matt. 21:13).

"Therefore behold, *I, even I, will* utterly forget you and forsake you, and the city that I gave you and your fathers, and will cast you out of My presence" (Jer. 23:39).

"Therefore thus says the Lord God: 'Indeed *I, even I, am* against you and will execute judgments in your midst in the sight of the nations" (Ezek. 5:8).

"Indeed *I, even I, will* bring a sword against you, and I will destroy your high places" (Ezek. 6:3).

"For *I will be* like a lion to Ephraim, and like a young lion to the house of Judah. *I, even I*, will tear them and go away; I will take them away, and no one shall rescue" (Hosea 5:14).

Jesus is much more than we have been taught. Jesus is all in all – and in Him all things consist! And in His right hand is power and justice and life to exercise mercy, judgment, justice, lovingkindness and righteousness in the earth (Jer. 9:24)! Jesus is the Righteousness of God, Jesus is "The Lord Our Righteousness" [14] and Jesus is Almighty God!

---

[14] Jer. 23:6. This is the name Jesus has given Himself for His millennium.

"He who has the Son has life; he who does not have the Son of God does not have life" (1 John 5:21).

Jesus is the Life. Without Jesus, you have no chance for life eternal, so if you want eternal life, then I suggest you begin spending less time on the things that don't matter or defending your denominational traditions and start spending more time with Jesus. Believing in Jesus is just not enough to guarantee eternal life... you must walk according to His way, which means you may need to throw away some man-made religious theology in order to know and understand who Jesus truly is, and in this manner you will be known by Jesus, as He expresses Himself living alive within you – and through you – as a manifest working of the Spirit of Jesus within you.

Faith does not just believe in Jesus as Christ; we must also come to understand Him and know Him as He truly is! We must believe He is who He says He is, and do what He tells us to do.

Faith is not *what* you believe – faith is *how* you live according to what you believe.

Jesus is Lord Jehovah

Let us go back to the scripture about Abraham and see another reality of Jesus – as Jehovah.

> "When Abram was ninety-nine years old, the LORD (*Jehovah*) appeared to Abram and said to him, "*I am Almighty God (El Shaddai)*; walk before Me and be blameless" (Gen. 17:1).

The word "LORD" in this scripture, and 6518 other times as well, is the Tetragrammaton *YHWH* (3068) translated as Jehovah (Ex. 6:3; Psa. 83:18; Isa. 12:2; 26:4) and also Yahweh, the Jewish national name of God. This name *YHWH* only appears in the Bible and its exact pronunciation is debated; however, the Lord revealed Himself to Abraham in Gen. 12:7 and then referred to Himself as

YHWH in v.8, so within this context, we can establish a direct correlation between Jesus and *YHWH* – as Lord Jehovah.

The word "Jehovah" occurs only four times in the Old Testament (KJV), but names associated with Jehovah occur nine times, including one very special name for Jesus: Jehovah Tsidkenu.

> "And God spoke to Moses and said to him: "***I am*** the LORD [*YHWH*]. ³ **I appeared** to Abraham, to Isaac, and to Jacob, as God Almighty [*El Shaddai*], but by My name LORD [*Jehovah*] I was not known to them" (Ex. 6:2, 3).

This is perhaps the most spiritually profound and significant scripture regarding the true identity of Jesus Christ, not only as the One who appeared to Abraham, but also as the One who spoke to Moses and established Himself as the Covenant Maker with all Judaism.

Taking into consideration all the terms which have been presented thus far regarding the identity of Jesus in the Bible, we can see many terms for God (*YHWH, El Shaddai, Jehovah, Yahweh, Adonai*) are associated with "the God" who appeared to Abraham, Isaac and Jacob, as well as 25 other times and places in the Old Testament. Jesus is God! Jesus is *YHWH*! The time has come for the church to lay aside its' disingenuous patriarchal understanding of Father God and footnoted lip-service to Jesus, and fully comprehend Jesus as *LORD* and *YHWH*.

> "That they may know that You, whose name alone is the LORD (*Jehovah*) are the Most High (*Elyon*) over all the earth" (Psa. 83:18).

> "Behold, God (*El*) is my salvation, I will trust and not be afraid; for YAH, the LORD (*YHWH Jehovah*)

is my strength and song; He also has become my salvation.'"(Isa. 12:2).[15]

"Trust in the LORD forever, for in YAH, the LORD (*Jehovah*), is everlasting strength" (Isa. 26:4).

Abraham saw *YHWH* and referred to Him as God Most High (*El Elyon*), as did Melchizedek:

> [18] "Then Melchizedek king of Salem brought out bread and wine; he was the priest of God Most High and he blessed him and said: "Blessed be Abram of God Most High (El Elyon), Possessor of heaven and earth; and blessed be God Most High, who has delivered your enemies into your hand." [22] "But Abram said to the king of Sodom, "***I have raised my hand to the Lord (YHWH), God Most High (El Elyon),*** the Possessor of heaven and earth" (Gen. 14:18, 22).

The compound *El Elyon* which appears in Gen. 14:18, 22 also appears in Psalm 78:35:

> "Then they remembered that God (*Elohim*) was their rock,
> And the Most High God (*El Elyon*) their Redeemer" (Psa. 78:35).

El Elyon is also identified with *YHWH* (Yahweh) in other verses as well:

> "The LORD (*YHWH*) thundered from heaven,
> And the Most High (*Elyon*) uttered His voice" (2 Sam. 22:14).

---

[15] YAH, or JAH, is a shortened word for Jehovah (3050) and also is found in Psa. 68:4, "Sing to God, sing praises to His name; extol Him who rides on the clouds, by His name YAH, and rejoice before Him."

> "For You, LORD (*YHWH*), are most high (*elyon*)
> above all the earth;
> You are exalted far above all gods" (Psa. 97:9).

Thus, Jesus is *YHWH, El Elyon, Elohim and Lord Jehovah* from everlasting to everlasting:

> "Blessed be the *Lord God* (*YHWH Elohim*) of Israel from everlasting to everlasting! Amen and Amen" (Psa. 41:13). "Before the mountains were brought forth, or ever *You* had formed the earth and the world, even from everlasting to everlasting, **You are God** (*El*)" (Psa. 90:2), "who led them by the right hand of Moses, with His glorious arm, dividing the water before them to make for Himself an everlasting name" (Isa. 63:12).

Jesus "appeared to Abraham, to Isaac, and to Jacob, as God Almighty [*El Shaddai*], but by My name Lord [*Jehovah*] I was not known to them" (Ex. 6:3)… yet the children of Israel were unable to perceive their true reality in relationship with God Most High [*El Elyon*] nor comprehend the reason for their existence on earth as an 'ecclesia' called out nation from out of all other nations… to be a special people upon the earth.

> "They do not know, nor do they understand; they walk about in darkness; all the foundations of the earth are unstable. [6] I said, "You are gods [*elohim*], and all of you are children of the Most High [*Elyon*]. [7] But you shall die like men, and fall like one of the princes" (Psa. 82:5-7).

Even though Jesus chose Israel from among all nations to make for Himself an everlasting name, Jesus (*YHWH*) was unknown to Israel (Ex. 6:3) and they rejected His parousia; yet it has always been Christ's intention to make Himself known "to those who love God, to those who are the called according to *His* purpose" (Rom. 8:28); it is for His reasons, His purposes in the earth and for His glory – that we are His "called, chosen and faithful" – His elect (Rev. 17:14).

> "But the *Lord* (*YHWH*) is the true God; He is the living God and the everlasting *King*. At His wrath the earth will tremble, **and the nations will not be able to endure His indignation**" (Jer. 10:10).

If you kept coming to people who disrespected you, disregarded you, refused to acknowledge you, mislabeled your title, minimized your true identity, refused to comprehend who you are and then rejected your message of life and hope that you bring so that all may come to the knowledge of the truth and attain eternal life, then let me ask you this: would you not also be indignant?

> "Blessed is the King who comes in the name of the Lord!' Peace in heaven and glory in the highest!" (Luke 19:38).

Back on point... the other names that Jesus uses to express Himself as *YHWH* Jehovah are:

1. Jehovah Jireh – The Lord Will Provide (Gen. 22:14)
2. Jehovah Rapha – The Lord Our Healer (Ex. 15:26; Psa. 103:3; 147:3)
3. Jehovah Nissi – The Lord My Banner (Ex. 17:15)
4. Jehovah Shalom – The Lord Is Peace (Judges 6:22-24; "Then the LORD said to him, "Peace be with you" v.23, and this phrase is widely attributed to Jesus which He spoke to His disciples after His resurrection, "Peace to you" (Luke 24:36; John 20:26). Jesus is also referred to as "The Prince of Peace" (Isa. 9:6) and "Lord of Peace" (2 Thess. 3:16).
5. Jehovah Sabaoth – The Lord Of Hosts (Heb. 6635; Gr. 4519) – and is equivalent to mean "Lord all sovereign" of hosts, masses, armies, etc. (Gen, 2:1; Psa. 33:6; 103:21; 148:2; Joshua 6:14; 1 Kings 22:19; Dan. 8:10-11; Jer. 33:22; Isa. 6:1-3; Rom. 9:29; James 5:4)

6. Jehovah Mekoddishkem (Qadash) – The Lord Who Sanctifies (Ex. 31:13)
7. Jehovah Raah – The Lord My Shepherd (Psa. 23:1; and Jesus refers to Himself as the Good Shepherd – John 10:11)
8. Jehovah Shammah – The Lord Is There, or The Lord Who Is Present (Ezek. 48:35; and He also refers to Himself as a God "who is near at hand" Jer. 23:23)
9. Jehovah Tsidkenu – The Lord Our Righteousness (Jer. 23:6; 33:16)

Jesus is the Righteousness of God and refers to Himself in this manner: "Seek ye first the kingdom of God and *His* righteousness" (Matt. 6:33).[16] Jesus is God, He is King of heaven and earth, and it is His righteousness that we need to seek and allow to become manifest within us.

This is Jesus, the living God who exists and affects His will, who makes covenants with men, who reveals Himself in the fullest sense as Lord Almighty, Sovereign Lord, Elohim, and Lord over all. He is the God who sees – and is seen. He has always been "the Father's *manifest* representative on earth, appearing for Him and as Him" [17] and yet, there are many religions and mainline Christian denominations that overemphasize the Father as Lord Jehovah much to the "indignation" of Jesus, who is *Lord God*, who was referred to by Abraham as *El Elyon* (Most High God; Gen. 14:20) and He calls Himself *El Shaddai* (God Almighty; Gen. 17:1).

Jesus is truly Lord, Jehovah, Lord of everything and *Adonai* "Lord over all," and yet the church's comprehension of Jesus is tempting the Lord's indignation by refusing to acknowledge Him as God Most High according to His truth and His testimony!

What more could Jesus possibly do to reveal Himself as "the Truth" to us?

---

[16] A comprehensive teaching about Jesus being the righteousness of God can be found in another book by the author titled: *EN* (sic).
[17] Conversation about Christology, by Robert (Bob) Luginbill.

I Am Who I Am

"I Am Who I Am" is one manner in which Jesus chose to express Himself, as '*HAYAH*', as God Himself, as the Existent One who is in divine control of all things (H1961-*hayah* = *to exist, be or become*), as the Lord God who is living and active and represents Himself as the God who keeps His covenant promises and works His will (Ex. 3:14). It is not that Moses did not know the Lord's name, or that Israel had forgotten what His name was, because even Moses knew the Lord's official name '*YHWH*' (Yahweh or Jehovah), as well as His proper (covenantal) name, '*Adonai*' (v. 4:10, 13).

The issue at hand is this: when Jesus tells you to do something, then do it – and do not get into a debate with God! Jesus told Moses, "I will send you to Pharaoh that you may bring **My people**, the children of Israel, out of Egypt" (Ex. 3:10), but Moses began to question the Lord – and make excuses for himself. Try reading the "five buts" of Moses with a straight face and tell me if you would not have become frustrated with Moses just like Jesus did.

1. "but who am I" (v.11)
2. but what shall I say *if* they ask, "What is His name" (v.13)
3. "but suppose they will not believe or listen to me" (v.4:1)
4. but "*O Adonai*, I am not eloquent – I am slow of speech and tongue" (v.4:10); and then here comes the kicker
5. "but *O Adonai*, please send someone else" (v.13)

   "So the anger of the Lord was kindled against Moses" (Ex. 4:14).

No kidding! Why God would put up with these disobedient excuses and only just get angry is the greatest show of mercy in the Bible! If it were up to me, I think I would have just knocked some sense into his head. This is Moses, the mighty man of God, who is telling Jesus to take a hike and find someone else to work His will.

Allow me some latitude to express this event from God's perspective. Jesus appears to Moses and introduces Himself as *YHWH* – "I am the God of your fathers… the God of Abraham" – this is the same Jesus who appeared to Abraham and spoke to him, and now Jesus appears to Moses and tells him what He wants him to do: bring *My* people out of Egypt.[18] So far – so good. If the Lord appeared to any of us and was to tell us something this profound and significant, we would probably ask the same thing that Moses asked next: "but who am I?" This is a very valid question considering the fact that you are having a conversation with an "Angel of the Lord" who appears as a Flame of Fire within a bush that does not burn. So, Jesus comforts Moses by giving him a miraculous "sign" that authenticates this calling as having been spoken by God (v.12). Still, no harm no foul.

"But" Moses then begins to bring hypothetical what-if scenarios that invariably "question" the sovereignty and majesty of the One who called Moses into service. From firsthand experience, when the Lord tells you what to do and you question it beyond the "first but," you will then face the consequence of what amounts to doubt and unbelief. When an angel appeared to Zacharias to tell him he would father John the Baptist (and this was just an angel) and he questioned the validity of the word given to him in "unbelief," the angel rendered him mute and unable to speak until the birth of John. When God tells you to do something – then believe – and do it!

Then Moses said to Jesus, "What shall I say when they ask, what is His name?" "And God said to Moses, "I AM WHO I AM."" Tell them, "I AM has sent me to you."

There seems to be some conjecture about this being a special name for God, but I can assure you that it is not. This seems more like a cryptic name that was given to someone who has begun to question the Lord God Almighty and Supreme Commander of heaven and earth. This appears to be the name the Sovereign Lord told Moses to 'put him in his place' though it seems without much effect.

---

[18] The children of Israel have always been Jehovah's (Jesus') chosen people.

God's official name is *YHWH* (v. 15) and Jesus tells Moses *that this is His name forever.* So, why did Jesus tell Moses that His name is "I AM?" Because "He is" who He says He is and He doesn't need to explain or defend Himself. And this is why Jesus kept telling us at least seven times that He is "I AM" in the gospel of John... b*ecause we remain clueless about "Who" Jesus really is*! Jesus always was and always is the Existent Preeminent One. Jesus is present perfect all the time, He is in Divine control of all things, He keeps His covenant promises and He always works His will to the glory of the Father.

- Jesus presented Himself before Moses as "**I Am** Who I Am" (Ex. 3:14)
- Jesus told the Jewish leaders: "Before Abraham was, **I Am**" (John 8:58)
- Jesus said, "**I am** the First and I am the last; besides Me there is no God" (Isa. 44:6)
- "There is none besides Me. **I am** the Lord, and there is no other" (Isa. 45:6)
- Jesus walked on water, appeared to the disciples and said to them, "**I am**" (John 6:20)
- "**I am** witnessing concerning Myself" (John 8:18; literal Greek)
- "**I am** the Alpha and the Omega, the First and the Last" (Rev. 1:11)
- "**I am** the First and the Last" (Rev. 1:17)
- "**I am** the Bread of life" (John 6:35, 41, 48, 51)
- "**I am** the Light of the world" (John 8:12)
- "**I am** from *above*" (John 8:23; *ano* (507) – meaning, *from the first*)
- "**I am** the Door of the sheep" (John 10:7, 9)
- "**I am** the Good Shepherd" (John 10:11, 14)
- "**I am** the Resurrection and the Life" (John 11:25)
- "**I am** the Way, the Truth, and the Life" (John 14:6)
- "**I am** the True Vine" (John 15:1, 5)

Jesus is all in all. Jesus is The Great **I AM**! Jesus is the all Existent One and is greater than we can ever imagine or perceive. "He who comes from above is above all... He who comes from heaven is above all" (John 3:31). Jesus can manifest Himself any way He wants, as a flame of fire or as a burning torch or as a pillar of cloud and fire or as a brilliant light to the Apostle Paul – and yet, Jesus desires to manifest Himself *to* every single one of us... as Immanuel within our heart. Jesus desires to abide within each and every one of us and He is speaking to you and me even now – at this very second. Will you turn aside to hear what He desires to say to you?

Moses asked the Lord Jesus, "Who am I" and what seems very characteristic of Jesus in the New Testament... He either answers a question with a question or He bypasses the question all together. In this instance with Moses, which is the same with you and me, it is not at all that important to Jesus if you know "who you are." *Who you are doesn't matter*! *It isn't about you*!!! What matters most is that you know Who the One "*is*" who speaks to you. Him you must know and understand. Him you must hear – and obey! Listen to Jesus!

> "But let him who glories glory in this, that he *understands and knows Me*, that *I am* the Lord, exercising lovingkindness, judgment, and righteousness in the earth. For in these I delight," says the Lord'" (Jer. 9:24).

Consider the conversation between Moses and Jesus as a very similar type of conversation that we may have with bank associates who try to authenticate our identity over the phone. There was this one time when a lady asked for my name, date of birth, social security number, address and phone number – and then she began to ask me a bunch of secret personal security questions that only I would know (because I had already given them the question to ask, as well as the answer). After much frustration from a barrage of endless questioning, I asked this lady, "Why don't you prove to me who you are over the phone and that you are actually calling me from my bank. How do I know that you are who you say you really are?" Well, she was perplexed at first, and then, indignant. I told her, "I know who I am, but how do I know who you are?" She shot back quickly, "I know who I am, but I am just trying to verify who you are." So I said, "I know who I am because I am who I am, so now prove to me you are who you say you are."

OK, so, how do you think this conversation ended? Yup, she abruptly cut me off and transferred me to her supervisor.

Well, this is the same type of conversation that Jesus had with Moses, so He gave him the "I AM" answer that was far less authoritative and much harder to authenticate (prove to others) regarding the validity of "*YHWH* sent me." Let me put it to you like this... if you have a personal relationship with the Lord, then you are always listening to hear His voice and you will obey the words He speaks to you (John 10:4, 27). Jesus knew that Moses (and the Israelites for that matter) did not have a personal relationship with Him; and He also knew that "He was unknown to them" and that they did not want to hear His voice. They had a theology that told them they had a relationship with God, but they did not have an experiential personal relationship built upon love and trust by hearing His voice with understanding that results in obedience.

How do I know this? Well, the answer comes after the third "but" by Moses: "But suppose they will not believe me?" (v.4:1) So, Jesus transforms the shepherd rod of Moses into a serpent, and then He transforms the hand of Moses into leprosy and back to health again before his very eyes. This would certainly authenticate the authority of the Voice who is speaking to Moses amidst the bush, however – the "buts" continue.

"Then Moses said to the Lord, "O my *Lord* (*Adonai*)... but I am slow of speech and slow of tongue" (v.10). Moses speaks this fourth 'but' and uses another name for God: *Adonai* (H*136*). The word *Adonai* is the word that indicates, "Lord par excellence" and "Lord over all" (Deut. 10:17; Joshua 3:11). The meaning of this word implies "Master" and this is the same term the Lord Jesus used to express Himself when He spoke of His covenant to Abraham (Gen. 17:2). Furthermore, it implies a relationship between a servant who has every right to expect to be completely protected and cared for by a master who has the ability to provide for the servant and who, therefore, expects faithful obedience on behalf of the servant to accomplish all that the master has commanded him to perform.

So, let me ask you this: do you think Moses is truly responding to Jesus as "Master" in a reverent and respectful manner, as one whose conscience dictates his actions must operate in a servant-obedient manner, or is he making excuses by pulling out the *Adonai* wild card? Well, Jesus tells him, "I will be with your mouth" but I do not think Moses noted the seemingly sarcastic tone in the Lord's voice. Moses tells Jesus the fifth and final but – "but *Adonia*, please send someone else" (v.13)... "So the anger of the Lord was kindled toward Moses" (v.14). Here is Moses, the law-giver for the Israelites, who gives Jesus five 'but' excuses – and yet he lived.

This has got to be the single greatest act of mercy, grace, longsuffering and kindness by God in all of humanity – and Moses lived to tell us about it! And this is the same Jesus who came back to His own people that He covenanted with, to *fulfill* (*teleo* – John 19:28, 30) the obligations and customary (*ethos*- Luke 22:37; John 19:40) requirements of the law – so that great grace could be made available for all people and to *accomplish perfectly* (*teleioo* – John 17:4, 23; Heb. 7:26) the work that Jesus was sent to do (to glorify the Father in the earth) – on behalf all men (*ethnos*) who are unable to accomplish that which was required under the law. Jesus gave us the Law, was born as a Man under the Law, satisfied the requirements of the Law, fulfilled the promises of the Law, fulfilled the letter of the Law – and then judged it by being illegally murdered by it... and then He disregarded it (rendered it obsolete; Heb. 8:13) by instituting a New Covenant that had only one commandment: "Love one another as I have loved you" (John 15:12). Love has always been the ways and means whereby we have dominion over the earth – in Christ's name.

"This is the work of God, that you believe in Him who He (the Father) sent" (John. 6:29) as the Holy One who is able to restore the divine relationship between God and man.

Jesus said, "I have manifested Your name" (referring to the Father – John 17:6) as a living manifest presence of God Himself so that the disciples would believe – without questions and without doubts. And this is the same truth that has already been spoken to each of us by the Holy Spirit – so that "we are all without excuse." You (yes, you) have already heard, so – why do you continue to doubt? The work of God is to believe that Jesus is God, so... how can it be any more complicated than that?

None of us get it right the first time. My walk of discipleship obedience to Jesus has had several hiccups, missteps and downsides, but never any backslides. So, let us consider this initial meeting between Jesus and Moses, who is considered one of the mightiest men in scripture, *but now*, we shall see him according to how he is remembered most – according to his faith.

This "But" story has a happy ending because that was who Moses *was*, as someone who ran from his murderous past in Egypt and became an excuse-maker in the presence of the Lord; however, this is not how the final pages of his life are recorded. There is a "new book" that is recording all the wonderful things you do – once you've returned to reason and you convert (turn to God and run with God)! This new book does not keep record of our previous failures or past sins – it only records *all* our acts of obedience and faithfulness, as Spirit-directed persons who walk according to the Spirit of God. This is the Book of Faith that records every remembrance of our faithfulness to Jesus (Heb. 11:23-29; Rev. 20:12).

Your page is still being written – "but" the choice is yours. All of our previous failures are not recorded – nor are our past sins remembered once we become a new creation in Christ! Jesus is not all that interested in your past – He is more interested in your future as a follower and disciple who listens obediently to the sound of His voice to establish the kingdom of God upon the earth. This is the Good News for those who desire to serve God and listen obediently to the words that Jesus Himself will speak to those who follow Him.

Who you were doesn't really matter to God – only who you are becoming…

…because every day is *a new day* "in the Lord." By grace through faith, newness happens.

Let me state this as emphatically as possible, with the blunt force of a sledgehammer gospel: when Jesus tells you to do something… then do it!!! Do not delay. Hear and obey (*shema*)! Hear and understand! Perceive and comprehend! Believe in Jesus fully, completely and wholeheartedly! Jesus is the key to understanding all that we are and all that He has planned for us. It's all about Jesus – and Jesus wants you to know and understand all mysteries in the kingdom, but we must dedicate our lives to loving Him – and then listen obediently to Him!

> ***"But let him who glories glory in this, that he understands and knows Me,***
> That I am the LORD [*YHWH*], exercising lovingkindness, judgment, and righteousness in the earth. For in these I delight," says the LORD" (Jer. 9:24).

Who is the Lord (*YHWH*)? Indeed, Jesus Christ in *YHWH*! Jesus is **LORD *God*** and we need to thoroughly comprehend and understand that Jesus is Lord, and **whenever we see the word "Lord" in the scriptures – we need to perceive this truth:** *Jesus is the Lord*! Jesus is "the Manifested One" who appears and who speaks on behalf of the Father as His representative.

Jesus is Lord!

It is well beyond the scope of this book to bring forward a comprehensive teaching about Jesus Christ, for this would in fact fill entire libraries, so I invite the reader to yield your will and ask Jesus yourself to reveal Himself to you under the guidance of the Holy Spirit.

Trinity Prelude

Before we begin to describe the Trinity, we must be absolutely certain in our mind that Jesus is God. The terms "God" and "Jesus" are synonymous. The Lord Jesus calls Himself "the Almighty" and "Lord God Almighty" in Revelation 1:8 and 4:8, and we have also learned that all the names of God in the Old Testament are, in fact, names attributed to Jesus and, therefore, Jesus is the God of Abraham, Isaac and Jacob – who appeared to all three.

Who, then, is the Father? This is an awesome question, indeed! We know that God is our spiritual Father, and He is regarded as one Person of the Trinity, but beyond that, the Father is only made known when referenced by Jesus – because only He can reveal the Father to us (Matt. 11:27). In nearly every instance, Jesus associates Himself as operating and abiding in Oneness with the Father... and doing only as the Father directs. In this regard, we see Jesus as the subordinate Son in terms of authority and duties assigned, as One having come from the Father to do His will (John 5:30; 6:38), but never subordinate in terms of relationship; the Son and Father are One. The subordinate role of Jesus on earth during His three plus years of Messianic ministry was intended to teach us and tangibly demonstrate to us, by example, how to live in subordinate authority within a divine personal relationship with the Father – in Presence and Spirit. Yet somehow, the church has made a big to-do about the Father while neglecting the supremacy of Jesus Christ, our Lord, as God Incarnate, whom God the Father established as Lord of heaven and earth, and is the only God this world has ever seen or heard.

> "For thus says the Lord, Who created the heavens, Who is God, Who formed the earth and made it, Who has established it, Who did not create it in vain, Who formed it to be inhabited: ***I am the Lord, and there is no other***" (Isa. 45:18).

What does Jesus Himself say about the Father?

"And the Father Himself, who sent Me, has testified of Me. You have neither heard His voice at any time, nor seen His form" (John 5:37).

The scriptures are very clear regarding the invisible nature of God (John 1:18; 6:46; Col. 1:15; 1 John 4:12), but this verse seems to contradict "the voice" we heard at Christ's baptism and again at His transfiguration. Bible scholars will say this verse is speaking only to those unbelieving Jews who were at Christ's baptism by John, or it refers to "the word of God" which they rejected as well, yet there is another explanation that will unify the following verses:

- "And suddenly *a voice* came from heaven, saying, "You are My beloved Son; in whom I am well pleased" (Matt. 3:17; Luke 3:22; at Christ's baptism)
- "And suddenly *a voice* came out of the cloud, saying "This is My beloved Son, in whom I am well pleased. Hear Him" (Matt. 17:5; Luke 9:35; at Christ's transfiguration)
- "Father, glorify Your name." Then a voice came from heaven, *saying*, "I have both glorified it and will glorify it again." [29] Therefore the people who stood by and heard it said that it had thundered. Others said, "An angel has spoken to Him." [30] Jesus answered and said, ""*The voice* did not come because of Me, but for your sake" (John 12:28-30).
- "For He received from God the Father honor and glory when such a voice came to Him from the Excellent Glory: "This is My beloved Son, in whom I am well pleased." And we heard *this voice* which came from heaven when we were with Him on the holy mountain" (2 Pet. 2:17, 18).

On October 12, 2015, Jesus spoke these words to me: "No one has seen the Father or heard His voice at any time." This was the second time in two weeks that He spoke this message to me, so I asked Jesus to explain this to Me… whose voice did we hear? And then the Holy Spirit brought understanding and said: "Mine." The voice absolutely came from heaven, but the scriptures never say it was the voice of the Father. The heavens parted, the Spirit descended like a dove and "then *a voice* from heaven" said, "This is My beloved Son, in whom I am well pleased" (Matt. 3:17; Mark 1:11; Luke 3:22; John 1:32 does not record hearing a voice).

This could have been the voice of the Father, and this is what the church teaches, but if no one has ever heard the Father's voice (and verily, we should take all of Jesus' words literally), then the scriptures also seem to indicate it was the voice of the Spirit. To be perfectly candid, I was perplexed, and remained perplexed for many days, so I waited and listened.

The idea of "the Father" is a New Testament concept that was presented by Jesus who never said, "I am the Son of God" during His earthly ministry except once to the Jews who were trying to kill Him (John 10:34-38).[19] Jesus never said, "I am the prophet – or Messiah – or Son of God" because His nature of meekness would not allow Him to claim "I am so-and-so" which, incidentally, is the nature of man. Jesus merely affirmed what other people claimed Him to be. His name for Himself was "Son of Man" and He used the term "Father and Son" in order to present to us the realized and realigned role for man, as one who is subordinate to God in authority, yet can become one in relationship with Him and perform His will regarding heavenly/spiritual matters.

Let me say this again: Jesus is the Almighty and He revealed Himself in physical form to patriarchs, prophets, and kings (Theophanies). Jesus is God Almighty, our Creator, who created everything, and He has always been in Divine Oneness with the Father, in Presence and Spirit, and yet... we know very little (if

---

[19] Jesus referred to Himself as "Christ" to the Samaritan woman (John 4:26) and as the "Son of God" to the man born blind whom He healed (John 9:35-37; the NU-text reads "Son of Man"); the Jews sought to kill Him because He "claimed" that God was His Father (John 5:17-19); and then confronted the Jews later in John 10:36. Jesus did claim this title Himself when the angel wrote to the corrupt church in Thyatira after His resurrection (Rev. 2:18).

anything) about the Father except for the testimony by Jesus, which is yet another reason why Jesus came to us: to teach us about the Father.

> "Even so, Father, for so it seemed good in Your sight. [27] All things have been delivered to Me by My Father, and no one knows the Son except the Father. Nor does anyone know the Father except the Son, and the one to whom the Son wills to reveal Him" (Matt. 11:26, 27).

The Father was made known to us through the Son – and only through the Son, who abides in Oneness with the Father as *Elohim*.[20]

The Father of the Son

The nature, identity and character of God was made known to us in the Old Covenant by God's fifteen names (El (4 variations – Elyon, Roi, Shaddai, Olam), Elohim, Adonai, and Jehovah (9 variations)) in addition to Lord (*YHWH*), yet the fullest realization of who God is – was best described by Jesus Himself as our "heavenly Father." God is our Father – and He is the Origin and Source of everything. OK, but what does that mean?

By Origin, we can say the Father is the impetus, originator, giver and source of everything whatsoever as coming *from* Him. The Origin '*ek*' denotes "the point whence motion or action proceeds,"[21] and thus, the Father is the "nourisher, protector, upholder" and Progenitor of a spiritual family for "those animated by the same spirit as Himself."[22] Our heavenly Father is the Origin of His family regarding those who walk according to the Spirit of God and have the love of God in them (1 John 4:7), and when we profess Jesus as Lord, then, by grace through faith, we are adopted into the Father's spiritual family.

---

[20] *Elohim* is plural
[21] Strong's Concordance, word study on '*ek*' (1537).
[22] IBID.

> "In this the ***love of God*** was manifested toward us, that God has sent His only begotten Son into the world, that we might live *through Him*" (1 John 4:9).
>
> "But whoever keeps His [Jesus'] word, truly the ***love of God*** is perfected in him. By this we know that we are *in Him*" (1 John 2:5).
>
> "He who does not love does not know God, for God is love" (1 John 4:8).

God is love. When we have the love of God in us, with Jesus as our Lord, then we will desire to do what God requires as those who claim to be members of His spiritual family.

> "And this is His commandment: that we should believe on the name of His Son Jesus Christ and love one another, as He gave us commandment" (1 John 3:23).
>
> "Jesus said to them, "If God were your Father, you would love Me, for I proceeded forth and came from God; nor have I come of Myself, but He sent Me" (John 8:42).

God is our Father <u>only</u> when we declare Jesus Christ is the Son of God... and Lord of all.

Our spiritual relationship with the Father is made manifest by the "love of God" in us and by our love for Jesus, which is revealed through us by our obedience to His commandments within the New Covenant established by Jesus. This is a monumental word of instruction, which forms the basis for our covenantal relationship with the Father *through* the Son whereby we may attain eternal life by faith in Jesus Christ and live as adopted sons and daughters of Abba, Father. This is the Good News! And this hope is by God's grace!

> "Therefore, having been justified by faith, we have peace with God *through* our Lord Jesus Christ, ² *through* whom also we have access by faith into this grace in which we stand, and rejoice in hope of the glory of God" (Rom. 5:1, 2).

In The Beginning

Before anything came into being, the Father existed in Oneness with Son and Spirit as *Elohim*.

Before any beginning occurs, there exists a source – as the origin of any beginning – that initiates an impetus to spark a beginning. Beginnings don't just begin; there is always an organizational thought, idea or plan that serves as an originating source of "intent with action" that produces a result called: the beginning. The Source and the Origin of everything – is God the Father – who is all in all.

> "There is one body and one Spirit, just as you were called in one hope of your calling; ⁵ one Lord, one faith, one baptism; ⁶ *one God and Father of all, who is above all, and through all,* **and in you all**" (Eph. 4:4-6).

Indeed, our heavenly Father is… everywhere, omnipresent, and all in all; and He is "in you all" i.e. every person. God our Father is already in us, but we oftentimes pretend that He is not really there by creating a separate reality within us that says He isn't. How preposterous!

God is everywhere, but some of us have bought into the illusion that we can declare Jesus as Lord, yet continue to compromise the truth found in the word of God as if God cannot see our actions or hear our thoughts. How utterly preposterous! He hears all our thoughts… and regardless of wherever we may try to go, God is there.

> "*If* I ascend into heaven, You are there; *If* I make
> my bed in hell, behold, You are there" (Psa. 139:8).

For thousands of years, we used the term "God" inclusively with broad brush-strokes to describe the Divine in an impersonal manner who seems far beyond human reach and comprehension, but nothing could be farther from the truth. Our terminology for God is often vague and ambiguous, but our heavenly Father has *always* been near at hand. Since God is everywhere, then there is not any place where He isn't – and since God is omniscient and all knowing, He can also hear our thoughts and feel our distress; therefore, the illusion created by the enemy that has convinced some of us that our God is remote, distant and aloof to our many concerns… could not be farther from the truth. God is our Father… and He cares for you!

This point is worth repeating over and over: God cares for you. During my walk of faith, I have had to revisit this truth of God on numerous occasions because I tend to focus more on my circumstances than His goodness… and this is where I continue to get sidelined and even drift into trouble. God loves us and cares for us without ceasing, but oftentimes – we get in the way, doubt His promises, vacillate in our trust of Him, and forfeit the assurance of faith thereby preventing the Divine relationship from taking hold and producing a noteworthy effect that changes our life – and produces godly fruit. When this happens, I typically take full control of the reins once again to fix or correct my mistake only to find I made it worse and then spend even more time and energy trying to correct my fixes. What sheer and utter madness!

Lord, I need more grace! And grace upon grace to trust you in everything!

Jesus came to us in the form of a Son and taught us about our heavenly Father so that we might understand and comprehend the relationship that God desires to have with us… as sons and daughters of our Father. God is no longer just a word relegated to generic terminology and religious phraseology; God is now a term that connotes "heavenly Father" and we, the church, need to use the terms Jesus and Father to break away from the generalities of God-talk that many people in the world espouse without any comprehension that comes from having a personal relationship with the Father and the Son.

Get personal! If the Lord is your God and is real in your life, then talk to others about Jesus and the Father as if Jesus is your best friend and closest companion; after all, isn't that what we profess, right? This world is dying in darkness without the knowledge they have a heavenly Father that loves them or Jesus, His Son, who came and sacrificed His life in order to tell us the truth about the Father. The Father loves us – period! He cannot love us any more or any less than He already does! The families of man need to be set free from the bondage of ignorance and indifference to comprehend the Father that always loves them regardless of what they may have done, and to believe in Jesus, His Son, who made a way for us to return home to the Father through faith in Him. There is a way of escape, but someone has to tell them.

What could I liken this scenario to? It is like having advance warning of a major storm but refusing to get out of the way; it is like the warning of Noah to his generation but they ridiculed the message and the messenger. If you heard a news report that a train carrying toxic chemicals had just tipped over and the wind is blowing your way, would you change the channel to watch a movie or would you go to bed early? If not, then why not? Why, then, do we treat the warning of eternal torment in hell with similar disregard? Jesus came to save us so that we may be reunited to the Father, but the consequence for our disobedience by refusing to hear His voice and doing what He tells us will be met with justice and judgment.

> "… and that every tongue should confess that Jesus Christ is Lord, to the glory of God the Father" (Phil. 2:11).

The problem that we apparently have within the church is moral relativism and Christian atheism. We boldly profess Jesus as Lord and stand on His holy word for salvation, but we imitate the sinful customs of this world by compromising the word of God that produces a form of atheistic unbelief which results in spiritual complacency. To profess Jesus as Lord means: He alone is sitting on the throne of your heart as Sovereign God, King, Lord, Master and Savior who calls each of us to walk according to the Spirit of God and imitate Christ Himself. Well, who is sitting upon the throne in your heart? Is it Jesus Christ, or are you sitting there to justify the lifestyle you cannot scripturally defend?

Origin and Source

Back on point....so, why is this beginning, origin and source so important for us? Because we understand from the previous chapters that Jesus is the Father's representative as Creator of all creation, and now we need to comprehend the nature of the Father as the One whom no one has ever seen or heard within the context of the Son whom He sent to redeem and save the world – and to reveal Himself to us.

Perhaps this example will help us comprehend the Father better: according to the Big Bang Theory, the universe began in an instant whereby an infinite amount of mass, energy, and motion became manifest and formed into galaxies, and the origin of this mass and energy that initiated this beginning came from out of "the Source," and through Whom the worlds were spoken into existence, Who was with God... and His name is Jesus: "The Word of God" (Rev. 19:13).

> "In the beginning was the Word, and the Word was with God, and the Word was God" (John 1:1)

It was through Jesus Christ, the Word of God, that the visible reality of the cosmos was created and physically formed according to the will of an invisible God. The Father established it – through His Son. Perhaps the most exquisite proof of the Trinity as the Oneness of Father and Son is found within the following verses:

> "For thus says the Lord, Who created the heavens, Who is God, Who formed the earth and made it, Who has established it, Who did not create it in vain, Who formed it to be inhabited: "***I am the Lord****, **and there is no other***" (Isa. 45:18)

There is one God in Oneness (Father, Son and Holy Spirit), but "the Lord" of heaven and earth is none other than Jesus!!! Why would the Lord (Jesus) refer to Himself in such a manner, "***Who is God,*** Who formed the earth and made it, who did not create it in vain" – unless it was exceedingly and abundantly clear *who* this "Person" is? Jesus operated in Oneness with the Father before anything ever was, created the physical reality in Oneness with the Father, and then manifested Himself to us as Lord, as Lord God, and as "the Lord your God" in a personal manner… who is *intimately* interested in having a personal relationship with us! Jesus is Lord – who works the will of God and speaks the words of God so that we may enter into a personal relationship with *Elohim*.[23]

Adding word diagnostics to this verse will help us understand the message even more…

> "For thus says the Lord [*YHWH*], Who created the heavens, Who is God [*Elohim*], Who formed [*yatsar*] the earth and made [*asah*] it, Who has established [*kuwn*] it, Who did not create [*bara*] it in vain, Who formed [*yatsar*] it to be inhabited: "***I am the Lord****, **and there is no other***" (Isa. 45:18).

Yatsar (3335) – "to form, mold, fashion…through the squeezing into shape" (i.e. as a potter)
Asah (6213) – "to do or make; and when used with '*bara*' it implies creation from nothing"
Kuwn (3559) – "to prepare, be established, be readied, being firmly anchored"

---

[23] ***Elohim*** is plural.

IMAGE

Bara (1254) – "to create out of nothing. God brought the object or concept into being from previously non-existent material..."[24] (All definitions from Strong's).

Perhaps the best way to describe creation with '*bara*' is... the Father established it by the thought of His intellect (commissioned it) whereby all creation was then formed, made and established by Jesus "***through whom***" all things were '*yatsar*' formed to be inhabited for His glory and came into existence... and "***in Him***, all things consist" and are held together.

Jesus is *YHWH* the Lord. When we read Isaiah 42:1-4, we see the Father talking about His Son as the Messiah, and then beginning in verse 5 through Isaiah 46:9, we see the revelation of Jesus as He expresses Himself in Oneness <u>as God</u> (*El*) in singularity – and <u>with God</u> (*Elohim*) in plurality:

> "Thus says God [*El*] the LORD [*YHWH*], Who created the heavens and stretched them out, Who spread forth the earth and that which comes from it, Who gives breath to the people on it, and spirit to those who walk on it;" "I am the LORD [*YHWH*], that is My name; and ***My glory*** I will not give to another" (Isa. 42:5, 8).
>
> [7] "Everyone who is called by My name, *whom I have created for **My glory**;* I have formed him, yes, I have made him." – [10] "You are My witnesses," says the LORD [*YHWH*], and My servant whom I have chosen, that you may know and believe Me, and understand that I am He. **Before Me there was no God [*El*] *formed* [*yatsar*], nor shall there be**

---

[24] Strong continues... "but the technical meaning of *bara* (to create out of nothing) may not hold true in these passages." Note: the author differs with Strong's conclusion on '*bara*,' because we need to see Jesus as Creator in Oneness with the Father, who says of Himself "Before Me there was no God [*El*] formed [*yatsar*]... nor shall there be after Me" (Isa. 43:10)

after Me. ¹¹ I, even I, am the LORD, and besides Me there is no savior"... ¹² "Therefore you are My witnesses," says the LORD, "that I am God [*El*]" (Isa. 43:7, 10, 11, 12).

⁶ "Thus says the LORD, the King of Israel, and his Redeemer, the LORD of hosts: '*I am the First and I am the Last*; besides Me there is no God [*Elohim*]."... ⁸ "Is there a God [*Elohim*] besides Me? Indeed there is no other Rock; I know not one" (Isa. 44:6, 8).

¹⁴ "They will make supplication to you, saying, '*Surely God* [*El*] *is in you*, and there is no other; there is no other God [*Elohim*].'" ¹⁵ "Truly You are God [*El*], who hide Yourself, O God [*Elohim*] of Israel, the Savior!" ¹⁸ "For thus says the LORD [*YHWH*], Who created the heavens, Who is God [*Elohim*], Who formed the earth and made it, Who has established it, Who did not create it in vain, Who formed it to be inhabited: "I am the LORD [*YHWH*], and there is no other." ²¹ "And there is no other God [*Elohim*] besides Me, a just God [*El*] and a Savior; There is none besides Me." ²² "*Look to Me, and be saved*, all you ends of the earth! For I am God [*El*], and there is no other" (Isa. 45:14, 15, 18, 21, 22).

And finally, the last time the Lord speaks to Isaiah using "*El*" in concord with "*Elohim*":

"Remember the former things of old, for I am God [*El*], and there is no other; I am God [*Elohim*], and there is none like Me..." (Isa. 46:9).

The Lord Jesus (*YHWH*) is *El* and *Elohim*, God in singularity and Lord God in plurality. His name is *Yahweh* and that is His name forever (Ex. 3:15), who reveals Himself in oneness of Father and Son as... the God who "is in you" (Isa. 45:14), the God who is "in you all" (Eph. 4:6), the God who created you for His glory, the God (Immanuel) who is *with* you… and the God who desires to have a personal relationship with *you* and abide (tabernacle) within you!

God is everywhere – and God is in you, and in you all. God is in us, and with us, and for us – without exception, but He is only "our Father" through faith in Christ in order that we accomplish the works of the Father on earth, to proclaim His kingdom and establish the dominion of Christ upon the earth.

When Jesus proclaimed, "I am in the Father and the Father is in Me" and "the Father is with Me" – likewise, we can boldly proclaim the Father is in us and the Father is with us… **but only** when we profess faith in Jesus as our Lord and Master. Jesus was not conveying some new spiritual teaching that only He had special privileged mystical access to; He was telling every one of us that we can ALL **profess this** because God is all and in all, but we can only **possess this** when God becomes *our* spiritual Father through faith in Jesus Christ. This wisdom is monumental for the world to understand – and comprehend! Professing it and possessing it are two different realities that are oftentimes combined within the greasy-grace gospel, which is no real gospel at all. And furthermore, grace is not the license to do what we want; grace enables us to manifest the attributes of God Himself in us and through us for His glory… not ours.

And "If God is for us, who can be against us?" (Rom. 8:31).

Jesus told us numerously that He only does the works of the Father. And just like Jesus, who came in human flesh to serve as our example and living proof of God 'in us-with us-for us,' such that we can also do the works Jesus did – for the glory of the Father – because the Holy Spirit is operational in us. God desires to be our heavenly Father with all the rights and privileges as sons and daughters of the Father, but Jesus must be Lord of our life *AND* the Holy Spirit must be operational within us to guide us and empower us to do the greater works of Jesus our Lord.

We were saved for this purpose… not to get heaven, but to do the works of the Father on earth. The blessing and inheritance you receive in the life hereafter is predicated upon these works born out of a divine relationship with the Father through His Son and the indwelling Holy Spirit.

The Father is glorified *through* His Son and then the Son is glorified by the Father (with the glory that He had with the Father before the world was). This is the earthly template that Jesus taught us: glorify God through the Son – and then the Father will glorify Himself through us because of His Son. And God our Father gets all the glory – through His sons and daughters according to grace. Amen.

Therefore, since God is in everyone regardless of whether they are saved or not, we must "Love your neighbor as yourself" – for such is the kingdom of God. And since God is in all, and in you all,[25] then Jesus, being one with God, is within us as well – whereby we are all without excuse; *however, the promise of eternal life is only validated and fulfilled when you declare Jesus as Lord and place Him upon the throne of your heart as Sovereign Lord and Master of your life!*

We do not invite Jesus into our heart, as if we can exercise any control over Jesus to do this-or-that; Jesus is already ready there, but you must get off your heart-throne and exalt Him upon it. When Jesus breathed the "breath of life" into man (Gen. 2:7), He filled us with the essence of Himself: "I am the way, the truth and *the life*. I am the bread *of life*. I am the resurrection and *the life*."

"I AM… *the Life*."

God is everywhere; Jesus is everywhere. They are all in all! Verily, we cannot deny the existence of God nor escape the Presence of Jesus even if we tried! But the enemy has tricked us to

---

[25] And also "*in all y'all*," so as not to leave out any of our brothers and sisters living in America's deep south.

think They are not "in our midst" in order to keep us separated from having a personal relationship with them.

> "Can anyone hide himself in secret places, so I shall not see him?" says the LORD; "Do I not fill heaven and earth?" says the LORD" (Jer. 23:24).

When Jesus preached "The kingdom of God is at hand," He was telling us that God Himself in Christ Jesus has come to us and manifested Himself "in our midst." The Lord of heaven and earth manifested His promise to be Immanuel: God with us... and He has always been in our midst and near at hand!

> ***"Am I a God near at hand," says the LORD,***
> ***"And not a God afar off? (Jer. 23:23)***

Jeremiah recorded this prophetic utterance from the Lord Jesus. When we look up the meaning of "at hand" we see the Hebrew word '*qarob*' (H7138, coming from the word '*qarab*' H7126) which means, "near in place, kindred or time: – allied, near of kin, neighbor, them that come nigh at hand."[26] Jesus is the God we serve who is near at hand *and* regards us as kindred family.

Many years ago I heard the testimony of a Papua New Guinea tribesman who was converted to faith in Christ after fighting against it for a long time. In His testimony, he professed boldly, "This Jesus... you cannot get away from Him." Indeed! He is everywhere!

Is Jesus still *just* the Son of God in your mind – or has revelation truth concerning Jesus as *Elohim*, God Almighty and *El Elyon* (God Most High) – as *the Life* – become manifest in your heart and mind?

By the thought of the Father's will and intellect, everything was purposed, planned and established – ***in Christ Jesus and for His***

---

[26] Strong's Concordance.

glory. The Father operated in Oneness with the Son before the beginning even happened in order to initiate "In the beginning, God" (Gen. 1:1), and "from out of" their Oneness... Jesus spoke the thoughts of the Father and by His Word the worlds were created whereby all creation came into existence *through* His official capacity as: the Word of God.

How can the church continue to talk about Jesus in humanly terms as *just* a radical teacher or revolutionary thinker, as *just* an enigmatic prophet or charismatic preacher who died upon a cross and rose from the grave to save us from our sins? Jesus always had the authority to lay His life down and pick it up again (John 10:17), and yet, many perceive the Son of God as a "less-than" version of Father God, who 'kinda-sorta' hangs around in Oneness with God as a second lieutenant... and then bypass His Divinity by offering all prayers and thanksgiving to the Father with little more than a footnote of acknowledgement to Jesus our Lord, our Creator... who is Lord of Heaven and Earth, and Lord of the prayers we pray.

If we haven't been taught the full revelation message of Jesus Christ as LORD OF ALL, then we haven't heard the full message!

On this side of God's throne (and the Big Bang) – it's ALL about Jesus!!!

Jesus *is YHWH* of Heaven and Earth – to the glory of the Father!!!

Jesus is the *IMAGE* of the invisible God and "*THE*" instrumentality of the Father!

Jesus is exceedingly more than we will ever comprehend, but the church seems to have minimized the message, marginalized the Messenger and watered-down the true identity of Jesus Christ... who is the Father's only manifest representative the ***universe*** has ever seen or heard! ***And furthermore – the universe is under His command!***

Jesus is the covenant maker and covenant keeper; Jesus is the promise maker and promise keeper; and Jesus is coming back to judge the living and the dead. Are you ready for it?

When Jesus tells you to do anything – then you had better do it! His words are not an optional invitation to "pick-and-choose" what you want to believe; His words are commands! Do them! And if you call Jesus Lord, then you must become His disciple...

> "Not everyone who says to Me, 'Lord, Lord,' shall enter the kingdom of heaven, but he who does the will of My Father in heaven. ²² Many will say to Me in that day, 'Lord, Lord, have we not prophesied in Your name, cast out demons in Your name, and done many wonders in Your name?' ²³ And then I will declare to them, '*I never knew you*; depart from Me, you who practice lawlessness!'" (Matt. 7:21-23).

"I never knew you" is a very important concept regarding true faith. So much so, that there are numerous scriptures which all say the same thing (Matt. 7:21-23; 25:12; Luke 6:46; 13:25-27; John 10:14; 1 Cor. 8:3; 13:12; 2 Cor. 5:12; Gal. 4:9; 2 Tim. 2:19; Nah. 1:7; Mal. 1:60). Ponder this: it is more important that Jesus knows you than how much you know about God. Selah.

When Jesus says He is the *only* Door to the Father – you better believe it!

Who, then, is the Father? Can you describe Him for me? If you were to ask theologians who the Father is, even they stammer through the answer, and for this reason Jesus came and revealed the love of the Father to us as a spiritual Father who desires to have a personal relationship with us. Prior to Jesus, God was known by many names, and yet, we know very little about the Father other than what Jesus taught us.

How can we describe the Father whom no one has ever seen or

heard? [27] Indeed, we cannot! Only Jesus Christ, the Son of God, is able to describe the Father and declare Him to us because ***only Jesus has seen the Father*** (John 6:45). He is the only person to ascend into heaven (John 3:13) and His witness and His testimony is true. Christ put on flesh to make the Father known to us in a corporeal manner so we might tangibly touch and hear and see what prophets, kings and priests desired to know: the Living God who loves us – and can be experienced.

The Father is a New Covenant concept that is rarely mentioned in the Old Testament because the revelation of the Father was made known to us only through revelation by the Son of God, Jesus Christ. Jesus was sent to earth by the Father, as our Redeemer and Savior, to redeem creation and take away the sin of the world so that the kingdom of God could be restored to its pre-Adamic state. Within this significant work of God, Jesus revealed His identity as the Messiah and Son of God by many miraculous works so that all who repent and return to God, through faith in Him, may inherit life eternal.

> "And this is eternal life, that they may know You, the only true God, and Jesus Christ whom You have sent" (John 17:3).

God is Spirit. God is invisible, incorporeal, not needing anything, self-existent, the Origin of and the Source for everything. Jesus and the Holy Spirit, being co-Existent and eternal with the Father, proceeded forth from the Father to make manifest the reality of the

---

[27] We can describe the Father by His attributes and works evidenced in the scriptures. God our Father is: Spirit (John 4:24), Omnipotent (Matt. 19:26), Omniscient (Matt. 10:29), Holy (John 17:11), Righteous (John 17:25), Loving (John 3:16; 17:23), Good (Matt. 6:26, 28-30; 10:29, 30), Perfect (Matt. 5:48), Glory (Eph. 1:17), Provider (Matt. 6:32, 33), Protector (John 10:29; 17:11), Blessor ((Eph. 1:3), Comforter (2 Cor. 1:3), Merciful (2 Cor. 1:3), the Father of all life (John 5:26), the Father of our Savior (1 John 4:14), the Father who taught the Son (John 8:28), the Father who draws men to Christ (John 6:44, 45), the Father who reveals truth to men (Matt. 11:25; 16:17; Luke 10:21), and most importantly… He is the Father to those who believe through faith in the Son (Gal. 3:26; Eph. 2:18; Rom. 8:14; 1 John 3:1) Who delegated all power and authority and dominion to the Son.

Father known to us (John 8:42; 15:26). By word and revelation, and by the physical incarnation of Jesus Christ as our Lord and Messiah, the glory of God was revealed to us (John 11:40; Acts 7:55), and in Christ "dwells all the fullness of the Godhead *bodily*" (Col. 2:9; 1:19). Jesus Christ and "the Holy Spirit of God, by whom we were sealed for the day of redemption" (Eph. 4:30), have been declaring the things of God and doing the will of the Father, and making Him known, as His manifest representatives upon the earth since the beginning.

When the Father wills to make known His purpose and plan, He communicates to us through Jesus and the Holy Spirit, as His two intercessors unto mankind (Rom. 8:26, 27, 34) who are doing the will of God to save us and make us one with the Father. When the inward knowledge of the Father is made known to us, we can give testimony for this message revealed to us by the Spirit, "For it is not you who speak, but *the Spirit of your Father* who speaks in you" (Matt. 10:20).

Thoughts Beget Words

When it comes to words and pattern languages, there is always a thought that precedes the utterance, and this is especially true with man as well. The Divine conversation with man and all creation originates in 'ratio' before an 'oratio' utterance,[28] which we clearly see expressed regarding the '*logos*' and '*rhema*' of God; a Divine thought (*logos*) is followed by an utterance (spoken and unspoken *rhema* words). Within the context of creation, we see the thoughts of God to "make and orchestrate" all things according to His will and plan, whereby the manifestation of His thought is followed by all things being created and formed by the hand of Christ our Creator.

"The creative thoughts of God and the creative power of His word always precede creation. In this manner, "word is two-fold: λόγος ἐνοιάθετος – word conceived; and λόγος προφόρικος – word

---

[28] "Listen" by the author.

uttered. The λόγος ὁ ἔσω and ὁ ἔξω, ratio and oratio – intelligence and utterance."[29]

Are we able to hear God's voice? This is not a yes or no question. When we hear "the voice of God," we say this within the context of hearing a message from God through Jesus or the Holy Spirit, which is most often by thoughts and words with understanding placed within our mind. The word translated as "hear" in John 5:37 is '*akouo*' and literally means: to audibly hear; but there are two main types of hearing:

1. The sensational hearing of a sound, the sensational perception of sounds without the attentive hearing (or discerning) of the words or messages
2. The audible hearing of the message, words or thing perceived (Strong's)
3. And the third type, apart from the hearing by ears, are thoughts heard and understood within the mind of the inner man

The word-thought conceived (*logos*) precedes the word-revealed manifest expression (*rhema*).

> "He who does not love Me does not keep My words; and the word which you hear is not Mine but the Father's who sent Me" (John 14:24).

By this verse, the Lord Jesus tells us that the spiritual words we hear belong to the Father as having come from Him. And this is what Jesus meant in John 6:45-46[30] which could be interpreted to indicate our ability to hear the Father's voice, yet Jesus Himself tells us plainly that it is the *Spirit* of the Father that we hear.

---

[29] "Listen" by the author; from Matthew Henry's Commentary on the Whole Bible, an exposition on John 1:1; Volume VI, p. 848; MacDonald Publishing Company, McLean, Virginia

[30] (John 6: 45-46). "It is written in the prophets, 'And they shall all be taught by God.' Therefore everyone who has heard and learned from the Father comes to Me. ^{46} Not that anyone has seen the Father, except He who is [παρὰ τοῦ - *with from*] God; He has seen the Father" (Verse 46 is exclusive to Jesus only).

Regardless of our understanding or doctrinal interpretation regarding who is saying what, the Father is credited with and given honor and glory for all divinely-inspired words, which are delivered to us by Jesus and the Holy Spirit. And there are also two other people groups who deliver the words of God as well: the host of heaven and the host of earth. Angels are the host of heaven and their name in Greek '*angelos*' means: messenger; and the sons of men were created as messengers for the earth as well – to declare the word of the Lord.

Jesus and the Holy Spirit operate in Oneness with the Father, acting in one accord, in union, in communion, in concord, in unity – being distinct yet abiding as One – in Trinity Oneness. And they declare the words of God and perform His will, to the glory of the Father.

> "Now to our God and Father be glory forever and ever. Amen" (Phil. 4:20).

The Trinity

The Trinity is a divine mystery such that there is no earthly example whereby we may comprehend it, nor any earthly equivalent which may greatly illuminate it; the Father, Son and Holy Spirit are coexistent with one another at all times – as God '*Elohim.*' Man, as a finite created being, struggles with this concept quite often because, for all of us – there is a beginning and an end of days. Every aspect of our life can be inserted into a timeline of our personal history; however, such is not the case with God Almighty – who is the Existent One, who has always been, always is, and forever will be… without beginning or end.

It is within this realization of time bounded on all sides by eternity that we find Jesus, once again, in oneness with the Father – at the center of it all. Jesus proceeded forth and came from the Father, having always been with Him in all regards – and abiding in oneness *of* Him – and we need to perceive Jesus as the manifest, visible expression of God our Father whom no one has ever seen or heard.

We understand that Jesus was sent by the Father as our redeemer and savior, yet somehow we seem to misunderstand why He was *sent forth from* the Father as His representative – to appear for Him and as Him. In this regard, Jesus is not a mystical prophet as some have come to perceive Him; Jesus is the manifest expression of God who is representing the Father and manifesting the love of God and the way of love to us – by word and example.

Jesus, the existent and Preeminent One, was sent from the Father.

Jesus was conceived and born to Mary after being overshadowed by the Holy Spirit,[31] whereby Jesus didn't begin His life in a manger; He always was, is and will be! In this capacity, Jesus became the only begotten Son of the Father, being one with Him and being sent from Him to become the only visible manifest expression of God the Father (Isa. 43:10), and being sent, therefore, to do His will.

Jesus is God eternal, yet became manifest unto us… as a Man constrained by time.

We live within a physical world where many of our most important decisions are predicated upon the physical reality we see and sense, yet there is an even greater reality which we cannot see, and it is from this vast invisible reality that the physical reality, through Christ, was created and became visible.

> "For by Him all things were created that are in heaven and that are on earth, visible and invisible, whether thrones or dominions or principalities or powers. All things were created through Him and for Him" (Col. 1:16).

---

[31] "Thus, the real Father of Christ's body was the Holy Spirit, and the real miracle was not the Savior's birth, but His supernatural conception." Willmington's Study of the Bible; p. 649. Refer to: Luke 1:35; Matt. 1:18-20.

> "By faith we understand that the worlds were framed by the word of God, so that the things which are seen were not made of things which are visible" (Heb. 11:3).

It was difficult for me to perceive this message initially because I was taught to perceive the Father as Creator rather than Progenitor. Even though I have written about it often, and in this regard I am not unlike many others who know it and profess it, but somehow, I needed to comprehend it at a deeper level. This truth needed to become ironclad in my mind.

- The Father is – the Origin and Source of everything, _from Whom_ the Son proceeded forth to manifest Him, manifest His love, and do His will
- The Son is – the Father's representative as Lord of heaven and earth, the One _through Whom_ all things and the cosmos were created and formed, to the glory of the Father
- Everything that is physical and visible… proceeds *from* the Origin and Source which has never been seen or heard
- Through Jesus, everything from the Father came into existence, including man, and _through Jesus again_, by grace through faith, we can return home to the Father

The Father is the Origin and Source, and Jesus is the Instrumentality of God through whom the Father established as the nucleus of it all! Jesus is the Divine Conduit through whom the worlds were created and He is the **only** Door through which we may return to the Father (John 10).

We came to earth from the Father through Jesus – and we will return to the Father through Jesus! Wow! We truly are spiritual beings sent from the Father to do His will on earth, and through faith in Jesus, who is the Resurrection, we will be raised to newness of life through Christ by the power of the Spirit! Does this put Jesus into full perspective? It is **all** about Jesus!

Jesus is the Door! Jesus is the Gate for the sheepfold. Jesus is the Divine conduit through whom all of the Father's purposes and plans have been revealed. Through Jesus, the Father was made known to us, and by faith in Jesus Christ, we can return to the Father in Oneness with Him through Jesus. Jesus is the GATEWAY through whom everything exists!

And Jesus has been given all authority from the Father as Lord of Heaven and Earth, in this phase of eternity… as well as the Regeneration of all things in the New Earth.

Jesus is more than just our Savior and Redeemer, as if that is all we need Him for so that we can escape planet earth; He is Lord of heaven and earth and He has called each of us to take up our cross and advance forward into the darkness with the light of Christ to establish the kingdom of God within the midst of the enemy's strongholds throughout the earth. We are ambassadors and kingdom builders for the sake of Christ and God our Father.

This is not a casual affinity that I have for Jesus; I am obsessed in my love and my affections for Jesus, and I am compelled to follow Him and do whatever He says. He is everything and He is MY EVERYTHING because I thoroughly know and comprehend that JESUS IS LORD of everything – and apart from Him, nothing else really matters (myself included).

Jesus proceeded forth from the Father to manifest that Expression which resides in the Origin – as God in Oneness … as one extension of His glorious expression. Everything that we attribute to the Father has been manifested by the Son and continues to be expressed today through the Spirit of God in us who guides us into all truth.

It was through Jesus, who is God Almighty and the Creator of all things, that Jesus came to manifest our heavenly Father in such a tangible manner that we might eagerly desire the divine relationship with our Father restored. What greater love can there be than this – that God would personally demonstrate to us how much He loves us… in the form of His only begotten Son.

"For God so loved the world that He gave His only begotten Son, that whoever believes in Him should not perish but have everlasting life" (John 3:16).

Jesus, who is God, who is One in being with the Father, was sent, and in Oneness with the Father, God came to remind us how much They love us.

Read that again! Jesus came to earth as Lord of heaven and earth, as the Messiah, as the Christ, and as the Son of God to teach us how to be sons of God, having written history and then inserted Himself into history itself by the Spirit to show us the way back home to the Father. This is a complex heavenly transaction, so allow me some latitude to explain this mystery within the next four sections...

Father and Son Oneness

The Father and Son are One God, as the Jewish Shema states:

> "Hear, O Israel: The Lord our _God_, the Lord is *one*!" (Deut. 6:4; _Elohim_ *is plural*)

And other verses as well...

> "And the Lord shall be King over all the earth. In that day it shall be— "The Lord is *one*," *and His name **one**"* (Zech. 14:9).[32]

> "Thus says the Lord, the King of Israel, and his Redeemer, the Lord of hosts: '***I am*** the First and I am the Last; **besides *Me* there is no _God_**' (Isa. 44:6; _Elohim_).

---

[32] "*One*" is '*echad*' (259) "stresses unity/oneness but recognizes diversity within that oneness" Strong's. A union of two separate entities united into oneness (i.e. used for man and woman (Gen. 2:24).

> "***I am One*** who bears witness of Myself, and the Father who sent Me bears witness of Me" (John 8:18).[33]

> "***I and My Father are One***" (John 10:30).[34]

Jesus said, "I am One" and "I and My Father are One" – always and eternally Existent, in uninterrupted Oneness.

> "Yet for us there is one God, the Father, *of whom* are all things, and we for Him; and one Lord Jesus Christ, *through whom* are all things, and through whom we live" (1 Cor. 8:6).

In the scripture above, the Apostle Paul nailed it perfectly, and yet, some of the disciples seemed to have trouble understanding Jesus as Lord God of the Old Covenant; however, that was the first century church in transition away from Judaism, so let me ask you a direct question: are there two God's in the Bible – one for the Old Covenant and one for the New Testament – or is there only One God? If you answer "only One," then the same God who administered both Covenants is Jesus Christ – in Oneness with the Father, who was sent to teach us "the Way."

Father *IN* the Son

The Oneness, unity and insolubility of the Father and Son will become increasingly evident by these "in Me" verses:

> "Do you not believe that I am in the Father, and the Father in Me? The words that I speak to you I do not speak on My own *authority;* but **the Father who dwells in Me** does the works" (John 14:10).

---

[33] "*One*" is ὁ (3588) – *ho*; and is typically translated "the." The Greek says, "I am ὁ witnessing concerning Myself."
[34] The word "*One*" is ἕν (1520) – and is the neuter form of εἷς (one, primary numeral). Strong's Concordance.

"Believe Me that ***I am in the Father and the Father in Me***, or else believe Me for the sake of the works themselves" (John 14:11).

"...but if I do, though you do not believe Me, believe the works, that you may know and believe that ***the Father is in Me, and I in Him***." (John 10:38)

"I do not pray for these alone, but also for those who will believe in Me through their word; [21] ***that they all may be one, as You, Father, are in Me, and I in You***; that they also may be one in Us, that the world may believe that You sent Me. [22] And the glory which You gave Me I have given them, that they may be one just as We are one: [23] ***I in them, and You in Me***; that they may be made perfect in one, and that the world may know that You have sent Me, and have loved them as You have loved Me" (John 17:20-23).

"At that day you will know that ***I am in My Father***, and you in Me, and I in you" (John 14:20; "am" was added and should read: "I in My Father, and you in Me").

Jesus abides in the Father and the Father dwells in the Son. This is easier to comprehend when we perceive them in this manner: *as tabernacles for each other*. On earth – Jesus is the Tabernacle for the Father who dwells in Christ and manifests Him; and in heaven – the Father in glory is the Tabernacle for the Son. This is perhaps the only explanation that makes sense to me in order to comprehend what Jesus says, "You, Father, are in Me and I in You." They are Tabernacles for each other.

And They want to tabernacle "with" the sons of men, as the scripture says:

> "Thus says the Lord: "Heaven is My throne, and earth is My footstool. Where is the house that you will build Me? And where is the place of My rest" (Isa. 66:1).

> "Jesus answered and said to him, "If anyone loves Me, he will keep My word; and My Father will love him, and *We* will come to him and make Our *home* [*mone*-abode] *with* him" (John 14:23)

The word '*mone*' (abode) was also spoken by Jesus in John 14:2, "In my Father's house are many abodes," which has been translated – mansions. If we take the translation that we are accustomed to and insert it into verse 17:23, do you see your purpose on earth within a much grander and glorious plan by the Father… "And We will make our mansions *with* them." How incredibly marvelous is our divine calling as sons and daughters of the Most High God!

Not only are they One in each other, on earth as it is in heaven, they desire to be One in us! And it gets even better than this! The Father and the Son want to manifest themselves in you, in unity of the Spirit, to become Christ's likeness and kingdom ambassadors on the earth.

This is our chief aim in life: to turn back to the Lord, keep our eyes upon Jesus, do what He tells us, tell others about the hope of salvation which you have, establish his kingdom on earth with the dominion and authority He has given us, persevere with joy to the end – and then our soul will return to Him who created us… and we will be with Jesus for all eternity.

> "When Christ *who is our life* appears, then you also will appear with Him in glory" (Col. 3:4).

When we talk about our life on earth, it is usually in terms of owning things and bettering this life we have, but this is part of the grand illusion; our life belongs to Jesus … He is "our life" because He is "the Life." Jesus said, "I am… the life" (John 14:6), such that the life we have was given to us from the Father through Christ Jesus and it belongs to God – we are merely stewards and caretakers of His life within us during our brief sojourn on earth. When we die, the life we had, as well as the spirit that was given to us to help our soul with this journey, will return to God who gave it. Even the molecules in your body belong to God; when you die, your body will return to the earth from whence it came (and the earth belongs to the Lord also). The only part of you which is really you… is your soul, so… do you know where your soul is going?

Father *WITH* The Son

The Father was *in* His Son *and with* His Son throughout His earthly ministry

> "And yet if I do judge, My judgment is true; for *I am not alone*, but ***I am with the Father who sent Me***" (John 8:16).

> "*And **He who sent Me is with Me**. The Father has not left Me alone*, for I always do those things that please Him" (John 8:29).

> "Indeed the hour is coming, yes, has now come, that you will be scattered, each to his own, and will leave Me alone. And yet I am not alone, because ***the Father is with Me***" (John 16:32)

> "And whatever you ask in My name, that I will do, ***that the Father may be glorified in the Son***. If you ask anything in My name, I will do it" (John 14:13, 14).

That the Father may be glorified in the Son… is because the Father was with/in the Son. The Father and Son were never alone – and they have never left us alone or abandoned us either.

"And lo, I am *with you* always, even to the end of the age. Amen" (Matt. 28:20).

Jesus said, "I am *with* the Father who sent Me," and "I am *in* the Father and the Father is in Me." The Father and Son operated in Oneness so perfectly that Jesus said in truth: "I and My Father are One." This is why Jesus told us that He alone '*oida - knows the Father perfectly*' (John 8:55). The Father dwells *in* the Son as Jesus Christ, and the Son abides in the Father as *El Elyon* – God Most High. They are Tabernacles for each other.

In Heaven, Jesus is at home on the Father's throne, and on earth, the Father abides with the Son. They are tabernacles for each Other depending upon which reality they manifest.

Jesus appeared as God in Oneness of Father and Son in the Old Testament – and then manifested Himself as Lord in Oneness of Son and Father in the New Testament. Think about this for a moment before reading any more.

Let me say this another way: "The Lord our God, the Lord is One" (Deut. 6:5). ***The Lord Almighty is One who expresses Himself in the Old Covenant as the Father in oneness with the Son – and manifests Himself as the Son in oneness with the Father dwelling in Him in the New Covenant. The Father and Son are one expression manifesting – Oneness.***

God reveals Himself in Oneness of Himself, and uses the revelation of the Son to make Himself known as our heavenly Father and manifest Himself within all His beloved – you and me – through Jesus Christ our Lord. He manifests Himself in us, with us and through us – according to the Spirit of life in Christ Jesus. Thank you, Jesus!!!

The plurality of God that we see in Deut. 6:5 is the Oneness of God *with His Spirit.* They are One *in* each other – and They are One *in* you… when you believe! The hearty-cry of Jesus for us is that we would be one with Him and the Father – "*that they all may be one, as You, Father, are in Me, and I in You.*" They want to be

One in us and with us so that They may establish the kingdom of heaven on the earth through us with the indwelling Spirit! We should fervently desire to be spiritual tabernacles and living temples for the Father, Son and Holy Spirit in order to continue in the Father's work upon the earth – and by doing so, we are promised an eternal inheritance.

> "He who overcomes shall inherit all things, and I will be His God and he shall be My son" (Rev. 21:7).

When the Lord says He desires to be *with* us, this is not something to be taken lightly. He is Immanuel: **God with us**, and His plan of salvation and redemption is to establish the kingdom of God in us and through us. When we profess faith in Christ, we place Jesus upon the throne of our heart-home (abode) as Lord and Master whereby "They" initiate an aggressive kingdom-building program within us that begins by the Holy Spirit transforming us into the image of Christ by the renewing of our mind so as to "have the mind of Christ" and therefore – think like Jesus. They want to build a *"mansion"* within us so that They may be with us always *and* accomplish all the works which were predestined for us in Christ before the foundation of the world. **God is with us!!!**

We were created on purpose for this purpose!

> "And they shall call His name Emmanuel, which is translated, God *with* us" (Matt. 1:23).

"The word "with" is *'meta'* (3326) meaning: "joined with, accompaniment amid" with us on our sojourned life. From Enosh to Jesus to the Holy Spirit's presence today, we see our Triune God joined with us and *alongside us* every step of the way. He knows that we are dust and He knows fully the predicament we are in before we even call upon His name – because He is *right there beside us, in us and with us* every step of the way."[35]

---

[35] Excerpt taken from "Listen."

Jesus, the only begotten Son of the Father, came to earth, sent by the Father, being born as a Child. Jesus created history and then was inserted into the history He created by the Spirit, as a beloved and only begotten Son of the Father... as Immanuel: God with us.

> "For unto us a Child is born, unto us a Son is given; and the government will be upon His shoulder. ***And His name will be called*** Wonderful, Counselor, Mighty God, ***Everlasting Father***, Prince of Peace" (Isa. 9:6).

This scripture is read every Christmas during our reenactment of Christ's birth in a manger to Joseph and Mary, but have we ever studied the words within the context of Jesus as "Everlasting Father" being born as a Child, and given as a Son. Or perhaps these scriptures:

> "You shall call Me, "My Father," and not turn away from Me" (Jer. 3:19).

Jesus has always been the Father's representative on earth, appearing as Him in every regard, speaking His words and manifesting the Father on earth who abides in Him and dwelled with Him at all times. We might be somewhat confused by these scriptures, yet that is to be expected because They express themselves as One God in Oneness within a perfect and mysterious Triune relationship – which requires faith to understand! Another reason we have difficulty comprehending this is because God is infinite in nature; when He declares things, those things *are true at all times*, in all past, present and future realities – at the same time.

Jesus expresses Himself as "the voice" in the Old Testament and then manifests Himself as "the Word of God" in the New Testament. Jesus is "the voice" we hear, which is why He said this about the Father, verily, "You have neither heard His voice <u>at any time</u>, nor seen His form."

> "No one has seen God at any time. The only begotten Son, who is in the bosom of the Father, He has *declared* Him" (John 1:18).

> *Jesus is*
> *the Word of God*
> *through Whom words of God were spoken*
> *and became manifest.*

Jesus is the final authority on the word of God as the Word of God. Amen! And Jesus is still speaking the words of God to us today through His Holy Spirit. The Bible (as the written word of God) is not the final authority on the Word of God – Jesus is! Jesus will always be the final authority to make manifest the words of God and the will of God – in the church age – and the kingdom age that is upon us now.

> **Jesus is "the Word of God"** (Rev. 19:13). Amen!

> "In the beginning was the Word, and the Word was with God, and the Word was God. He was in the beginning with God. *All things were made through Him, and without Him nothing was made that was made.* In Him was life, and the life was the light of men. And the light shines in the darkness, and the darkness did not comprehend it" (John 1:1-5).

> "*For He whom God has sent speaks the words of God*, for God does not give the Spirit by measure" (John 3:34).

Jesus is the "mouth of God" who speaks the words of God – and it is within this unified concept that we hear messages from God our Father through Christ Jesus our Lord, who has also commissioned the Holy Spirit to speak on His authority… and now the time has come, once again, for the church to focus on the authority of Christ as Head of His Church!

Father *SEEN* as the Son

Whenever Jesus speaks about His unique and intensely personal '*oida*' relationship with the Father, He reveals Himself as the Son of the Father. At least 56 times, Jesus identifies personally with God as "My Father" to accomplish one of His primary missions upon the earth: to show us the way – i.e. how to live in love as sons and daughters of God our Father. However, it seems no one comprehended His message.

> "Then they [Pharisees] said to Him, "Where is Your Father?" Jesus answered, "You know neither Me nor My Father. If you had known Me, you would have known *My **Father*** also" (John 8:19).

If they had known '*ginosko*' Jesus, then they would have '*oida*' (perceived) the Father as well, but Christ's message gets even more profound than this: "If you've seen Me, you have seen the Father." The word "see" '*theoreo*-2334'(v.12:45) and "seen" '*horao*-3708' (v. 14:9) means: tangible sight that one sees and experiences with the eyes as a spectator!

> "And he who sees Me sees **Him** who sent Me" (John 12:45).

> "If you [disciples] had known Me, you would have known My Father also; **and from now on you know Him and have seen Him**. Philip said to Him, "Lord, show us the Father, and it is sufficient for us."
> ⁹ Jesus said to him, "Have I been with you so long, and yet you have not known Me, Philip? **He who has <u>seen</u> Me has <u>seen</u> the Father;** *so how can you say, 'Show us the Father'?* ¹⁰ Do you not believe that **I am in the Father, and the Father in Me**? The words that I speak to you I do not speak on My own *authority;* but the **<u>Father who dwells in Me</u>** does the works. ¹¹ **Believe Me that I am in the Father and the Father in Me**, or else believe Me for the sake of the works themselves" (John 14:7-11).

IMAGE

They saw God!!! Jesus, literally, is the image of the Father who was dwelling within Him!

> "He is the image of the invisible God, the firstborn over all creation" (Col. 1:15; see also 2 Cor. 4:4)
>
> "If you had known [*ginosko*] Me, you would have known [*oida*] My Father also; and from now on you know Him and have ***seen*** [3708 *beheld*] Him" (John 14:7).

By stringing all these scriptures together, it could be construed that Jesus is the Father, which is one conclusion which I and others have come to – but I could not reconcile the chasm between "He who has seen Me, has seen the Father" and the "My Father" verses – until years later. These "My Father" verses have been used to debunk the "God only" theology that cults use to diminish the deity of Jesus Christ. Thus, more wisdom and understanding from God was necessary.

When Jesus used the term, "My Father," it is literally πατέρα μου "the Father of Me." Jesus is not *just* claiming God as His Father, nor is He *just* making a tangible association to the Father; Jesus is saying He is in direct personal relationship with the Father whereby He is One with the Father much like the hand on your body is yours: They are indivisible, inseparable and One! Even if your hand is removed, it is still your hand. I hope you can perceive this because this is a very important point. At no time were the Father or the Son separated. Theirs is a union and unity in Oneness that is not severable! They are always *EN* Oneness with the Other.

Jesus identified Himself as coming from the Father and, like Jesus, '*who we are*' can only become known when our identity remains in oneness with the Father by having a personal relationship with Jesus. "Who" we claim to be is miniscule compared to "what" God created us to be – and we are no different than Jesus in this regard. "As He is, so are we in this world" (1 John 4:17).

We are to be imitators of Christ, and this is what Jesus was teaching us: what comes out of Me is because the Father is in Me. The works I do, the words I say, the miracles that happen, the image I manifest – "are" the evidence of My Father in Me. And this truth applies to you as well!

The Oneness of the Father and Son in the person of Jesus Christ is a poetic and pragmatic mystery of love incarnate… and They want to reveal the mystery of this love in us. Jesus is God. God is our Father. The Father dwells in Jesus, and Jesus abides in the Father – and they are One. *The Son and the Father are Elohim*! And (now get this) mankind was created as *elohims*, a little lower than the angels, like *gods*, in the image of our Creator according to *His* likeness (Psalm 8:5; 82:6; John 10:34). If you felt a spiritual tug in your soul when you read these words, then this is because the spirit within you gave witness to this truth! You were created and sent to earth by Jesus to be His image bearer and to do the will of the Father, in the similitude of Christ Himself, just like Jesus (as He is) – according to His image (Gen. 1:26-28).

> "Love has been perfected among us in this: that we may have boldness in the day of judgment; because as He is, so are we in this world" (1 John 4:17).

The Express Image

> "God, who at various times and in various ways spoke in time past to the fathers by the prophets, ^{2} has in these last days *spoken to us by His Son*, whom He has appointed heir of all things, through whom also He made the worlds; ^{3} *who being the brightness of His glory and the* **express image** *of His person*, and upholding all things by the word of His power, when He had by Himself purged our sins, sat down at the right hand of the Majesty on high" (Heb. 1:1-3).

This is the finest exposition to describe the relationship between

IMAGE

the Father and the Son in all scripture. The Greek writer of Hebrews describes Jesus as the "express image" of God the Father and uses the word *'charakter'* (5481) only once in all of scripture to convey an extremely important point. No other word more excellently describes the Son of God in relation to the Father than this.

Embodied within the meaning of this word expresses more than just the visible image of an invisible God; Jesus is not merely a copy, duplicate, reflection, facsimile, similar type or comparative essence of the original which is God, but infinitely more so… Jesus is the exact representation and character of God Himself whereby He Himself manifests the Father in every aspect as being equal to and operating in oneness with Him in every regard. There is nothing lacking in Jesus concerning the fullness of His being in relation to God, nor is there any diminishment of God in relation to Jesus being His express image. They are One! The Expression and the Manifestation of God's character were revealed in Divine Fullness and Perfection within the Oneness of the God-man, Jesus Christ.

No other earthly examples of *'charakter'* exist! So unique and extraordinary is this unified expression of God's character and nature being manifested perfectly in Oneness with the other that there could not possibly be another observable likeness or image within all known creation – except by Jesus Himself. By the power of His Word, Jesus made the world and all creation, yet He reserved within Himself the only begotten expression of His Father in Oneness with Himself – being made manifest in Jesus Christ: the Son of God. The human mind cannot fully comprehend this aspect of our God in Triune Oneness whereby words and expletives fall eternally short of hitting their intended mark to describe God from a human-based perspective. It would be like trying to put a garment around the elemental nature of light which cannot ever be contained.

Jesus is the express image of God.

No other created thing can possibly manifest the physicality and spirituality of God Himself except Jesus Christ. No person can ever profess having this Divine Charakter [sic] except Jesus! And it perplexes me beyond intellectual reason why anyone would want to follow after anyone or imitate a second-rate spiritual person who was created by Jesus... instead of emulating Jesus and becoming His disciple. Incongruous! Irrational! Incomprehensible! Inconceivable! Contemptible! And utterly inept! Jesus Christ Himself, through whom we were created as His image according to His likeness as elohims in the image of Elohim Himself, who dwells in Oneness with the Father, loves us more than we will ever comprehend, and yet, we have been exchanging the glory of His image and likeness within us to seek after other self-proclaimed divine wannabes! Anathema!

We have thoroughly forgotten who we are – and "Who" created us on purpose for a purpose!

Those who profess Jesus Christ as the Son of God are being revealed as sons of God for such a time as this! We were created as His image bearers so that we might also be "conformed to the image" of Jesus Christ!

> "For whom He foreknew, He also predestined to be conformed to the image of His Son, that He might be the firstborn among many brethren" (Rom. 8:29).

No one who professes Jesus as Lord God Almighty is chicken liver or second-rate to anything or anyone; you are the head and not the tail; you are more than conquerors through Christ Jesus; you are mighty ones in Christ who are being activated into divine service to become the exact image of Jesus Christ that He created you to be. How excellent and praiseworthy are the feet of him who brings good news – regardless of what your status or employment position in this life might be. You are ambassadors and servants of the Most High God... and it's high time we started acting like it!

Let Jesus be Christ in you – so that you may be His unique manifest expression upon the earth!

No one will ever be like you because Jesus created you to be a very unique expression of His character being revealed in you, with you and through you – to the praise of His glory. The time has come for us to stop bemoaning and trivializing who we are in Christ! If Christ is in you and the Father abides in you, then it's about time that we own this:

> "He who is in you is greater than he who is in the world" (1 John 4:4).

The time is now at hand for the saints of God Almighty to begin taking back the territory that was stolen from them and returning it into the kingdom of our heavenly Father. Satan stole our inheritance and birthright through lies and deception… and it's about time we manifest the righteousness of God to recover the kingdom of heaven that violent men have been plundering in order to establish the kingdom of God in the midst of His enemies.

Jesus is the only one of His kind, and yet… He created us as His image bearers to become like Him in every respect in order to represent Him in every regard. Once we acknowledge Jesus as Lord of heaven and earth, then Jesus will baptize us with the Holy Spirit whereby the Spirit manifests Himself in us to become the likeness and representational impress of our Lord and Redeemer, and then… the Spirit empowers us to continue the work of Christ upon the earth.

We were created, redeemed, saved, sanctified, baptized and commissioned so that we may represent Christ – and continue His work to restore the kingdom of heaven on earth. It is impossible to conceive of any calling or earthly position with greater importance than this: to be a disciple of Jesus and bear His image.

However, it seems man keeps searching high and low to find God so we can see Him, yet He has been waiting for us to enter in and find Him waiting for us in our heart. This world seeks to find proof of God expecting Him to manifest Himself by some tangible, observable event to prove to all "Ahah – I exist," but the only proof of God's existence has already been placed within our heart... and the only proof of our relationship to Him is by the fruit we produce through faith. We become the manifested proof of God – and we manifest our invisible Father by what flows out of our heart; it either looks like the world to glorify self or it glorifies our heavenly Father.

This is the manifest fullness of the Father's work through the Son, who resided *in* His Son and *with* Him throughout His earthly life in the flesh (1 Tim. 3:16). Jesus meant every word He said with specificity, "I only say and do what I see and I hear" because the Father and Son abided in uninterrupted intimacy since before the beginning – in Oneness – in flesh as well as spirit.

- "Most assuredly, I say to you, the Son can do nothing of Himself, but what He sees the Father do; for whatever He does, **the Son also does in like manner**" (John 5:19).
- "When you lift up the Son of Man, then you will know that I am He, and that I do nothing of Myself; but as My Father taught Me, I speak these things" (John 8:28).
- "I speak what I have seen with My Father, and you do what you have seen with your father" (John 8:38).
- "For I have not spoken on My own authority; but the Father who sent Me gave Me a command, what I should say and what I should speak" (John 12:49).
- "And I know that His command is everlasting life. Therefore, whatever I speak, just as the Father has told Me, so I speak" (John 12:50).
- "Do you not believe that I am in the Father, and the Father in Me? The words that I speak to you I do not speak on My own authority; but **the Father who dwells in Me does the works**. [11] Believe Me that I am in the Father and the Father in Me, or else believe Me for the sake of the works themselves" (John 14:10, 11).

Jesus did not only come to earth to exactly represent the Father and to appear for Him, He also manifested the Father to appear as Him and was the exact representation and *image* of Him whereby the works Jesus did were "exactly" identical to those of the Father dwelling in Him. His words and His works were the same as God's! (John 5:19; 14:11) The Father told Jesus what to say and what to do, and when we get to this level of intimacy with the Father, like Jesus, then the only things that come out of us (or come through us) will become the only testimony we need that God our Father is dwelling within us. No other proof is necessary!

I want to live like that!

Jesus did not come into the world to condemn it (John 3:17), but to save as many souls alive as possible. Jesus is the Son of God, sent as the only Son from the Father as His representative, appearing for Him and as Him, who, though being the fullness of God Himself, did not act on His own authority. Jesus acted under the authority of His Father, who was sent to lead as many souls home as possible by turning them around so they may be united with their heavenly Father. And this command from the Father which was given to Jesus – was given to the sons of men as well. We were sent, by grace, to save as many souls alive as possible.

And just like Jesus, who did everything by living out of Oneness with the Father dwelling within Him, likewise… we are to live out of this Oneness, in Presence and Spirit, by asking Jesus, the Lord of glory, every step of the way regarding what we are to say and what we are to do. It is very easy to succumb to human effort, human ingenuity and human traditions to operate according to our own wisdom and understanding, as though we are the lord of our own soul to live according to self determination and thus satisfy our own program of self-righteousness and personal self glorification. This is the way of the world, but it is certainly not the way in the kingdom of God!

We were all created as vessels in order to host the Presence of God in us. To the extent that we empty ourselves (this earthen vessel) is the extent to which the Lord can use us as a gateway for heavenly things to pass through. Jesus emptied Himself and then only said and did what the Father instructed; likewise, when we empty ourselves – we can also do the same mighty works that Jesus did… but we must allow our vessel to be emptied first.

Just as Jesus emptied Himself, not regarding who He is (as Lord God) but of His will, so also we must empty our earthen vessels of agendas, attitudes, opinions, preconceptions, biases and every other human convention to become completely empty and open so as to allow heavenly things to come into us without them being corrupted by us (or polluted once again by the cares of this world). Jesus did not empty Himself of His Divinity or His Glory – He never operated from them in order to become an "empty vessel" just like you and me, thereby becoming our example for living like sons and daughters of God according to the spirit – being partnered with the Spirit.

If we completely emptied our earthen vessel of everything, including sinful junk as well as our theology – I mean ALL of it – and then asked the Lord God to be sovereign in all that we think, say and do, and then fill us with the Holy Spirit, then… what would you look like and what would you do? We would look just like Jesus – according to His likeness that we were created as – and we would do the works of the Father and do no works other than His!

This is the message that Jesus taught us throughout His entire life: believe My words and do My works. The kingdom message from heaven is all about how many great things we can do for God once we surrender our will and empty this vessel, but the worldly message we hear is about how little we do because the enemy said we can't. We are already *elohims* (like gods) according to the likeness of Jesus, our *Elohim*, but the enemy will do whatever it takes to minimize this truth and diminish His message and promises to us in order to marginalize the works of God on the earth (John 10:34).

This is the example Jesus taught throughout His entire life: imitate My example. Jesus is God, in whom the fullness of the Godhead with the Holy Spirit dwelt bodily, and the Spirit of the Lord was with the Lord Jesus (Luke 4:18) even before His baptism in the Jordan by John. The baptism by John was to satisfy all legalistic righteousness under the Law, and the events that happened which spectators saw and heard were done for our benefit only; Jesus did not need the confirmation of the Holy Spirit upon Him as a dove to tell Him He was the Messiah, nor did He need "a voice" from heaven to tell Him that He was the Father's beloved Son. These events were witnessed for our benefit and were written down for our benefit – that we may believe! Believe the message and believe the example! Jesus already knew who He was – with the Father dwelling in Him and the anointing of the Holy Spirit upon Him. Jesus came to earth as a man, like us, and became an empty vessel, as an example for us, in order to demonstrate to us what it is like to have the Father dwelling in you, the Holy Spirit flowing through you, the anointing upon you to perform God's greater works through you – and finally – the glory of God being revealed in you as you sojourn upon the earth – right now. This is not just a future promise but a present tense actionable decree by the Lord Jesus! (John 17:22).

The pearl of great price is this truth which has been hidden within all of us in the hope that we seek and find it, but we will never find this pearl until we sell everything we have and empty our "vessel" in order to purchase "the pearl of great price."

The reason why we haven't been able to see this happen on earth yet is because the enemy has conditioned us to believe we are wretched sinners with a sinful nature and that we will always be "less than" vessels on account of sin; however, Jesus called us to believe His word and become His disciples. The past doesn't matter, nor is it remembered *if* you have been forgiven – therefore, the only thing that matters is this: who you are becoming NOW!

So, whose testimony are you going to believe? We have all adopted and then elevated the doctrine of sin far above the doctrine of grace and greater works – so I ask again… whose testimony are you going to believe? If Jesus is your Lord, then follow Him!

Hear Him! Do what He says! Stop believing the lies of the enemy! Fear is faith in reverse!

If Jesus did it – so can *we*!

Jesus lived His life as an example for us so that we might say and do the exact same things Jesus did while upon the earth – and to proclaim the same message He did: "Repent – the kingdom of heaven is at hand." When we repent, and operate according to the Spirit as Jesus taught us, then truly – "the kingdom of God has come upon you" (Matt. 12:24-30; Mark 1:15; Luke 9:2), and the light of this truth is now radiant within you, so now, go ye therefore into the world and preach this good news as lights in this world to disperse the darkness – and "be" the salt of the earth to change lifeless water in wells upon the earth into springs of living water (2 Kings 2:20; John 4:13, 14; 7:38; James 3:11).

We are more than just human beings; we are image bearers created in the likeness of Jesus Himself to do the will of the Father and have dominion over the works of the enemy!

If the Sovereign Lord is truly within us, then we are His hands and feet, and the works that are being done by us are actually the result of His works of grace being done through us – by Him! When we pray and lay hands on someone and they are healed, it is not us doing it, nor is this power ours – it is God within us and it is God releasing His power through us; we are merely gateways and conduits of His glory, power and grace. God alone is Almighty, and this is why we are to give God all the glory for any good that we do… because it is His goodness being done in us and through us – according to His great power at work in us (Eph. 1:19; 3:7, 20).

This is the truth! Walking in the light of this truth and living according to it – is saving faith for you and multitudes of souls as well. This truth is liberating!

Many have been deceived by a lie from the enemy that there is another way or some alternative to living in oneness with the

Father to recover the glory that was stolen from us. This is the lie of our adversary, the devil, whose work on earth is to keep us separated from the Father. By believing this lie, we have all entered into a less-than version of who we are in Christ whereby we delivered the glory that was placed within us into the hands of someone who promised us immediate glorification. We were bamboozled! We traded our divine heritage and divine birthright to attain something that we already possessed, but we surrendered it into the hands of someone who wanted to enslave us from ever getting it back – by deceiving us to enter into sin that separates us from the Father *and* keeps us separated from the truth. Apart from living in Presence and Spirit, in oneness of the Father, we will always be incomplete... and this was the plan of the enemy all along: keep us doubting, keep us separated and keep us cursed.

Since Jesus is our Lord and Master, then we must follow Him, hear His voice, and only say and do what we see and hear Him say and do. We were called by Jesus to be His disciples and to imitate Him. This is an instrumental point to the church, who tries to imitate the Father whom they have neither seen nor heard. Jesus is our Lord! "Hear Him!" Follow Him!

When the Son speaks on behalf of the Father, the Father is magnified by the Son – because they speak as One. When the Son does the will of the Father, the Son glorifies the Father and the Father is glorified in the Son – because they are One. When the Son rejoices in the Spirit, the Father is exalted by the Son – because they abide in Oneness, always and eternally, except once...

Once Upon A Cross

Please understand this next point: the Father was abiding *in* the Son and *with* His Son the entire time Christ lived on earth. There never was a moment when the Father and Son were not in union and Oneness with each other – except during the final moments of Christ's earthly life. We need to stop and reflect upon this mystery within the context of Christ's crucifixion.

Jesus and the Father knew exactly what was going to happen during this time, and so did Satan. Jesus was sent to redeem us and set us free from the bondage of sin and the penalty of sin, which is death; there was a plan of salvation and redemption, and it required Jesus to offer His life as a living sacrifice in order to pay the ransom.

> "For even the Son of Man did not come to be served, but to serve, and to give His life a ransom for many" (Mark 10:45; Matt. 20:28).

When Jesus identified Judas Iscariot as His traitor, He told Satan (after he entered Judas): "What you do, do quickly" (John 13:25). There was an agreement, a predetermined act of redemption in which the life of the Son was to be exchanged for the prisoners being held captive to sin; everything was known by the Son in advance… and He willingly and obediently went to the cross anyway. And Satan knew this as well, which is why Jesus told him, "What you do, do quickly."

As we read these next three verses, I would like you to see Jesus in transition during the final moments of His life as He is preparing to leave the disciples He loves and this world we know in order to return to the Father. Now, let me ask you this: how can Jesus indicate not being One *in* the Father and One *with* the Father in some near-future event such that He had to "return"? Because it has to do with where Jesus is going (Hades). In preparation for this moment, Jesus also gave instruction to His disciples regarding how to pray in His absence…

> "Little children, I shall be with you a little while longer. You will seek Me; and as I said to the Jews, 'Where I am going, you cannot come" (John 13:33).
>
> "And in that day you will ask Me nothing. Most assuredly, I say to you, whatever you ask the Father in My name He will give you. [24] Until now you have asked nothing in My name. Ask, and you will receive, that your joy may be full" (John 16:23, 24; in that day refers to the period of time while Jesus was in the tomb).
>
> "Now I am no longer in the world, but these are in the world, and I come to You. Holy Father, keep through Your name those whom You have given Me, that they may be one as We are" (John 17:11).

Jesus is getting everything in order because He has nearly finished the work the Father sent Him to accomplish; He is going to the cross to finish God's work. This was all part of God's plan of redemption, and we need to see the redemptive work of Jesus on the cross from a much larger perspective in terms of "why" Jesus was sent to redeem us, ransom us, rescue us and deliver us?

Nothing is too difficult for God, so why did Jesus have to suffer and die in order to save us from sin and death? To answer this question, we need to understand the big picture of redemption itself, because it involves something more than just saving man from sin and death. Man was created and sent to have dominion over this world in which Satan rules as a prince of rebellion, but man was deceived into delivering over to Satan the glory and the authority that God had given them. What began as man's dominion mandate in the Garden to take back and redeem the world from Satan's dominion became a rescue and recovery mission for the Lord Jesus. The plan also involved recovering that which was stolen from God in heaven by Satan which resulted in his expulsion from heaven; Satan received God's glory (worship) and then kept it for Himself whereby iniquity was found in him.

And then he instigated a rebellion in heaven against God with the glory that he stole from God. Christ's mission was manifold and predetermined, and it didn't just include saving man and restoring the glory of God in man; it also included taking away the sin of the world, triumphing over Satan, recovering what was stolen by him, saving mankind and restoring the glory of God in heaven and the earth as well.

Redemption is made known to us through two related words: *'apolutrosis'* (629) and *'lutrosis'* (3085-a ransoming) are both translated "redemption in the sense of deliverance" as a "releasing for payment of a ransom" and indicates the act of freeing and releasing "prisoners" by paying a ransom price; it includes the act of buying back (family lands and members) by paying a ransom such that those persons and lands are "totally set free, never to be sold again." [36]

If everything belongs to God, then why would He have to pay a ransom to redeem and buy it back? And more so, who had it and how did they get it? This was stolen from God by Satan and was being held captive by him. So, why didn't God just go and get it back? Well, that is exactly what He purposed to do, and the will of God determined the host of earth (aka the sons of men) should recover it and give God the glory in it.

With this understanding of redemption and the culmination of God's work through Christ's life, I am about to share with you my understanding of the big picture regarding our salvation. I cannot prove (from one scripture) that a deal was made between the Father and Satan in order to redeem us and purchase us back, but it involved the Son in Oneness with the Father, and the shedding of His blood and the forfeiture of His life by willingly laying it down. This was a hard bargain, indeed, but God so loved us that He agreed to the terms and sent His only Son whereby the purchase price for our redemption was the Son Himself who successfully ransomed all flesh back to the Father; however, there was just one

---

[36] Strong's Concordance.

catch... anyone desiring to return home to the Father must profess unyielding faith in Christ and declare obedience to Him. This seemed like a coup-de-teat for Satan to get God to deliver up His Son in order to recover His kingdom on earth for a bunch of disobedient sheep that he was convinced he could keep from declaring unyielding obedience to Christ, but he was yet unaware of God's secret weapon.

Everything that happened during the life of Christ was predestined and purposed in order to restore the kingdom of God; Satan thought he had tricked God into forfeiting the life of His Son – because they are One – but Satan, who was blinded by sin, was completely unaware of God's secret weapon:

RESURRECTION AND THE REGENERATION

Prior to the crucifixion, during the crucifixion and after the resurrection, three events occurred that will help shed light on this matter which occurred within the final moments of Christ's life on earth.

Three More Scriptures

Luke 22:41-42 – "And He was withdrawn from them about a stone's throw, and He knelt down and prayed, [42] saying, "Father, if it is Your will, take this cup away from Me; nevertheless not My will, but Yours, be done."
- This confirms His humanity
- Jesus, being fully aware of the disciple's close proximity, personified the heavenly example of prayer in the midst of suffering unto death for the sake of the kingdom whereby "He learned [taught them] obedience by the things He suffered" (Heb. 5:8)
- Jesus demonstrated the ultimate cost of surrendering our free will is the only way we can do the will of the Father; Jesus knew what was going to happen, and likewise, we can petition the Lord to see "if" another alternative might be possible

Matt. 27:46 – "And about the ninth hour Jesus cried out with a loud voice, saying, "Eli, Eli, lama sabachthani?" that is, "My God, My God, why have You forsaken Me?"
- This confirms His suffering
- In every aspect of His humanity, Jesus showed us that He truly understands the human condition, including our suffering; when we think God has forsaken us, it is then that we may thoroughly comprehend and be encouraged by the very real fact that He is "with us" and is walking alongside us – and even carrying us every step of the way
- Jesus is God, so how can God forsake Himself? This cry from Jesus upon the cross was not an indication the Father turned away from Him on account of our sin placed upon Him, but rather, Jesus cried out to God, "why have You forsaken Me" because at no other time during His life was Jesus ever separated from the Father. Never ever! The Father did not abandon the Son, He *'egkataleipo'* (1459) *left Him behind*, and in so doing, to suffer the consequence of fulfilling the ransom agreement and purchase price. They are *in* One another – as tabernacles in/with the other – except in this moment
- Jesus did not say, "My Father, My Father" which indicates Jesus understood His Father perfectly, who was always with Him in uninterrupted relationship with Him.
- Jesus was confirming to us the extent of His suffering by pointing us to recall Psalm 22,[37] whereby He also validates Himself as the Messiah by the seemingly exact manner in which His death fulfilled prophecy

---

[37] This is a standard technique used to recall scripture. We do the same thing when we quote Psalm 23, "The Lord is my Shepherd" whereby we recall from memory, "I shall not want.[2] He makes me to lie down in green pastures; He leads me beside the still waters.[3] He restores my soul;" And again, "Our Father"... we recall the remainder of the verse "Who is in heaven, hallowed be Your name" (Matt. 6:9).

- "When you lift up the Son of Man, then you will know that I am *He*" (John 8:28); these events foretold by Jesus proved that Jesus is Messiah and the Son of God

John 20:17 – "Jesus said to her, "Do not cling to Me, for I have not yet ascended to My Father; but go to My brethren and say to them, 'I am ascending to My Father and your Father, and to My God and your God.'"

- This confirms His bodily resurrection
- He declared He would die and rise again whereby He proved His Divinity
- He is telling us that He is separated from His Father and will be ascending to the place where He will be *reunited* in/with His Father on the throne in heaven
- Jesus is God, yet He refers to the Father as *His* God and *His* Father as "the Origin" of everything, including Himself. Once again, Jesus is teaching us to refer to God as "our Father" within the context of having a personal relationship *with* Him, not just as an act of faith to an obscure God that does not speak, but as a way of life within a divine personal relationship whereby we might also refer to Him as "*our Father* in heaven" – in Presence and Spirit!
- Jesus did not refer to His Father as "My Lord" because Jesus is our Lord who represents the Father. Jesus expressed Himself as having a Divine relationship with the Father, and likewise, the Father speaks of His Son in similar manner: "For David himself said by the Holy Spirit: 'The Lord said to *my* Lord, "Sit at My right hand, Till I make *Your* enemies *Your* footstool"'" (Mark 12:36; Psa. 110:1) which makes two statements of fact:
1. David regarded "the Lord" and referred to Him in personal terms as "my Lord"
2. "The Lord" in glory revealed Himself and manifested Himself to David within a personal relationship in a new and experiential way that David could comprehend

In life, and even death, Jesus continued to teach us about the nearness of God and what the attributes of the kingdom of heaven are like. God has always been with us and in us, even for those who do not know Him to help them in their time of need – even at the hour of their death, yet for those who profess Jesus as Lord, God adopts as "our Father" according to faith, and when we breathe our last breath… the Father will leave us behind for just a little while like He did with His Son, and the life-giving spirit within us will return to/with God who gave it.

Jesus was teaching us everything we need to know about life, death and life eternal – and He used His life as an example so that we may understand what is happening to us on earth. And in His hand are the keys of Hades and of Death, so we can rest assured that there is not any place where we will ever be out of touch with Him. For the unsaved, these words are meaningless ramblings, but for those who have put their hope and trust in Christ, we should be encouraged and strengthened in our spirit to know that wherever we go and whatever happens to us, Jesus is there to help us – and even carry us – and that everything is going according to plan.

The Blood Price

All three of these scriptures are highly significant because they all deal with the intimate personal relationship between the Son and the Father, and doing the will of "My God and your God." Within the larger context of Christ's redemptive work on the earth, we need to perceive the will of God in this moment which consummated a deal that God made with Satan to redeem all creation, including the earth, after man's fall from grace in the Garden of Eden.

Now, let's connect a string of events beginning in the Garden that includes the story of Job, which is an interesting narrative that does not seem to fit logically into the rest of the biblical narrative, yet *must be integrated* in order to comprehend the big picture of man upon the earth.

- Satan deceived Adam and Eve to doubt who they are, to act independently of God, and to "deliver" their authority whereby Satan took captive the glory residing within them

- Jesus was tempted by Satan in the wilderness to doubt who He was and fall into the same trap. Satan told Jesus he would deliver these kingdoms and "all this authority and their glory" to Him if He would bow down and worship him, indicating "All this authority I will give You, and their glory; *for this has been delivered to me*" (Luke 4:6) – which was delivered to him by Adam and Eve in the Garden. Jesus overcame Satan's temptation and accomplished what no other Person could in order to set the stage for the redemption and the restoration of the kingdom.
- The life work of Jesus successfully accomplished the will of God whereby "All authority in heaven and earth was delivered" to Jesus by the Father (Matt. 28:18), including the authority that mankind had delivered to Satan. By this act, the kingdom was restored into the authority of Christ, which He delivered back to us before His ascension, yet there was one more act that needed to be fulfilled in order to consummate the deal God made with Satan: paying the ransom price to redeem (purchase back) that which was stolen and taken captive by Satan
- Now consider the story of Job; he was a man like no other on the face of the earth who feared God (*Elohim*) in righteousness. Satan wanted to sift him, and God relented. Satan was interested in a "flesh for flesh" deal in order to take Job's life, but the Lord (Jehovah) would not allow it, whereby God put limits on this test and said, "You cannot take his life." [This, it seems, *in the sole opinion of the author*, did not satisfy the deal that Satan wanted to make with God, so God allowed a new redemption price that did satisfy the deal, not because God was beholden to meet all of Satan's demands, but rather, so the enemies of God could not charge God with error (Deut. 32:27).]
- This time, the purchase price was determined by Satan and God agreed to it: the flesh for flesh of God Himself. For the sake of mankind, God was willing to allow the shedding of His Son's blood to pay the ransom price in order to restore man's relationship with the Father. Can

you comprehend this monumental sacrificial act of love on God's behalf? Do not consider this lightly! Hebrew sacrifices merely postponed the atonement of sin, and the sprinkling of blood provided a temporary peace offering that allowed the punishment to pass over until the sacrifice of "The Holy One of Israel" paid the debt in full (Lev. 17:11; Col. 1:4; 1 Pet. 1:2; Rev. 5:9)

- Satan's logic was to entice God into giving up "flesh for flesh" and "blood for blood" whereby He would be able to take away God's kingdom from Him by sacrificing the life of His Son and heir of the kingdom (the earthly type and shadow is Abraham and Isaac).
- So Jesus, the Predetermination of God, was sent by the Father to pay the ransom price at the cost of His own life through the shedding of His Own blood. This would fully consummate God's agreement with Satan and "finish" the deal. Jesus knew from the beginning that He was "the Sacrificial Lamb" of God and His life was going to be taken from Him (John 1:29, 36; Heb. 2:14-17)
- At this point in the story, it seems God [from Satan's perspective] was put in a lose-lose situation such that the life of His Son would be forfeited to purchase back mankind so they could complete their dominion mandate on earth, but God had a secret weapon that Satan was unaware of called – THE RESURRECTION. Jesus said regarding His life, "I have power to lay it down, and I have power to take it again. This command I have received from My Father" (John 10:18), yet Satan, being blinded by sin, could not comprehend the mystery of God's plan, otherwise... "They would not have crucified the Lord of glory" (1 Cor. 2:8)

God's plan of redemption for – and reconciliation with – man, and the restoration of the kingdom, was all based upon His plan of resurrection... and the regeneration with "all things" becoming new again (Rev. 21:5) Saints, if you haven't yet understood the mystery of God, then perceive it now: the resurrection of your life is His life being raised up in you again on account of His great love for you whereby God will include you in the regeneration of all things – because you have been declared His sons and daughters according to faith in Christ! This is God's *imputed* work of grace that He predestined for everyone, but is only *imparted* to those who bow the knee to Christ and declare Jesus is Lord.

And if Christ is in you, then "the resurrection and the life" is in you as well (John 11:25).

This is the big picture concerning the redemption of man and the significance of the blood price.

Now, let us look at the events surrounding the crucifixion and death of Jesus Christ whereby He satisfied the blood price that was agreed upon between God and Satan. In order to understand this, we need to look at the events leading up to His death – and the words He said during His final moments:

- While Jesus was upon the cross, the Oneness of Father and Son was maintained – even during the brutal torture. The Father was abiding in Jesus and with Him the entire time, which was necessary in order to satisfy the agreement by the shedding of God's blood
- When the life of Christ Jesus had been sacrificially offered to satisfy the agreement, having been consummated upon the cross, the Father left Jesus, which was a pain greater than the suffering He endured in the flesh
- Jesus cried out to His Father, "My God, My God, why have You forsaken [left behind] Me." At no other time during His life was Jesus ever separated from the Father. Never ever! They are *in* One another – except in this moment (Matt. 27:46)
- Jesus received the sour wine offered to Him by the soldiers and then said, "***It is finished!***" (John 19:30) What was finished? What agreement was fully and completely and perfectly consummated with nothing left undone? The purchase price for our redemption *and* our salvation – was

the blood of Christ being shed once for all – for payment of the ransom *and* the remission of sins! (Matt. 26:28)
- "Now it was about the sixth hour, and there was darkness over all the earth until the ninth hour. ^{45} Then the sun was darkened" (Luke 23: 44, 45).
- Then Jesus said, "Into Your hands I commend My spirit" (Luke 23:46) whereby Jesus placed His spirit (small 's') into the hands of His Father. This was a monumental spiritual transaction occurring in the heavenly realm in which angels from both camps watched over and served as witnesses on behalf of both God and Satan.
- "And bowing His head, He gave up His spirit" (John 19:30)

Jesus died! And at that moment, something miraculously and supernaturally wonderful began to occur:

> "Then, behold, the veil of the temple was torn in two from top to bottom; and the earth quaked, and the rocks were split, ^{52} and the graves were opened; and many bodies of the saints who had fallen asleep were raised; ^{53} and coming out of the graves after His resurrection, they went into the holy city and appeared to many" (Matt. 27:51-53).

If you were an eyewitness to these events, you might have responded in like manner:

> "So when the centurion and those with him, who were guarding Jesus, saw the earthquake and the things that had happened, they feared greatly, saying, "Truly this was the Son of God!" (Matt. 27:54).

The veil of separation between the Father and His children was torn in two from above (*anothen*) by the Spirit of God. Now, therefore, there is no longer anything that keeps us separated from the love of God – except the lies we chose to believe whereby we maintain the gap of separation by our doubt and unbelief. There is nothing more to be done because – Jesus did it all! If you want your relationship with your heavenly Father restored, then call upon Jesus, believe in Him whom the Father sent, and trust in Jesus Christ with the fullness of your attention and affection.

This truth is paramount. There no longer exists a wall of separation between us and the Father; there is an open '*dianoigo*' heaven that allows us unrestricted access to the Father through Christ Jesus. The only separation that currently exists between God and man is the doubt in our mind created by lies that we continue to believe, such that we continue to enforce this separation through unbelief even though we have been set free to walk in liberty *and* abide in love as sons and daughters of God our Father through faith in Christ Jesus.

God loves us more than we will ever know; He loves us despite what we have done or whatever lifestyle we may be trapped in because – God is love! Our heavenly Father has always loved us and this is the love that I have been called to testify and write about. There are no conditions or restrictions on His love; God is love. In this regard, God does not love as we understand love because – He doesn't have love, per se… **He is love**. Any love that exists within the cosmos comes to us as this expression of who the Father is! In this regard, He cannot love us any more or any less than He already does, nor can you do anything to minimize His love for you or do anything to earn back His love because the fullest expression of love and the very essence of love itself – is God Himself. God *is* love! And God loves you!

Yet for centuries, many people and religious institutions viewed God as stoic, detached and aloof, being disconnected and seemingly indifferent to our sufferings, but this is the lie that the enemy wants us to believe. If our spiritual adversary, the devil, can prevent us from truly comprehending so great a love as this, then he can silence the love relationship the Father desires to have with every one of us. So God sent Himself, as the manifest expression we know as Jesus, to act as the Father's representative,

IMAGE

appearing for Him and as Him, to show us how much the Father loves us – from our side of heaven's door.

How far would you go to prove your love for another person? How much suffering and indignation would you willingly allow done to yourself to prove your love for another person? Could you do what Jesus did to prove how great your love is? Jesus did this on behalf of the Father; He acted on behalf of the Father's great love for us and obediently surrendered Himself to be the ransom for us and redeem us (purchase us back) so that we may be united – once again – to the Father who loves us with a never-ending love. Jesus did it all for love!

We have been redeemed, reconciled to the Father, and saved – on account of faith *in* Christ.

Everything that has been written about in the scriptures, the Psalms, the Prophets and the gospels was written for one reason: that we may believe Jesus is Lord, the Son of God, and Christ our Redeemer and Savior!

> "Jesus answered and said to them, "This is the work of God, that you believe in **Him** whom He sent" (John 6:29).

> "Then He said to them, "These are the words which I spoke to you while I was still with you, that all things must be fulfilled which were written in the Law of Moses and the Prophets and the Psalms *concerning **Me**"* (Luke 24:44).

Jesus left nothing undone. All was fully accomplished in Himself... all we ever had to do was connect the dots to perceive the trail that leads to faith in Jesus Christ as Lord God Almighty!

> "Now the Son of Man is glorified, and God is glorified in Him. [32] If God is glorified in Him, God

will also glorify Him in Himself, and glorify Him immediately" (John 13: 31, 32).

It's all about Jesus – and God Himself is glorified in the Son! Amen!
Just like a coin, God is One with two sides that operate in oneness, not as two persons, per se, but as two expressions of the same Oneness. Doors also has two sides, both to enter and to exit that operate in oneness… and thus, Jesus calls Himself "the Door" through Whom everything must go through:

> "Then Jesus said to them again, "Most assuredly, I say to you, I am the door of the sheep. [8] All who ever came before Me are thieves and robbers, but the sheep did not hear them. [9] I am the door. If anyone enters by Me, he will be saved, and will go in and out and find pasture" (John 10:7-9).

Doors and coins have two sides – and Jesus is the only side we can experientially see, hear and touch until we get to the other side. Two sides of the same God, *Elohim* (Father and Son) who is One with His Spirit.

God had to express Himself in two ways for this reason: on account of His holiness. If God were to manifest Himself in the flesh only, then we would disregard His holiness as just another person appearing with flesh and spirit claiming divinity, which would have violated His law, but His manifestation after the resurrection… and before, in His Theophanies, is proof positive that Jesus is God Almighty; He is the Preeminent One who is before all things and sovereignly rules as Lord of heaven and earth.

Jesus is Who He claims to be: the Gateway to the Father because all things from the Father came through Jesus and He Himself is the only way back to the Father. Amen!

Therefore, through faith in Jesus Christ, who is our Gateway to the Father, we have become like Jesus as gateways of grace to each other with the Spirit of Christ dwelling within us. How absolutely wonderful and marvelous is the mystery of God revealed in Christ – and the mystery of the Father revealed in Christ... so that we might be restored to the Father within the divine relationship of Christ in us – our hope of glory – and then help others to come into this salvation truth! Totally awesome, indeed!

This final question is vitally important: ***do you have a personal relationship with Jesus***? Most of us were taught to believe in God and Jesus, whereby we made a profession of faith and have been baptized; however, this is merely your faith in a theology – but it does not constitute having a personal relationship with Jesus. Do you see the difference? Do you know and understand Jesus? Do you obey His commands? Do you hear His voice, follow Him and obediently do what He tells you? Do you perceive Him as a Friend? *Do you love Jesus – I mean, do you really truly love Jesus with all your heart and soul and the fullness of your being?* It is not enough to just believe this truth; "even demons believe and tremble" (James 2:19). Jesus is calling everyone to enter into a personal relationship with Him *and* become His disciple.

Don't read another word of this until you settle this in your heart with Him:

> Jesus is Lord – but is He *your* Lord and *your* God?

> "How long will you falter between two opinions? If the LORD *is* God, follow Him" (1 Kings 18:21).

God revealed Himself in "the" manifest expression we know as Jesus Christ so that we should have a real, tangible, personal relationship with a Person and not a theology, philosophy, religion, tradition, statue, graven image or invisible ghost. Jesus was revealed in the form of a Son, so that everyone who chooses to imitate Christ and become His disciple... *shall* be adopted sons and daughters by God, live as children of God, and then return to the Father in oneness with Him.

Jesus wants us to enter into a personal relationship with Him whereby His Spirit speaks kingdom truth to us within the uninterrupted flow of an open heaven – through the gateway of our mind.

> "None of them shall teach his neighbor, and none his brother, saying, 'Know the LORD,' for all shall know Me, from the least of them to the greatest of them" (Heb. 8:11).

Jesus Himself is the voice talking to us – and He is our teacher who instructs us in the way to go. We do not need to consult neighbors and brothers... we need the witness of the Holy Spirit who dwells within us to confirm the Word of the Lord that was planted within us long ago, as we are guided by His Holy Spirit into all truth and righteousness. Jesus said He will do this for everyone who seeks Him diligently with all their heart, soul and mind, and He is doing it even now as I write these words for Him. Jesus desires to speak with each and everyone one of us, so... why do you continue to stand in doubt and unbelief? Why do you procrastinate? Jesus desires to do this! Jesus wants to manifest Himself in you and through you as His heavenly representative upon the earth and establish you as one of His gateways of greater works.

I Am With You – here and now

"I am with you, here and now... and I have been with you always."

"I have always been present among you, in Presence and Spirit, but man continues to forget Me and prefers to live apart from Me.

'I walked in the Garden with Adam and Eve, and they abided in Me, and then they did something that created a separation between us, and then they did something to reinforce the separation: they chose not to repent and then entered into sin. They left the oneness in Me, and the Spirit and Presence of Me, to enter into something that separated them from Me. This was their choice. I never left them... they walked away from Me and the consequence of maintaining their attitude of unrepentance was walking within a reality called earth where I am not ever-present.

'The first generation of man continued to reinforce this separation, as well as take all credit for My goodness and My glory which their hands performed, until I found one remnant living in oneness with Me and was perfect in his generation. So, I delivered him and made a covenant with him and his family because he chose to honor and reverence Me, to remember the way of the Lord and to walk in it, which I memorialized with a rainbow.

'As the families of man increased upon the earth, they began to increase the separation between Me and them, thinking once again that I am not with them here and now... in Presence and Spirit. So, I called one man to walk with Me so I could lead him from Ur to a special place where I could manifest My presence to him for all future generations to see and understand... that I am the God who loves everyone with an unrelenting love. Yet once again, they began to forget the way and lose remembrance of Me, so they became slaves to a nation that did not know or understand Me or My ways.

'As the families of man continued to increase upon the land, thus having lost nearly all remembrance of Me and failing to acknowledge My goodness and grace, or to give Me glory in all things, I called the generations of Abraham to come out of Egypt and by many signs and miracles I hoped they would remember Me and My goodness. I sent My Presence and Spirit to tabernacle with them on their journey, but they walked in rebellion to Me, so I established a permanent presence among them so they might always know and never forget that I am with them always as "the Lord your God." I called them to be My covenant people and to listen to My voice and walk in My way, but they rejected My invitation, so I gave them over to a Law having many requirements. I told them to eradicate the people of the land because those people did not want to know Me and I did not want them to be distracted by the lostness and forgetfulness of many nations that were already in the land.

'And then I saw one among many shepherds who remembered and acknowledged Me and lived out of My Presence and Spirit, so I caused My Spirit and Presence to come upon him, and I established a covenant with him, and he delighted himself in Me. His lovingly-reckless worship of Me set the stage for a new revelation of life with My creation that could live without the veil of separation between us. I was his delight – and He became My delight, as a man after My own heart, and I decreed that there would always be one from among his lineage who would sit upon My throne.

'The people whom I called as My namesake began to focus on the many requirements and ordinances instead of Me, whereby they preferred to live in faithfulness to an institutional religion instead of a personal relationship with Me in Presence and Spirit, so I sent Myself to them, as an only begotten Son from Me. I purposed to show them, guide them, help them to remember and lead them in the right way to demonstrate to them My great love for them as Immanuel: God with them… in Presence and Spirit. I never left, so I manifested Myself in a manner that all people could comprehend, as someone like them with meekness, of low estate, as Incarnate Immanuel, but they rejected My testimony because they preferred to live separate from Me… preferring obligatory sacrifices instead of loving obedience.

'My plan since the beginning has always been to remove this self-imposed veil of separation between *us* so that *We* may, once again, walk with each other in the Garden – in Presence and Spirit. So I established a New Covenant that rendered the Old covenant of Moses obsolete so that a new beginning should be established; and I sent My Spirit to remain with those who remember and acknowledge Me and desire to live according to the way I personally demonstrated: the way of love.

'Those who walk in the way of love will desire to acknowledge Me and reverence Me with their life-giving love, and I will put My Spirit in them and they will live out of My Presence. There is no place where I will not manifest Myself to them as I teach them to remember the days of old, and My Spirit will guide them into all truth with understanding and comprehension.

'I never left you! My kingdom is all around you and the kingdom of God is already within you. Stop striving to attain what you already possess! If you have separated yourself from Me, then you cannot profess what you do not possess; you are unable to enter into My heavenly reality because you continue to reinforce the veil of separation that I removed once and forever by My sacrificial act of Love on the cross. It is no longer there, but you continue to perceive it and teach others to perceive it. And you teach them also that My Presence and My Place is in the cosmos far beyond their reach, and yet, I am in you all and with you because I never left you. I am the One who established covenants and tabernacles so that you would always know that I am ever-close to you, always… but you prefer to abide in sin and the traditions of your fathers that reinforces the separation between us rather than living out of My Presence.'"

> "I am with you always, even to the end of the age" (Matt. 28:20).

"Your home is ready. Now is the time to return and – enter into Me."

> *"Enter into My Presence…in oneness with Me… in you."*

The Message

Where, if you can find it, does it say that God ever separated Himself from humanity? Contrary, "I Am" is always calling us to turn away from darkness and return to His glory and light. Just as Jesus said "My Father is in Me" and "He is with Me" is the same message for every one of us today because – this is the truth!

God is in us!!! God is with us!!! God is for us!!! I never left you!!! You are not alone!!!

What part of this do we not understand??? When the Lord says, "I am with you always," it doesn't mean only sometimes when we are walking with the Lord and pursuing righteousness... it means always! He never left us or abandoned us. Never ever!!! The God who loves us with endless passion is always with us – even to the end of the age.

The problem we have is not what we believe or that we don't believe ... the problem is we don't fully and completely believe what we do believe!

God is in us. God is everywhere and He is already in us. We do not have to go anywhere or go into any special building in order to find God; the kingdom of God is neither up nor down... but in. The God who is all in all – is already within you. "The kingdom of God is in you" (Luke 17:21). "He put eternity in your heart" (Eccl. 3:11). Why do we insist on making this too difficult to understand? You don't have to act special in order to get God's attention... you already are special... and He loves you with a never-ending love!

"I am with you always" (Matt. 28:20).

"I will never leave you nor forsake you" (Heb. 13:5)

Imagine a new way of living... knowing that God is always in you and with you.

Imagine a new way of living... in the love of God... and nothing else!

Unfortunately, our adversary has created an ***alternate reality*** in this world that exists apart from God – and this eternal kingdom is called Hell. Many times I have seen this alternate reality in operation, and every time I see someone who disregards Jesus as Lord and ignores the kingdom of God is yet another person that has adopted this alternate reality within their mind that erringly considers themselves as the Lord of their life that gives them license to do whatever they want. "If everyone is doing it, then it must be right" is one explanation... or perhaps it is mass delusion within this great illusion caused by the spirit of darkness to condemn many to eternal separation.

Unfortunately, we spend more time holding onto the things that reinforce the separation between us and God... and the love that He wants to manifest in us and through us. Why do we profess our love for God yet prefer living with enforced restrictions that reinforce the separation... rather than living in a love and trust relationship with an awesome, gracious, good and loving God who delights Himself in oneness of presence within us – in liberty – with freedom from sin.

Stop hanging on to the old way. Let go and trust in the Lord with all your heart and mind.

The God who loves us with a relentless love is the Father of the prodigal son, who waits with never-ending patience for the faint glimpse of a home-bound son or daughter coming from afar as their head pops up just above the horizon. God never stopped waiting!!! The past becomes irrelevant in the arms of His presence because all He wants is the separation to end... and to embrace us with the love He has always had for us.

Come home...He says... come home.

We are only complete... when we abide in the oneness of Him who loves us with a never-ending love.

God never stopped loving us. Never. The illusion on earth regarding the mystery of man is hereby corrected: God never left us. Never. He has given us the key to unlock the kingdom of God within us so that we may all live in love according to the Spirit of Love, Truth and Grace – but we must enter into this oneness by rejecting and removing the wall of separation caused by unforgiveness that we continue to enforce. We must enter into faith – through Christ Jesus.

Repent – and believe!

Jesus said, "I am the Door of the Sheepfold," but it must be unlocked from your side of the door.

> "Grace, mercy, and peace **will be with you** from God the Father and from the Lord Jesus Christ, the Son of the Father, in truth and love" (2 John 1:3).

Love is the Message

We were never intended to live life apart from the Lord. Life in Him is how we were intended to live life, and apart from Him we begin to die until we experience death.

This life is temporary and we are all in transition as sojourners between two places, between what was… and what will eternally be. Life as we know it, here and now is – is one season of eternity on earth, and the tempest coming against our soul needs to endure and persevere by faith, with hope and love in Christ Jesus… "and the greatest of these is love" (1 Cor. 13:13).

Love is the message. Jesus came to show us in manifest tangible ways concerning how much God loves us like a Father. God loves us more than we can imagine because He is love; this is the love of God who commissioned the Son to tell us about the Father's great love for us, which He purposed since the beginning. Message received!

> "For God so loved the world that He gave His only begotten Son, that whoever believes in Him should not perish but have everlasting life" (John 3:16).

Sons and daughters of the Most High God, we need to own this truth:

> "I will be a Father to you, and you shall be My sons and daughters, says the Lord Almighty" (2 Cor. 6:18).

Jesus is Lord Almighty and Lord God Almighty (Rev. 4:8; 11:17; 15:3; 16:7; 21:22). In this context, God expresses Himself as both a Father and as Son in order to teach us how to live in relationship with Him – as His sons and daughters. God manifested Himself as a Son, so that through Christ Jesus, we may have access to the Father and give thanks to God the Father through the Son... and reverence the God of Heaven.

This was the main problem within Judaism... they *were not* living as sons and daughters to a God they '*oida*' knew and loved as Father; they were living as faithful Jews to the teachings, doctrines and traditions of priests according to the Law, but they were dishonoring God – in spirit and in truth. So, **God sent His Son** to teach us how to live like His children according to faith – and according to love!

> "A son honors his father, and a servant his master. If then I am the Father, where is My honor? And if I am a Master, where is My reverence? Says the Lord of hosts to you priests who despise My name. Yet you say, 'In what way have we despised Your name?'" (Malachi 1:6).

In what way had Israel despised His name? They offered "defiled food" on His altar and rendered the table of the Lord "contemptible" (v.7). Israel showed utter contempt toward the Lord God by dishonoring Him as not worthy to receive all honor, glory, reverence, and respect – and then disregarded the Lord's covenant by polluting it with blemished sacrifices, so Jesus came Himself as a Son to teach us how to honor and serve God "our" Father ... by exemplifying the role of a son by becoming an obedient Son.

> "He who has My commandments and keeps them, it is he who loves Me. And he who loves Me will be loved by My Father, and I will love him and manifest Myself to him" (John 14:21).

> "If you keep My commandments, you will abide in My love, just as I have kept My Father's commandments and abide in His love" (John 15:10).
> "And whatever you do in word or deed, do all in the name of the Lord Jesus, *giving thanks to God the Father **through** Him*" (Col. 3:17).

Lord of Heaven and Earth

> "No one has ascended to heaven but He who came down from heaven, *that is,* the Son of Man <u>who is in heaven</u>" (John 3:13).

God manifested Himself in Oneness as Father and Son in heaven – and on the earth. Let me rephrase this: both the Father and Son are in heaven and the earth. And you ask, "how is that possible?" The reason we have problems understanding the truth of God is because we have manufactured many manmade doctrines to support the theology we want in order to believe in the god we want in order to live in the heaven we want. If you want to know about heaven from the perspective of Jesus Christ, who is God eternal, who is in heaven even while He Himself lived upon the earth, then read: "Here: The Kingdom of Heaven is." Heaven and earth are "*in*" the same place in the kingdom of God, but they exist as separate realities.

Wherever Jesus is… the kingdom of heaven is at hand; here now is!

If you protest this teaching, then let me ask you… as you are reading this: where is Jesus right now? You will rightly say that He is sitting at the right hand of God in heaven, and that is absolutely correct… but isn't He also abiding within your heart through faith in Him? And if Jesus is abiding in you, then the Father is also abiding within you as well. So, then, how can They be on the throne in heaven *and* dwelling in your heart on earth at the same time? Because heaven and earth are "*in*" the same place in regard to God's Presence in the kingdom of God, but these places exist as separate realities in regard to man in "this world."

Jesus Christ, the Messiah and Holy One of Israel…is the mystery of God revealed in Christ Jesus – as God in diversity and "Oneness"– and there is no other. Do you '*oida*' perceive and thoroughly comprehend it now? Jesus is the Lord our God.

> "For the Father loves the Son, and shows Him all things that *He Himself* does; and He will show Him greater works than these, that you may marvel" (John 5:20).

And for what purpose does Jesus reveal the Father to us? Exactly!… "what" is the correct answer, which we understand as the glory of God residing in men whom God regards as adopted "sons of God" through faith in Jesus Christ (John 17:22-24).

> "And whatever you ask in My name, that I will do, that the Father may be glorified in the Son" (John 14:13).

> "And the glory which You gave Me I have given them, that they may be one just as We are one" (John 17:22).

Jesus is the Holy *One* of God, the Righteous *One*, the Holy *One* of Israel, the **One** "who was and is and is to come" – Lord God Almighty! The glory that was stolen from the Father and stolen from us in the Garden by Satan was delivered back to Jesus, and this authority was then returned *back to us* to act on His behalf. The glory of God and His authority was returned to us 2,000 years ago, but we have chosen not to walk according to this truth.

God manifested Himself in the flesh and we know Him as Jesus Christ, and the Father was manifest *in* Jesus the entire time as well. What an incredible mystery, such that Jesus said, "Nothing is too difficult for God." God can appear wherever He wants, whenever

He wants, and "however" He wants to whomever He wants. God appeared as a Man and manifested Himself as Jesus Christ – as One Person in Oneness… as Father and Son – in Divine Presence; and the Spirit is manifest as well, whereby "God" always reveals Himself in Presence and Spirit – to make us one with the Father as adopted sons and daughters in His kingdom.

God Himself came to earth and the fullness of the Godhead dwelt in Jesus bodily, ***but God only reveals Himself to us as our Father through faith in Christ Jesus.*** Apart from faith in Christ, God cannot be our spiritual Father.

Anyone who suggests they have a personal relationship with God "the Father" apart from Jesus Christ has made an impossible claim and has been deceived by the anti-Christ to believe in the Father apart from Jesus Christ. Anyone who claims to have seen the Father or heard His voice without acknowledging Jesus as *Lord of all* has been deceived by the father of lies who masquerades as an angel of light (2 Cor. 11:14). You cannot have a relationship with the Father apart from Jesus Christ. Theirs is an absolutely incredible mystery of Oneness, indeed!

> "Whoever denies the Son does not have the Father either; he who acknowledges the Son has the Father also" (1 John 2:23).

> "Whoever transgresses and does not abide in the doctrine of Christ does not have God. He who abides in the doctrine of Christ has both the Father and the Son" (2 John 1:9).

Through Christ, the Father was made known because Jesus, being God, was also manifesting our Eternal Father – and One in being with Him. Now do you see it? This is absolutely beautiful what God accomplished *in* One Man, Jesus Christ of Nazareth.

> "You shall call Me, "My Father," and not turn away from Me" (Jer. 3:19).

The Father sent Himself with/in the form of His Son, hoping we would surely respect the Son... but we know how that worked out.

> "Hear another parable: There was a certain landowner who planted a vineyard and set a hedge around it, dug a winepress in it and built a tower. And he leased it to vinedressers and went into a far country. ^{34} Now when vintage-time drew near, he sent his servants to the vinedressers, that they might receive its fruit. ^{35} And the vinedressers took his servants, beat one, killed one, and stoned another. ^{36} Again he sent other servants, more than the first, and they did likewise to them. ^{37} Then last of all he sent his son to them, saying, 'They will respect my son.' ^{38} But when the vinedressers saw the son, they said among themselves, 'This is the heir. Come, let us kill him and seize his inheritance.' ^{39} So they took him and cast him out of the vineyard and killed him" (Matt. 21:33-39).

Now, let me try to explain the logic of God in this manner:

- Jesus is One with the Father, who was sent as a Son
- Jesus is Lord Almighty and King, who was sent as a Subordinate Subject
- Jesus is Master (Adonai), who was sent as a Servant
- Jesus is God our Lawgiver, who was sent as Israel's Messiah under the Law

Yet somehow, we only see Jesus as the Son of God as a less-than version of His Divine Fullness.

There was a TV show called "Undercover Boss." I know very little about this show as I rarely watch the glowing amusement box, but this show is about "the big boss... the CEO top dog" of the company who takes the role of a new employee to experience the organization from the entry level perspective... and is often amazed at what s/he finds. The boss never stopped being the bazillionaire boss even though "they" (as both boss and employee) inserted "themselves" into the entry level. Jesus is God; He is One with the Big Boss, who was inserted into our entry level – being born as a Child. Talk about condescension! And in this regard, we can see why Jesus says, "My Father is greater than I" (John 14:28). ***The expression is greater than the manifestation***!

Allow me to explain the mystery of God again, because the beauty, magnificence, awe-inspiring and sublime brilliance of God is absolutely marvelous to comprehend. When God came to earth, He didn't just reveal Himself in one way... He revealed Himself in multiple ways that are eternally timeless and exquisite: Messiah, Lord, Master, Savior, Christ, King, Teacher, Prophet, Father, Redeemer, Friend, *and as a Son*, but He only referred to Himself as the Son of Man. *The Lion and the Lamb came to earth – in the Oneness of Christ Jesus*!

> "Hear, O Israel: The LORD our God, the LORD *is* one!" (Deut. 6:4)

God is One, yet God expresses Himself in a multitude of ways – as expressions and manifestations – and as Spirit... in the oneness of One.

Jesus revealed Himself as the Son of/from God, yet this is only "one" of the manifest expressions of God's manifold nature expressed through Christ Jesus whereby He continues to reveal Himself to us – in a myriad of ways – even today. **God manifested Himself** – as "the Manifested One" Jesus Christ, and Jesus – as the Perfect Man, Jesus – as Eternal Father, Jesus as Beloved Son, Jesus as Messiah, as the Holy One of Israel, as Lord of the Gentiles, as the Ancient of Days, as the Lover of our soul, as well as all other 111 names to describe various expressions of His manifold *Charakter* [sic] so as if to say:

> "I manifest Myself because... I AM!"

IMAGE

This, my friends, is the most important statement of the entire Image Bearer series. Jesus is more than just "the Son of God" because Jesus is God Himself who came as a Son as our perfect example so that we may live like sons and daughters of the Lord our God... according to the manner in which we were created: in His Own image according to His Own likeness!!!

Jesus Christ is "the Manifested One."
And you are becoming one of God's manifested ones also ...
... because the hope of glory – Christ in you – is being manifested in you and through you.

Our true identity – is found in Christ.

And yet, the church regards Jesus as "just" the Son of God. Balderdash! And worse yet, we leave His body hanging upon a cross as emblematic of our true profession of faith in how we perceive Him: as a crucified Messiah accused of blasphemy by claiming to be the Son of God.

Jesus is God Almighty – He came unto us – and then we murdered Him!

And yet, the church offers desperate pleas to unregenerate sinners to simply believe in a watered down gospel so that we can boldly say, "we win souls for Jesus." Well, my friend, it isn't about you and your evangelistic soul-winning capabilities because this is the work of the Holy Spirit to reveal Christ to us; you are just a tool that He uses in His hand. The tool is worthless unless it is used by the Master according to His purpose and His will – to make disciples!

The church needs to get back to making disciples of believers.

The Father and Son have always abided in Oneness of authority and relationship at all times, with one possible exception being the crucifixion of Christ. Jesus is Jehovah Rapha – The Lord Our Healer, who was sent to save, yet He was bruised and beaten for our iniquity at the hands of sinful men. When we were murdering Jesus Christ upon the cross, at that moment, we were murdering God in Oneness of Father and Son as well. The Jews didn't just kill their One and only Messiah – they illegally convicted and then murdered the Chief Judge and Magistrate of the entire universe. We would do well to ponder this, in reverent fear, with fullness of conviction in our spirit – if – we have not declared Jesus as Lord and Master of our life… because His judgment is coming with great indignation.

So, why would God go to all this trouble just to save rebellious sinners?

He did it all for love!

He did it so that our relationship to God would be restored – with Christ our Lord *abiding in us* with the Father. Truly, the Father loves us beyond all human comprehension!

On October 12th, 2015, the Lord spoke John 5:37 to me, and also a second scripture: John 3:16. Most of us know it by heart, so allow me to show it to you in Greek:

"Οὕτως (Verily)[38] γὰρ (for) ἠγάπησεν (loved) ὁ (-) θεὸς (God) τὸν (the) κόσμον (world) ὥστε (thus therefore)[39] τὸν (the) υἱὸν (Son) τὸν (the) μονογενῆ (only begotten) ἔδωκεν (he gave), ἵνα (that) πᾶς ὁ (every-one) πιστεύων (believing) εἰς (in) αὐτὸν (Him) μὴ ἀπόληται (may not perish) ἀλλὰ (but) ἔχῃ (may have) ζωὴν (life) αἰώνιον (eternal)" (John 3:16). [40]

---

[38] (3689) '*ontos*' is translated, "really, certainly, indeed, verily" and (1063) '*gar*' is translated "for." Strong's.
[39] ὥστε (5620) '*hoste*' is translated, "so too, thus therefore; so that, wherefore, insomuch that, therefore." Strong's. This word stresses the importance of the previous statement: "God loved the world!" Thus therefore, He gave…
[40] God *gave* (1325) … and then in verse 17, God *sent* (649-*apostello*, to send out, the root word for apostle)… Jesus.

"Verily, for loved God the world, thus therefore the Son the only begotten He gave, that everyone believing in Him may not perish but have life eternal" (John 3:16).[41],[42]

*****

Jesus is God! Jesus is "from the Father" (John 16:28).[43] God so loved the world that... God, in Oneness of Father and Son, sent the Only Begotten One... as a Son... (ἐκ τοῦ) from out of Himself to teach us how to be sons of God. Jesus is more than *just* the Son of (τοῦ) God... Jesus is (παρὰ τοῦ - *with from*) God (John 6:46).[44] Jesus became the Son, the only Begotten One, sent τοῦ (of/from)(with the)(for)(as)(from) the Father... to remind how to live as sons of God.

*****

Allow me to put John 3:16 into a 'message translation' by the author:

> ***God so loved the world – that YHWH sent Himself as a Son – that everyone believing in Him may not perish but have life eternal!***

God sent Himself as a Son to teach us about Himself as Father – to become like Jesus, as sons of God. And because we love Jesus, we have access to the Father as adopted sons and daughters.

---

[41] Some cults do not accept Jesus as having come in the flesh, and some acknowledge Jesus as only just a man or an angel who was created by God, and yet this verse indicates Jesus is the "only begotten" Son of Him, which is confirmed in the scriptures.

[42] Please note: all scripture is inspired text, but red letters are not. These verses John 3:16-17 were not likely spoken by Jesus; any edition of the Bible that prints letters in red is an editorial decision.

[43] Jesus is "ἐκ τοῦ" Father and translated several ways, as "from; of the; out of the" or perhaps "from of the" Father.

[44] There are eighteen examples of "παρὰ τοῦ" in the scriptures which is translated "of/with/from" in various applications: "from the" Father (9x), "with -" God (2x), "with the" Father (1x), "from -" God (2x), "from the" Lord (2x), "from the [one]" God (1x, "from the" synagogue rulers (1x), "from -" Jason (1x).

The Father gave it all – and Jesus did it all... for love! "Greater love has no one than this, than to lay down one's life for his friends" (John 15:13).

God so loved the world... that He graced us with His presence.

The God of love with 111 names... reveals Himself and manifests Himself... according to love.

"The Lord our God, the Lord is One" (Deut. 6:4) – as one expression with many manifestations.

"I and My Father are One" (John 10:30).

The greatest gift of love and grace to mankind was not just the giving of Himself as an only begotten Son, but also, the sending of Himself with/in/as a Son to a world in desperate need of a personal relationship with God who is our Savior and loves us with a relentless love! Wow!

The God who lives forever and cannot die – was willing to die for us so that we may live forever with Him. What indescribably amazing love!

God demonstrated His infinitely great love toward us, as our heavenly Father – according to His Son's example – so that we may know how to live like sons and daughters of the Most High. This love is so grand and glorious that it is inconceivably beyond our comprehension, and yet, the most important thing that we will ever learn about our heavenly Father, who lives forever and loves us infinitely more than we will ever comprehend... is already:

- Living within us
- Feels our pain and suffering
- Hears our thoughts
- Understands our confusion
- Lives within our brokenness and despair

- And is willing to endure everything in this life "*with*" us, including our final moment leading up to death

Our heavenly Father is willing to go through all our worse human experiences "with" us so that we may come to the knowledge of this: "I love you... endure! I never left you! Patiently endure until the end." No greater love is this... than to lay your life down for your beloved ones.

It is impossible to understand or perceive why mankind has to go through all the painful experiences and junk we go through on earth[45]; however, God is in us, God is with us and God is for us every moment of every day. Our Father never left us... and His only thought for us is: "I love you... remember, repent, believe, endure! Come home!"

"I am willing to stay with you always, and never leave you, and I am willing to die with you; endure this life and get to the other side where I am waiting for you with open arms."

Since God is willing to live in you, and with you, and even die with you... are you not willing to endure this life for just a little while longer? Become a disciple of Jesus and follow Him because He is "the business end" of the Godhead and He alone knows the way to the Father. If you could understand your life within the context of the spiritual reality of eternity that is already within your heart, then consider this: this life represents only a small step forward on an eternal pathway thousands of miles long. The rest of your life is going to be fantastic without all the pain and problems of humanity's woes; are you willing to forfeit the most wonderful part of your life – as living in eternity with the Lord – by refusing to acknowledge the Father's love for you. Endure! And again I say... Endure! And remember!

---

[45] To get a better understanding of the reasons why we suffer, read "Commission."

Jesus came to reveal God as a Father to us and He continues to reveal the Father to us today.

> "These things I have spoken to you in figurative language; but the time is coming when I will no longer speak to you in figurative language, but *I will tell you plainly about the Father*" (John 16:25).

This is just one teaching that tells us about the Father – in Oneness '*in and with*' the Son at all times – who desires to abide in oneness "in and with" us also. Even though we have come to know and understand Jesus according to who He is… there is an even greater, unsearchable and inexhaustible aspect of the fullness of who Jesus truly is which we shall experience in the day of Jesus Christ (Phil. 1:6)… as well as a greater, unsearchable and inexhaustible understanding of who the Father is that we shall experience – once we get to the other side.

The Lord Is With You

Most of us listen to the nativity story every Christmas and yet somehow have never connected the dots of Jesus as being "called" Everlasting Father… ""For unto us a ***Child*** is born, unto us a ***Son*** is given; and the government will be upon His shoulder. ***And His name will be called*** Wonderful, Counselor, Mighty God, ***Everlasting Father***, Prince of Peace" (Isa. 9:6).

Now, I would like to highlight some words the angel Gabriel spoke to Mary:

> "Rejoice, highly favored one, the Lord is with you; blessed are you among women!" (Luke 1:28).

And much like Mary, by grace through faith, the Lord is also with us – every moment of every day. The angel of the Lord continues to declare the message of the Savior to be made manifest:

> "He will be great, and will be called ***the Son of the Highest***; and the Lord God will give Him the throne of His father David. [33] And He will reign over the

house of Jacob forever, and of His kingdom there will be no end." ³⁴ Then Mary said to the angel, "How can this be, since I do not know a man?" ³⁵ And the angel answered and said to her, "The Holy Spirit will come upon you, and the ***power of the Highest*** will overshadow you; ***therefore, also***, that Holy One who is to be born ***will be called the Son of God***" (Luke 1:32-35).

"***I am*** the Lord, your Holy One, the Creator of Israel, your King" (Isa. 43:15).

The heavenly wisdom contained within these scriptures is truly a mystery that only the Holy Spirit is able to unravel and bring revelation with understanding. Jesus, as we have already learned, is "Lord God, Almighty God and Lord God Almighty" who ***IS*** all power and might, and yet the Lord God (Himself) is going to give "the throne of His father David" to the Child born by Mary (i.e. Himself). It gets even more complicated than this! Jesus also described Himself as *El Elyon* (God Most High – Gen. 14:18; and in 17:1) and Jesus is "the power of God" made manifest (Matt. 22:29; 1 Cor. 1:25; 2:4; Rev. 4:11; 19:1). In effect, Jesus is the "power of the Highest" that overshadowed Mary to conceive a Child that would be named: Jesus. Jesus is the manifest expression of God in all manifold expressions, including the Incarnate Manifestation of the Savior born to Mary.

> "For by Him [Jesus] all things were created that are in heaven and that are on earth, visible and invisible, whether thrones or dominions or principalities ***or powers***. All things were created through Him and for Him" (Col. 1:16).

> "For since the creation of the world His invisible attributes are clearly seen, being understood by the things that are made, even His eternal power and Godhead, so that they are without excuse" (Rom. 1:20).

Jesus is God!!! Furthermore, Jesus is God our Creator! To keep this as uncomplicated as possible, we need to see Jesus our Lord ... as God Most High... as the Holy One who inserted Himself, in Oneness of the Godhead, into the fabric of time at just the right time to accomplish perfectly the will of God upon the earth. This mystery is supremely magnificent and sublime in all composition, complexity and truth wherein Jesus, the Lord our God, inserted Himself into the fabric of time according to His power as the Creator... in order to reveal Himself as our Savior and Deliverer. Jesus, who is the power of the Highest, created Himself "as" the Son of/from God... that we might "believe in Him who He sent." Jesus said:

> "This is the work of God, that you believe in Him whom He sent." (John 6:29).

Utterly amazing! Our loving gracious God sent Himself as a Son, in Oneness with the Father, to remind us who we are and to teach us how to become – and live – like sons and daughters of God Most High. So now, consider these words by a multitude of angels at our Savior's birth:

> "And suddenly there was with the angel a multitude of the heavenly host praising God and saying:
> [14] "Glory to God in the highest, and on earth peace, goodwill toward men!" (Luke 2:13, 14).

Glory to God in the highest... and on earth... PEACE... toward men of goodwill!

They were glorifying the Highest God... on earth! The Highest God came to earth ... to dwell as a man... to dwell among men for one season of eternity... just like us. Truly miraculous!

Selah! We would do well to meditate on this.

Perhaps the most perplexing scripture that I have ever encountered can now be understood within the context of the Lord God and His

Spirit sending Himself to do the one thing that only God Himself could do: unite the families of heaven and earth through the God-man, Christ Jesus!

> "Come near to Me, hear this: I have not spoken in secret from the beginning; from the time that it was, I was there. And now the Lord GOD and His Spirit *have sent Me*." (Isa. 48:16)

Jesus is the Lord God. The Lord our God wants us to thoroughly understand this mystery so that we move beyond the elemental teachings of Jesus as "just the Son of God" to embrace our high calling in Christ and to comprehend our positional place in Christ to have dominion over His enemies upon the earth – as the host of earth! Allow me to rephrase this scripture:

> "And now the Lord Jesus and His Spirit have sent... God in Christ Jesus."

Christ is in us *and* with us... and a new day is coming very soon when we shall experience the power of the Highest overshadowing us and flowing through us to tear down principalities and powers and strongholds to the glory of God in Christ Jesus! Glory to God in the Highest! And peace toward men of goodwill! Amen!

Christ In Us

A very popular Christmas song titled "Mary Did You Know" ponders what Mary may have thought regarding the Christ Child dwelling within her. Having just written the above message "The Lord Is With You," the Holy Spirit brought fresh revelation to me regarding Mary: she gave birth to Christ who was dwelling within her.

Mary, then, has become our earthly example and New Covenant archetype for all people who surrender their will and yield their life into the formative hands of the Holy Spirit. When we declare our obedience to Jesus, the Holy Spirit will come upon us... and the power of the Highest will overshadow us to indwell us in order to birth "Christ in us"… our hope of glory.

In this respect, Mary is "the" archetype of a new manifestation of God's manifold expression upon the earth – in mankind. Just as Christ was formed in her, likewise, Christ is being formed *in us*, by grace through faith, until Christ is fully formed within us and newness of the Spirit has birthed us to become a new creation "in" Christ upon the earth (whereby we are being formed, conformed and transformed into the image of Christ by the Spirit of Christ).

> "Everyone who is called by My name, Whom I have created for My glory; I have ***formed*** him, yes, I have made him" (Isa. 43:7).

> "My little children, for whom I labor in birth again until Christ is ***formed*** in you" (Gal. 4:19).

> "For whom He foreknew, He also predestined to be ***conformed*** to the image of His Son, that He might be the firstborn among many brethren" (Rom. 8:29).

When we yield to the purpose and plan of God, we will be overshadowed by the power of Christ and empowered by the Spirit of Christ to fill the earth with His glory… until… a critical mass has been achieved.[46] For Mary, Christ was dwelling in her bodily; likewise, for us through faith in Jesus, the Godhead dwells within these earthen tabernacles bodily – to the praise of His glory. In this respect, I rail at the term "Mother of God" attributed to Mary, as if the one giving birth is greater than the one being born, and yet the Catholic church has utterly and completely failed to comprehend an awesome and marvelous title that must be attributed to Mary as the first of many believers and brethren that is much great than that of mother: tabernacle of the Most High God. Mary was the first of many brethren – the archetype – of Christ in you!

---

[46] What this expression means has not been revealed to me. This is what I heard, so I wrote it.

Nearness to God *and* the kingdom of heaven... has never been more near at hand – than now!!!

> "I beseech you therefore, brethren, by the mercies of God, that you present your bodies a living sacrifice, holy, acceptable to God, which is your reasonable service. ² And do not be conformed to this world, but ***be transformed*** by the renewing of your mind, that you may prove what is that good and acceptable and perfect will of God" (Rom. 12:1, 2).

Elohim in Us

And now... for another layer in the revelation of God's mystery in Christ...

God Most High and Lord God are never manifest in the same place at the same time. God Most High *El Elyon* manifests Himself in His *glory* in Heaven as He rests from His work – and when God decides to work His work and accomplish His will, He leaves "His rest" *to manifest Himself* in the earth as Lord, Lord God, and Lord Almighty – through Christ Jesus.

God never divided or subdivided Himself into other persons; the Lord our God is One... on earth as it is in heaven! [47] They express Themselves according to the manner of Their manifestation.

Once we have declared Jesus as Lord and delivered our sovereignty to Him as our Master, God is now our spiritual Father whereby He converts our temporary dwelling (heart) into a *permanent* house (abode) firmly rooted and established within our heart and then – He enters into His rest within us. The Father's

---

[47] As a design-build contractor for 14 years, I would do planning and design in the evening, but in the morning, I would manifest myself on the job to work the work. I was the same person... performing two functions.

rest... is in us! When the Father's Presence permanently abides within us, we likewise can cease from our labors and enter into His rest because this salvation phase of our life with the Father is now complete; we are no longer striving... now we abide in Him as He abides in us! We have been saved, preserved in Christ and have been sealed for redemption by the Holy Spirit! Next begins the "dominion with a commission" phase of our life on earth whereby the Holy Spirit begins sanctifying us, changing us, renewing us, ***transforming*** us and manifesting Himself through us to save other souls alive and take back what the enemy has stolen from God. Our efforts from this point forward are done for our Father's glory through Christ Jesus our Lord by the empowering of the Holy Spirit. It is no longer you doing it – it is now *Elohim* doing it... in you, with you and through you, to the glory of God.

The Lord leaves His rest in Heaven – and then enters His rest within the permanent house (*mone*) They build within us (John 14:23). "Where is the house that you will build Me? And where is the place of My rest" (Isa. 66:1). Their place of rest is now residing within the heart-home we built and consecrated for Them to abide in, which successfully completes the Lord's plan of salvation for us – and now Christ *commissions* us to have dominion over His enemies with His authority residing in us and His power flowing through us by the Spirit of God. Wow, indeed!

"The kingdom of God is within you" (Luke 17:21).

We have been saved – in order to receive a commission from Christ – to complete the work of Christ – to have dominion upon the earth – with God abiding in us – in the name of Jesus – for His eternal glory.

If we say, "Oh yeah, I can see that now. How wonderful and marvelous is our glorious Father who resides within me. I am in the Father and the Father is in me. Awesome!" But (pause for a moment)... this revelation of the Father dwelling in us should also bring great conviction! Can we continue to live according to the ways of the world with all its' sinful and deceitful practices whereby we subject the Father of love, grace and truth who abides in our heart to experience these evil practices by us? He hears our thoughts and sees what we see and is subjected to any and all the sinful things that we do. (pause again). Do we disregard the Father's holiness with such contempt so as to imagine a separate reality in which His holiness abides within us while we rationalize our sinful thoughts to engage in sinful practices? Beloved – the Holy Spirit will hold us in contempt!

This is what I mean by Christian atheism; we believe it, but don't believe it enough to live it. If we were thoroughly persuaded and convinced by the truth of God, then we should live according to what we believe… and this way ***must*** look different than the manner of the worldly pattern.

How can we continue to live with this false perception of a dual reality within us, as if we can claim God as our Father but live like sons of Satan? Brethren, this is simply untenable! This is what the Bible calls lukewarm faith (because it cannot even be called authentic Christianity); we profess one thing by faith, but the reality of the life we live is dominated by the opposite reality of Satan's dominion at work in us and through us. Beloved – this must stop!

Who do you love more? What we love most … determines Who we love.

> "Do not love the world or the things in the world. If anyone loves the world, the love of the Father is not in him" (1 John 2:15).

Grace is not the license to do what we want; grace represents the attributes of God Himself that He wants us to manifest on the earth – in us and through us – for His glory.

> "For where your treasure is, there your heart will be also" (Matt. 6:21)

The only God anyone on this planet has ever seen or heard from is our Lord Almighty Jesus Christ! Jesus – is the Name above all names! And there is no one else!

It's all about Jesus – and the Father and Son get the glory![48]

God is Spirit

And now we shall learn about another aspect of God's nature. God is Spirit (John 4:24). When God is in residency on earth and manifesting His will, *Elohim* comes *with His Spirit*, yet when God is in residency in Heaven, He sends forth His Spirit to guide us and lead us into all truth – and the Spirit speaks on Christ's behalf (not on His own authority) and to work His will (John 16:13)! The Holy Spirit is known as the Spirit of God and the "the Spirit of Jesus Christ," whom Jesus sent forth from the Father for at least three reasons: as the guarantee of a better covenant, as the God who says "He will never leave us or forsake us," and as the administrator of His church – against which the gates of Hades shall not prevail. Jesus is preeminent and triumphant in life and death – and He came to offer us life eternal so that we may "enter into His rest" on account of our faith in Him and be received by Him "in paradise." [49]

> "We give You thanks, O Lord God Almighty, the ***One*** who is and who was and who is to come, because You have taken Your great power and reigned" (Rev. 11:17).

> "To him who overcomes I will grant to sit with Me on My throne, as I also overcame and sat down *with My Father* on His throne" (Rev. 3:21).

This teaching creates an open door for Judaism to comprehend their Messiah as "the One True Living God" and to embrace Jesus

---

[48] Unless we deliver this glory into Satan's hands again through disobedience and unbelief (read Galatians).

[49] Read "Here: The Kingdom of Heaven is" by the author.

Christ unbridled by any 'perceived' polytheistic constraints of a Trinity doctrine. It is hopeful that this teaching will initiate reformation and revival within both houses of faith whereby they now can come together in oneness to worship the Father in spirit and in truth – and in *dunamis* power – through faith in Jesus Christ!

We are standing at the precipice! The church age is over – the kingdom age has begun![50] *One kingdom, one God, one King, and one Lord – Jesus Christ!*

If we continue to see Jesus as just the Son of God instead of Almighty God, then the revelation of our true calling in Christ as "the church" will be forever minimized by a less-than version of our life in Christ; however, when we fully comprehend this teaching, the sleeping church will become radiantly alive with the Good News of Jesus Christ.

Jesus is Lord!

It is all about Jesus! Jesus is God, so why does the church talk so much about Father God yet so little about Jesus? *Because they do not know Jesus as YHWH and have taken Him for granted*! This must stop! The church, whose Head is Jesus Christ, **should be declaring Jesus is Lord** and making Him known as our Lord and our God in whom everyone can have a personal relationship. God is invisible, but Jesus was manifested so that we may see – and believe!

Declare Jesus to this dying world to help them see Jesus for who He really is and teach them the truth: apart from Jesus – you will never know God… because He represents the *One true God*!

If Jesus is your Lord and God, then use His name. Declare it and call upon it! The spirit of religion will do anything it can to

---

[50] Between every major spiritual shift, there is always a period of transition – and we are in transition now.

prevent people from using the "Name above all names" and keep this world enslaved to an impersonal noun. If you profess faith in Jesus as your Lord and Savior, then speak like a Christian and declare His name!

> "For this very purpose I have raised you up, that I may show My power in you, and that My name may be declared in all the earth" (Rom. 9:17).

Jesus is Lord God Almighty!

Jesus is Lord and God, who always is, was and forever will be – God Almighty!

If Jesus *is not your Lord and your God*, then stop calling yourself a Christian. Either you are His disciple or you're not. Either Christ is in you or He isn't. Either you hear His voice and do what He says or you don't. The time of being a member of a religion or a denomination in the church age is over; either you are His disciple in the kingdom age or you aren't. The time of play church and pretend church is over.

"As for me and my house we will serve the Lord" is a popular scripture that is proudly displayed within many houses, but believing in Jesus is not enough to profess living in service unto the Lord. The first half of this phrase is, "Choose this day who you will serve" (Joshua 24:15)… whereby this phrase is all about dedicating your life to serve Jesus. Do you serve Jesus as Lord – or do you merely believe? Faith is living according to what you believe, so if you believe in Jesus, then serve Him according to faith… "for whatever is not from faith is sin."

You are either all in – or all out! Attention!!! Do you believe in a theology that says Jesus is Lord – or do you have a personal relationship with Jesus and you have lovingly declared Him *your* Lord and *your* Master? Jesus is not interested in fans, spectators or passive admirers – He is seeking disciples who diligently seek Him and desire to worship the Father in spirit and truth.

Jesus was sent to be our Lord and Savior. Jesus is God – and *Jesus is **the only** begotten Son of the Father*. There are *no other "sons"* that the Father *has sent* to "represent" Himself; He Himself is *the* only One! Any religions or traditions that say they are from God or teach the ways of God by claiming to be prophets of God but do not honor and reverence Jesus as Lord are, simply, false teachings. Jesus proved His Divinity by His bodily resurrection (John 20:17) and no other prophet has ever done this – nor is able to do this.

If you *believe*, then settle it between you and Him, and enter into a covenant with Him. Stop running to pastors, priests, rabbis, and other such teachers for "their" opinion because they, most likely, are the same ones who have gotten this spirituality thing backwards and have turned your personal relationship with God into a religion in which you must pay to attend the man show.[51] Enough is enough! The *new earth* reality is based upon the relationship of one, i.e. you and Jesus, and it begins by making a solemn declaration in your heart to covenant with Him – and mean it! If Jesus is your Lord, then listen to Him and allow His Spirit to teach you and guide you in what you need to know.[52]

A *new earth* revival has begun – and it begins in the power of One!

Like all other names for God, we must reverence His name "Father" with great respect and, in holy fear, never profane it; therefore, we should never call anyone by His name, for this

---

[51] This teaching is not to be construed as the tearing down of any tradition or unique expression of faith. The organizational and built environment already exists as "the church," so there is no need to leave a church to build another building. Changes in organizations, much like people, begin from the inside out, as works of God's grace.

[52] If you want more information about how to hear the voice of Jesus, then read "Listen" by the author. This book and all others in this series are available for free. "As freely as you have received, freely give." Charging money to help people hear God's voice sounds almost as preposterous and paying men to hear His voice for you, but that is what some of us do on Sunday morning... we pay admission to hear entertaining words from a duly appointed listener of God's voice to preach a message to us instead of listening ourselves.

reason Jesus taught us: "Do not call anyone on earth your father; for *One* is your *Father*, He who is in heaven" (Matt. 23:9).[53] Anyone who calls themselves by God's names are inserting themselves between God and men... and we know that there is only "One" mediator between God and man: Jesus Christ (1 Tim. 2:5). Regardless of "what" your traditions teach, we would do well to heed these words of Jesus Christ: call no man Father... or do we desire to put the Lord to the test?

> "When the Son of Man comes in His glory, and all the holy angels with Him, then He will sit on the throne of His glory. [32] All the nations will be gathered before Him, and He will separate them one from another, as a shepherd divides *his* sheep from the goats. [33] And He will set the sheep on His right hand, but the goats on the left. [34] Then the King will say to those on His right hand, 'Come, you blessed of My Father, inherit the kingdom prepared for you from the foundation of the world...'" (Matt. 25:31-34).

Food for thought: if your heart has become impassioned for the people of this world who are lost and do not know the truth about Jesus, then take one year of your life to become His disciple... and then dedicate another year of your life to disciple someone else.

The Forgetful Prince

Imagine if you will, coming from a royal family, but you became separated from your family soon after birth and you have no recollection of your true family of origin. Your past has become obscured and you must now seek and find your origin without the help of anyone. All you have is this small nagging feeling that was planted deep within your soul that there is something marvelous and wonderful about your family of origin. Despite many attempts to forget and move on, the thought remains: you have a father that

---

[53] This teaching applies to spiritual leaders only, not as a father to his children within the family relationship.

loves you beyond measure and he has been waiting for you to find him. He cannot come to you, and there are forces at work that are diligently keeping you separated from your Father and preventing you from ever finding out who you really are ... so now, what do you do?

This story is analogous to who we are as sojourners and man's spiritual reality having been sent to earth. We have a heavenly Father who keeps calling out to us to come home, but all we can remember is the faint recollection of His deep love that created a void within us that only He can fill. It is a profound mixture of "Job" and "The Prodigal Son." Our sole purpose in life is to make contact and embrace the oneness of who we are in relation to Him. Nothing else matters.

God has been calling out to us since the beginning to be His ecclesia – His called out ones from the darkness into His light, but it seems man continues to perceive God as a spiritual concept rather than the reality of being a Father to us all – who is already in us all. We believe in God, and yet, we struggle to perceive Him in relational terms, so we restrict our understanding of Him to rational terms as separate, apart and distinct from us. "God" in heaven never left us and has never forsaken us on the earth; the God of heaven is our heavenly Father and has expressed Himself repeatedly through His Son in order that we may seek, find, understand and comprehend the great message of heaven and earth: God loves us! Through truth, change and oneness – our eternal homecoming is through faith in Christ Jesus. Christ is the Door to the Father; seek and find the Door! And then... enter *EN*!

God, in oneness of Father and Son, has been reaching out to us since the beginning, and has been speaking one simple message to us: We love you... turn around... come home.

Grasshoppers and Ants

> "It is He who sits above the circle of the earth, and its inhabitants are like grasshoppers, who stretches out the heavens like a curtain, and spreads them out like a tent to dwell in" (Isa. 40:22). [54]

Many years ago, I heard a missionary teach about his trip to a primitive culture. After much time of teaching about Christ, he grew frustrated because they still could not comprehend the mystery of Christ. It happened one day, while he was watching the construction of a roadway through the forest that he came upon an anthill – in the direct path of the road. The ants were scurrying about their business, oblivious to the eminent destruction about to occur... and then the idea came into his mind: "What if I could become an ant and tell them what is going to happen. Surely, then, they would listen and be able to get out of the way." And then the lightbulb went on in his mind; this is exactly what God did in order to tell us about the danger, show us the way – and save us. Later that day, when he told this story to the tribe, they embraced Christ immediately; they comprehended God's ways in the story about the ants.

> "Go to the ant, you sluggard! Consider her ways and be wise" (Prov. 6:6).

Does this make sense to you? Why else would God, who created the universe, come to earth in the form of a human being, over and over, in order to tell us, again and again, parables and stories about the kingdom of heaven? We refused to listen then, so why should we pay any attention to someone who professes to be the Messiah today? Why would God Himself come to earth in human form just to take away the sin of the world? God could have snapped His fingers and all problems would have disappeared, with heaven and earth restored in an instant, so why did God go to all this trouble just to conquer sin and death? There had to be more to the plan of

---

[54] Isaiah describes the "circle of the earth" over 200 years before Plato theorized it. Consider how he knew.

God according to the working of His will in Christ Jesus. Yes, indeed – much more.

He did it all for love! And He did it to show us the Way and manner in which we are to live – as sons and daughters of God as we have dominion over the earth – according to His teaching! Doing it all – in love!

> "And because you are sons, God has sent forth ***the Spirit of His Son*** into your hearts, crying out, "Abba, Father!" (Gal. 4:6).

Who, then, is the Holy Spirit? That is an excellent question which the church seems silent on. This will be explained soon, but all I will say at this point is: God is One... *with* His Spirit.

> "But he who is joined to the Lord is one spirit with Him" (1 Cor. 6:17).

> "And now the Lord God and His Spirit have sent *Me*" (Isa. 48:16).

What God has been saying (the expression) represents how He is going to work (manifest) His work on earth – *with* His Spirit. We can see the operation of God very clearly now, as God and His Spirit prevailing upon the earth... ever since the beginning... in Presence and Spirit:

> "In the beginning, *God* created the heavens and the earth... and *the Spirit of God* was hovering over the face of the waters" (Genesis 1:1-2).

> It's all about Jesus – and God gets the glory!

Expression and Manifestation

We believe in One God, who expresses Himself *and* manifests Himself – in Oneness.

"In the beginning, God" expressed Himself. The first expression of who He is became manifest through His creation, and man became another expression as well. The "Living God" of all creation (versus false gods that cannot talk or live or visit men) never exhausted His ability to infinitely express Himself, and every person is a unique, exquisite and wonderful expression of who He is as He manifests His glory and Himself in you, with you and through you. One day, we shall all be utterly amazed when we finally learn about the incredibly awesome expression that He planned for each and every one of us, but somehow... somewhere... we settled into a belief and then a lifestyle of "less than" rather than living out of His Presence and Spirit.

The expression always precedes the manifestation. At the beginning of anything is the thought of His intellect and – from God's thoughts – the manifestation proceeds "from out of" the expression. This is an incredibly important point to perceive – ***the expression precedes the manifestation*** whereby the experience proceeds from out of the expression; the '*ratio*' precedes the '*oratio*' – and '*logos*' (thoughts conceived, expression) precedes the '*rhema*' (utterance, manifestation).

We see this in its truest sense when we recall the story about Jericho. The Lord told the Israelites to march around that city once a day for six days, but on the seventh day – do it differently and march around it seven times... and then God manifested His might. The expression, followed by obedience, resulted in manifestation whereby the walls of Jericho crumbled. (Joshua 5:13; 6:1-5)

How is this different from what we are doing today? It seems an entirely devout group of Jesus followers are seeking manifestations of His power and glory without comprehending the reason why the expression must come first. This has been my observation of the Holy Spirit renewal movement over the past 30 years; we have been seeking the spiritual gifts (manifestations) of the Spirit without comprehending this expression (the what for *and* why). If the manifestation is there but the expression remains veiled, then somewhere, somehow, we misunderstood the message that is supposed to proceed from out of the expression. Were these manifestations intended to magnify the superiority of the Christian faith over other faiths, or certain ministers above other ministers? Or – is the manifestation intended to glorify Jesus through His church?

The gifts are manifested to glorify Jesus – through His body... which is the church.

We are not supposed to be celebrating the glory of any church or a specific outpouring in a place when God's manifest power and glory should be released everywhere through His church; we are supposed to be celebrating the glory of Jesus as "the manifestation of God's Presence" that proceeds from out of this unique expression of Who He is. Jesus is the expression and the church is the manifestation that proceeds from out of Christ Himself! Got it? Great!

If the church does not glorify Jesus, then why on earth does the church exist? The church has gotten stuck in promoting the salvation message at the expense of denying Jesus the glory of His unique expression that He Himself called "the church." We are the ecclesia, we are His "called out ones" from within many nations and tribes to hear His voice, who must then report back to our *ethnos* people groups the good news of Jesus Christ; however, the message most people hear today is "God this" and "Father God that" rather than Jesus is LORD GOD ALMIGHTY, who was and is and is to come!

We are here to glorify Jesus! The church is here to glorify Jesus!!! If we (the church) is the manifestation of Jesus Christ upon the earth and we do not even regard Him as God Almighty, then what on earth are we doing? It seems we have lost the true expression of our faith that can only be found in Christ alone – and we have lost our sense of purpose as well. We keep running from one new spiritual party to another manifestation of glory without understanding the expression is what Jesus wants us to seek: Jesus is the manifest expression! We are chasing after the glory cloud hoping the manifestation returns again and again so we can flop around like fish, but I tell you the truth... Jesus is seeking those who will worship the Father in spirit and in truth because He wants to express Himself in advance of the manifestation. Jesus wants us to walk with Him and become "His manifest expression" so that wherever we go, we manifest His glory and power and exalt His name above every name because – it's all about Jesus!

However, we have become a culture of glory chasers. We chase after the manifestation when Jesus clearly wants us to seek Him, to host His presence and to live according to the Spirit so that He may release His glory – in us and through us. Jesus is the expression, the manifestation, and the only manifest expression of God Himself... whereby Jesus told us, truly, "You have neither heard His voice at any time, nor seen His form" (John 5:37). God our Father does not speak, nor does He have a form – because God expresses Himself only through the voice of Jesus and manifests Himself only through the Holy One of Israel: Jesus Christ.

Any teaching or tradition that does not regard Jesus in the fullest sense of who He is – is diminishing the Divine reality of His glory, majesty and preeminence over all creation, as well as His Divine manifest expression through His very tangible body upon the earth... His church.

Wake up, church! Wake up, sons of God! The time has come upon us now to manifest the glory of Jesus through the church. Did you not perceive that He was manifesting Himself in the church (the expression) and now Jesus is about to manifest Himself through His church with greater works? The church is woefully unprepared for the next manifestation of His expression... because it will come as a tsunami wave of inexpressible grace.

Greater grace, greater works... and greater glory... is coming soon.

Many movements have come and gone during the past 50 years,

and many ages as well, which served as types and shadows preceding the next manifest expression of Jesus as He expresses Himself in the earth yet again. All previous movements are coming into alignment, including the new age movement, wherein, this time... it will herald Jesus Christ as Lord God Almighty.

Jesus will obtain the glory in everything – to the glory of the Father. Amen!

> "***And now the Lord God <u>and His Spirit</u> have sent Me***" (Isa. 48:16).

The Spirit of Jesus Christ

By now, we should know who God is, right? We understand Jesus is the manifest reality of God's incarnate expression upon the earth, appearing for God and as God, yet there is another Person of the Godhead that I would like to introduce to you, whose name is "the Holy Spirit."

> "***Come near to Me, hear this: I have not spoken in secret from the beginning***; From the time that it was, *I was there*. And now the Lord GOD ***and His Spirit*** have sent Me." [17] Thus says the LORD, your Redeemer, the Holy One of Israel: "I *am* the LORD your God, who teaches you to profit, who leads you by the way you should go. [18] Oh, that you had heeded My commandments! (Isa. 48:16-18)

Jesus has never spoken in secret, but the reality of His identity is often hidden within the scriptures for seekers of truth to find! Not hidden *from* us, but hidden *for* seekers of truth to find (Prov. 25:2). So now, allow me to express the reality of God within the context of the above scripture: Jesus is speaking this to the prophet Isaiah, in Oneness of the Father and Son, with His (Holy) Spirit. He says of Himself, "I am the Lord your God" who is being "sent" as an action by "the Lord God" and "His Spirit" (Isa. 48:16-18)!

To put this into context, let me remind you that Jesus never referred to His Father as Lord God, not once, and Jesus never prayed "to" the Father (He always said, "And I will pray the Father"), so this scripture is very complex and is impossible to comprehend without help from "His Spirit."

For example, we know that Jesus Christ is "the Lord God" who abides in Oneness with (and as) the Father, so there will be some scriptures that are impossible to comprehend because they refer to the Lord God in Oneness, within past, present and future tense because Jesus operates within the spiritual reality of Life eternal as "the God of the living, not the dead."

> "The Spirit of the Lord God is upon Me, because the Lord has anointed Me to preach good tidings to the poor; He has sent Me to heal the brokenhearted, to proclaim liberty to the captives, and the opening of the prison to those who are bound" (Isa. 61:1).

Three things are revealed from both of these verses: 1) Jesus is both "Lord God" and "the Lord your God," 2) the Sovereign Lord (Father and Son) sent "the Lord your God" (Jesus) and 3) Jesus was sent *with* "His Spirit." This makes absolutely no earthly sense to the natural mind of man which is why we need the Spirit to guide us into all truth. Yet this third point is what I want us to key into. To Whom does the Spirit belong? If the Lord God calls the Spirit "His Spirit," then to whom does the Spirit belong… to the Father *or* the Son?

We shall soon learn that the Holy Spirit is from God and is delegated to speak on behalf of the Son, and also the Father and the Son in Oneness, as "the Lord your God" – for the Spirit does not speak on His own authority. Now, let's look at several passages of scripture to confirm this:

- The Holy Spirit has names that are attributed only to Jesus: "the Spirit of Christ" (Rom. 8:9); "the Spirit of Jesus Christ" (Phil. 1:19); "the Spirit of Jesus" (Acts 16:6); and

"the Spirit of His Son" (Gal. 4:6) because it is the Spirit of Christ who reveals Christ to us.
- The "Spirit of *your* Father" is a term that is found only once in the scriptures, and it pertains to the inner witness of hearing from the Father within a divine personal relationship with Him (Matt. 10:20). This is highly significant, especially when we pay careful attention to what Jesus said about the Holy Spirit: "But the Helper, the Holy Spirit, whom *the Father will send **in My name***, He will teach you all things, and bring to your remembrance all things that I said to you" (John 14:26).
- The birth of Christ came about (to Mary)… "*through* the Holy Spirit" (Matt. 1:18-20)[55]
- When John the Baptist proclaimed the coming of the Messiah, he said of Jesus: "This is He who baptizes with the Holy Spirit" (Matt. 3:11; John 1:33), so then, the Baptism of the Holy Spirit is commissioned by Jesus Himself.
- In Romans 8:9, there is an interesting correlation between the Holy Spirit and Jesus: "But you are not in the flesh but in the Spirit, *if* indeed the Spirit of God dwells in you. Now *if* anyone does not have the Spirit of Christ, he is not His"
- The Spirit is often referred to as "the Spirit of God" and, since we also know Jesus is God, it is not surprising to see these next couple terms used in context with Jesus: "the Spirit of Jehovah" (Isa. 11:2); "the Spirit of the Lord Jehovah" (Isa. 61:1)
- Jesus is Lord, and the "Spirit of the Lord" is mentioned 28 times
- Jesus is the One, true living God (Jer. 10:10), and "The Spirit of the Living God" (2 Cor. 3:3) helps mankind realize the truth regarding who Jesus is… as the Manifested One

---

[55] "The Savior was begotten by the Holy Spirit. Thus the real Father of Christ's body was the Holy Spirit, and the real miracle was not in the Savior's birth, but in His supernatural conception." Willmington's Guide to the Bible, p.649; Section 5.E.1

- And finally, Jesus is the only mediator between God and man, yet Jesus *and* the Holy Spirit are referred to as our "intercessor" (Rom. 8:26, 27, 34; Heb. 7:25)

More specifically, pay attention to what Jesus tells us about the Holy Spirit:

- "However, when He, the Spirit of truth, has come, He will guide you into all truth; for ***He will not speak on His own authority***, but whatever He hears He will speak; and He will tell you things to come. ¹⁴ He will glorify Me, for ***He will take of what is Mine*** and declare it to you. ¹⁵ ***All things that the Father has are Mine***. Therefore I said that He will take of Mine and declare it to you" (John 16:12-15)
- "But when the Helper comes, *whom **I shall send** to you from the Father*, the Spirit of truth who proceeds from the Father, He will testify of Me" (John 15:26; both Jesus and the Holy Spirit proceeded from the Father and speak under His authority – John 8:42)
- "But the Helper, the Holy Spirit, whom *the Father will send **in My name***, He will teach you all things, and bring to your remembrance all things that I said to you" (John 14:26)
- "Nevertheless I tell you the truth. It is to your advantage that I go away; for if I do not go away, the Helper will not come to you; but if I depart, ***I will send Him to you***" (John 16:7)
- "*For He whom God has sent speaks the words of God*, for God does not give the Spirit by measure" (John 3:34)
- "But you shall receive power when the Holy Spirit has come upon you; and you shall be *witnesses to **Me*** in Jerusalem, and in all Judea and Samaria, and to the end of the earth" (Acts 1:8).

Jesus, in Oneness with the Father, told us, "the Father will send (the Holy Spirit) ***in My name***" (John 14:26), "*whom I shall send to you from the Father*" (John 15:26), and again, "***I will send Him to you***" (John 16:7). Jesus is telling us, in addition to the inner witness we have by the "Spirit of your Father" that Jesus will send an outpouring of the Spirit to us after He is reunited with His Father in heaven; therefore, the Holy Spirit speaks on behalf of Jesus – and the Holy Spirit will manifest Christ *in us* to continue His work upon the earth.

> **"Now the Lord is the Spirit; and where the Spirit of the Lord is, there is liberty"** (2 Cor. 3:17).

Jesus came to reveal the Father and declare His word to us (John 1:18; 17:26); likewise, the Holy Spirit was sent by Jesus to reveal Christ to us and declare His word:

- "He will glorify Me, for He will take of what is Mine and declare it to you" (John 16:14)
- "All things that the Father has are Mine. ***Therefore*** I said that He [Holy Spirit] will take of Mine and declare it to you" (John 16:15)

And yet, the institutional church has no clue who the Spirit is, who He is subordinate to, or Whose words He speaks. The Spirit is best known as the Spirit of God because He comes of/from God, and as the Spirit of the Lord because He comes of/from Jesus, yet we see in the above verses that Jesus is the One who sends the Holy Spirit while on the throne "in Oneness" with the Father, so that He (i.e. the Holy Spirit) is given without measure and continues to do the work of Jesus upon the earth.

And this same Jesus "Will baptize you with the Holy Spirit…"

> "And He [Jesus] is before all things, and in Him all things consist" (Col. 1:17).

Our understanding of who Jesus is resonates within the very core of who we are. Our inner man is constantly searching, hungering and seeking the One who completes us and makes us alive in oneness with the Father again. If we have professed faith in Jesus as Lord and Christ, then by grace through faith, we are born again (becoming anew by the Spirit). We are disciples following Jesus Christ, Who is our Lord and Savior, and is also "the One" person of the Godhead who created everything before the beginning, and in Christ Jesus "all things consist!" As it says concerning Jesus:

> "He who comes *from above* is above all; he who is
> of the earth is earthly and speaks of the earth. He
> who comes from heaven is above all" (John 3:31).

"He who comes *from above* (*anothen*) is above all." Jesus told us in John 3:3, 7 that we must be born *again* (*anothen*), anew... from above; and when Jesus was brought before Pontius Pilate, Jesus told him, "You could have no power at all against Me unless it had been given you *from above* (*anothen*)." Jesus is God. Jesus is not sort-of like God, as a Lieutenant who came to earth and received a reward for dying on the cross to save us. Jesus is the Lord of Glory, in Oneness with the Father, and Jesus is both God and Christ! And He made you!

"And He [Jesus] said to them, "The Son of Man is also Lord of the Sabbath" (Luke 6:5). Now, read Genesis 2:1-4 to see Jesus operating as "God" our creator (v.1) and then revealing Himself as "Lord God" of heaven and earth (v.4). Could Jesus really claim that He is "Lord of the Sabbath" unless – this is true? The clues were there all along...

The Spirit with the One

The doctrine of the Trinity is not that difficult to believe, which is why it is so easily believable, *but* if we believe the Holy Spirit is also God, then there should be some evidence within the scriptures that the Holy Spirit is also worshipped; I searched and could not find any reference (but I will discuss one instance of importance later on). It is, however, the work of the Holy Spirit to inspire us to worship God:

> "For we are the circumcision, who worship God in
> the Spirit, rejoice in Christ Jesus, and have no
> confidence in the flesh" (Phil. 3:3).

> "But the hour is coming, and now is, when the true worshipers will worship the Father in spirit and truth; for the Father is seeking such to worship Him. ^{24} God is Spirit, and those who worship Him must worship in spirit and truth" (John 4: 23, 24).

Perhaps the most interesting aspect of Jesus is *nowhere* found in the book Revelation: the physical appearance that John knew. When Jesus reveals Himself to John, the disciple whom Jesus loved (John 13:23; 19:26), who was an eyewitness to both the Transfiguration and the Resurrection, John should have recognized Him, but He didn't. Seven times Jesus reveals Himself, but never as Jesus "according to the flesh":

1. Rev. 1:12-14 – "and in the midst of the seven lampstands One *like* the Son of Man" whose head and hair "were white like wool." There is no doubt that this is Jesus, but John does not seem to recognize Jesus when He reveals Himself as "the Ancient of Days" (Dan. 7:9, 13)
2. Rev. 4:1-3 – "and behold, a door standing open in heaven... and behold, a throne set in heaven, and One sat on the throne. And He who sat there was *like* a jasper and a sardius stone in appearance; and there was a rainbow around the throne, in appearance like an emerald." Here is Jesus as we are to envision Him now, as He is in heaven 'according to His glory' in Oneness with the Father and abiding with Him, because He reveals Himself as "the Lord of Glory" (1 Cor. 2:8; James 2:1)
3. Rev. 5:6 – "and behold, in the midst of the throne and of the four living creatures, and in the midst of the elders, stood a Lamb as though it had been slain, having seven horns and seven eyes, which are the seven Spirits of God sent out into all the earth." This image of Jesus is a clear and unveiled message that John himself can identify with, whereby Jesus reveals Himself as "the Lamb of God" who took away the sin of the world! (John 1:29)

4. Rev. 14:1 – "and behold, a Lamb standing on Mount Zion." Jesus is revealing Himself by various images to communicate who He is in glory – who is worthy to receive worship… "Yet I have set My King on My holy hill of Zion. I will declare the decree: the LORD has said to Me, 'You are My Son, today I have begotten You" (Psa. 2:6, 7), whereby Jesus reveals Himself as the One who is worthy to stand upon God's Holy Mountain, i.e. "His dwelling place" (Zech. 14:4-9; Psa. 132.13; Isa. 8:13-18; John 4:21)
5. Rev. 14:14 – "and behold, a white cloud, and on the cloud sat One *like* the Son of Man, having on His head a golden crown, and in His hand a sharp sickle." Jesus reveals Himself as "the Lord of the Harvest."
6. Rev. 19:11 – "and behold, a white horse. And He who sat on him was called Faithful and True, and in righteousness He judges and makes war." Jesus reveals Himself as "the Conquering King" and as the One who sits as Judge upon the judgment seat of Christ.
7. Rev. 22:16 – "I, Jesus, have sent My angel to testify to you these things in the churches. I am the Root and the Offspring of David, the Bright and Morning Star." Jesus concludes the revelation of Himself *in Word only*, as the Word of God (Rev. 19:13), not in prophetic physical form, by declaring more names attributed to Him of which these are just a few of over 111 names for Jesus in the Bible… with 42 in Revelation alone. [56]

---

[56] There are at least forty-two names for Jesus in Revelation: Jesus Christ (1:1), the Faithful Witness (1:5), the Firstborn from the dead (1:5), the Ruler over the kings of the earth (1:5), the Alpha and the Omega (1:8); the Beginning and the End (1:8; 21:6; 22:13), the Almighty (1:8), the First and the Last (1:10, 17), Son of Man (1:12; 14:14), He who lives (1:17), He who has the keys of Hades and of Death (1:18), Son of God (2:18), He who has the key of David (3:7), the Amen (3:14), the Faithful and True Witness (3:14), the Beginning of the creation of God (3:14), One sitting on the throne (4:2), Lord God Almighty (4:8), O Lord (4:11), the Lion of the tribe of Judah (5:5), the Root of David (5:5), the Lamb (5:6, 8), the living God (7:2), our God (7:10), Him who lives forever and ever (10:6), the God of the earth (11:4), the God of heaven (11:13), our Lord and of His Christ (11:15), Lord God Almighty (11:17), Child (12:4, 5), King of the saints (15:3), The One who is and who was and who is to be (16:5), Lord of lords and King of kings (17:14), the Lord[our God (19:1), the Lord God

Jesus revealed Himself to John seven different ways: as the Ancient of Days, the Glorious One, the Lamb of God, the King on God's holy mountain (Zion), the Lord of the harvest, the conquering King, and finally... as the Word of God. Jesus operates within dynamic fluidity rather than static reality[57] and can appear however He wants to whoever He wants, so when people describe seeing the face of God in a vision, dream or whatever, we can be sure that they have seen another aspect of Jesus because... Jesus is the only one who has seen the Father (John 6:46)... and He is the only visible manifestation of God that can be seen.

In conclusion, John never saw Jesus "according to the flesh" as He remembered Him, but he somehow recognized Jesus in the manner which he knew Him on earth, which I am of the opinion was by the nail prints in His hands. Jesus manifested Himself in various unmistakable ways – as prophetic images of God and Christ to communicate a very clear message: Jesus is Lord God Almighty and He is seated upon the throne in Heaven! Jesus is our Lord, Redeemer and KING! However, John never saw an image *like* Jesus sitting upon the throne of His Father that he would have recognized. He saw a glorious image, much like what Ezekiel saw:

> "Like the appearance of a rainbow in a cloud on a rainy day, so was the appearance of the brightness all around it. This was the appearance of the likeness of the glory of the Lord. So when I saw it, I fell on my face, and I heard a voice of ***One*** speaking." (Ezek. 1:28)

Omnipotent (19:6), Faithful and True (19:11), The Word of God (19:13), Almighty God (19:15), KING OF KINGS AND LORD OF LORDS (19:16), Christ (20:4), the Root and the Offspring of David (22:16), the Bright and Morning Star (22:16).

[57] Static reality represents those things in the physical dimension which seldom change or change very slowly. The spiritual dimension, however, is always fluid and changes often and quickly at times, hence, dynamic fluidity represents those elements that change often, especially the things of the Spirit.

Just as the Apostle Paul taught us that we should no longer regard Jesus in the flesh because he (like Ezekiel) experienced the brilliance of His glory (2 Cor. 5:16, described above), now we should likewise regard Jesus according to His glory. The problem we have in the church is: we still think of Jesus in static realities as physical and unchanging when He is Spirit and can manifest Himself in an infinite number of physical manifest expressions; we need to perceive Jesus according to dynamic fluidity as One who can manifest His presence however He wants.[58]

Now consider this: after His resurrection, Jesus appeared unto many, but His countenance (appearance) had changed and they did not recognize Him, so do we think the Lord Jesus will appear in a manner that we will comprehend with our eyes – or – shall we perceive Him by the inner witness of our spirit with the Holy Spirit?

Yet this creates an issue to resolve in determining who the "seated One" on the throne is in Rev. 5:1 and 5:7. So I asked Jesus why He didn't reveal Himself in the manner which we know Him best, and He gave me this understanding, "I do not want to be remembered in My humiliation. I was treated with utter contempt, tortured, humiliated, ridiculed, scoffed at, insulted and murdered upon a cross. Think of the most embarrassing moment of your life – and then being made a public spectacle for all to see." All I could do at that moment… was repent. Forgive me, Jesus!

Back on point…

> "And I saw in the right *hand* of Him who sat on the

---

[58] Just as Jesus manifested Himself many times to John, as well as many times to others throughout human history, it should not surprise us whatsoever to see ourselves in this same manner. Our expression – as a living soul – was clothed in human flesh and yet our expression over time has been revealed as many manifestations: infant, baby, child, adolescent, sibling, teen, young adult, adult, parent, grandparent, and yes… as an ancient one with many days. And, likewise, the jobs we performed and the services we provided to family and community increase the number and diversity of these manifestations through which people have known us and shall remember us by.

throne a scroll written inside and on the back, sealed with seven seals. ² Then I saw a strong angel proclaiming with a loud voice, "Who is worthy to open the scroll and to loose its seals?" ³ And no one in heaven or on the earth or under the earth was able to open the scroll, or to look at it. ⁴ So I wept much, because no one was found worthy to open and read the scroll, or to look at it. ⁵ But one of the elders said to me, "Do not weep. Behold, the Lion of the tribe of Judah, the Root of David, has prevailed to open the scroll and to loose its seven seals." ⁶ And I looked, and behold, in the midst of the throne and of the four living creatures, and in the midst of the elders, stood a Lamb as though it had been slain, having seven horns and seven eyes, which are the seven Spirits of God sent out into all the earth.
⁷ Then He came and took the scroll out of the right hand of Him who sat on the throne" (Rev. 5:1-7).

"Who" is "the seated ***One***" on the throne that is able to receive worship in Rev. 4:10? Clearly, at this moment, this is King Jesus in Oneness with the Father, and the words of worship by the twenty-four elders proclaim the works of the Son "created all things" and the works of the Father "by Your will they exist and were created" (v.11). This Person does not have a physical form that John can see, at least not yet anyway. Everyone in heaven has just finished prostrate worship (with face to the ground) and then… there is a subtle scene change when John looks up immediately following the heavenly worship of God, who is sitting in resplendent, radiant, glorious splendor, and sees…

"And I saw in the right hand of Him who sat on the throne a scroll" (Rev. 5:1). [59]

---

[59] Rev. 5:1 (Greek translation): "Καὶ (And) εἶδον (I saw) ἐπὶ (on) τὴν (the) δεξιὰν (hand [right]) τοῦ (of/from) καθημένου (sitting one - or - the one sitting) ἐπὶ (on) τοῦ (the) θρόνου (throne) βιβλίον (a scroll)…" It is important to note

John did not describe the rest of the body, nor did the Holy Spirit tell him to write it, so it is possible that this now-visible hand has extended *just beyond* the glorious image of the seated One on the throne. Why is this small detail so important? Because if the One on the throne is the Father, and Jesus is the Lamb that is now standing in the midst of the throne who takes the scroll from "the hand," then either the invisibility of the Father that Jesus taught us, whom "no one has ever seen" is in error (John 1:18; 5:37; 6:46; 1 John 4:12), or there is another explanation for the hand of God that is being revealed at this time. All I ask is that you keep an open mind regarding the work of the Holy Spirit upon the earth – and in heaven.

As I mentioned before, the Father and Jesus are never revealed in the same place except when they reside within tabernacles for the other; "I and My Father are One." The Father and Son are in Heaven, seated in glory, and whenever God leaves His seat of rest to work the works of God in heaven or upon the earth, He leaves the glory of His throne and reveals Himself in various ways to men. Can God be in two places at the same time? Certainly! But can God, who is One, be manifested as two persons in the same place? Certainly, that is, if we are able to comprehend God *and* His Spirit, such that "nothing is too difficult for God."

The Father and Son were enthroned in glory in Rev. 4:1-11, then the scene in heaven changed (Rev. 5:1), and then the One seated on the throne reveals a hand with a scroll. The Person with the hand cannot be Jesus because He is about to be revealed as the Lamb standing in the midst of the throne who takes the scroll out of the One who is seated on the throne. Ok, is there any other possible explanation for the hand of God that appears 'from out of' the radiance of the throne other than the Father? Let me remind you of four incidents:

---

the Greek word for "the one sitting" καθημένου is the exact same word that appears in 4:2 and also 5:7, but translated as "He" in 4.3 and "Him" in 5:1.

- Ezekiel had an experience with the Holy Spirit and he recorded this event: "He stretched out the form of a hand, and took me by a lock of my hair; ***and the Spirit lifted me up*…**" (Ezek. 8:3)
- Jeremiah was commissioned as a prophet by the Lord with an outstretched hand (Jer. 1:9)
- Moses praised the wondrous deeds of the Lord "by an outstretched hand" (Ex. 15:12)
- Belshazzar, King of Babylon, as he was about to use the golden articles of worship that his father, Nebuchadnezzar, had obtained from the Lord's temple, experienced this:

"In the same hour the fingers of a man's hand appeared and wrote opposite the lampstand on the plaster of the wall of the king's palace; and the king saw the part of the hand that wrote" (Dan. 5:5).

Daniel was called to interpret the message and its' meaning because they knew, from prior experience, that "the Spirit of God is in you" (v.14). Daniel came, and he saw, and he told them: "The fingers of the hand *were sent from Him*, and this writing was written," (v.24) which he then interpreted for them. Not an entire body was seen… just the fingers of the hand were visible, as *having been sent from* God. If God can send a hand to Belshazzar, then can He not also send a hand out of His Own glory as He stands as a Lamb before the throne?

Now consider this: the Holy Spirit manifested Himself as a Dove upon Jesus (John 1:32), the Holy Spirit manifested Himself as the hand of God to King Belshazzar, the Lord spoke through Balaam's donkey (Num. 22:28-35, which I believe was the voice of the Spirit), and the Lord continues to manifest Himself and speaks to us through His Holy Spirit, so then, is it possible the hand in Rev. 5:1 is God's hand being manifested by the Holy Spirit? I believe that this is a very genuine possibility whereby the scripture is true… "You have not seen the Father at any time."

So now, pay careful attention to what the four living creatures and twenty-four elders and host of angels say about the Lamb in Rev. 5:8-14 that culminates in them worshipping the Lamb. This may be a very subtle and insignificant detail, but the *One* who is seated on the throne is neither worshipping nor receiving worship; all worship is directed toward Jesus, the Lamb of God, who is standing before the throne, in Oneness with the Father. The evidence points to the Spirit of Glory being on the throne (1 Pet. 4:14) – Who abides in Oneness with the Father and Son *yet does not receive worship*. The Holy Spirit is God – in Oneness – but does not receive worship!

There may be other examples whereby this can be explained, yet I do not know of any.

Here is John, the disciple whom Jesus loved, who gave us the testimony of Jesus as well as the best description of the Father who, until John's gospel, was barely known to man. His testimony regarding the Father and the Son is reverently regarded as "inspired text" and I also regard it in that same manner. Jesus is seated in glory with "our Father" and "His Spirit," thereby authenticating the Oneness of God – with His Spirit – not as three persons, per se, but as One expression with many manifestations.

The outcome of this teaching should inspire the church to teach all disciples of Jesus to become more passionate about who they are in Christ and to thoroughly comprehend their earthly mission to have dominion as they proclaim "Jesus is Lord" – according to the Spirit, in love!

> "But you have an anointing from the Holy ***One***, and you know all things" (1 John 2:20; this name is attributed to the Holy Spirit).

We desperately need the Holy Spirit to guide us into all truth and the knowledge of Christ whereby Jesus, our Lord and Teacher, will teach us all things and reveal the mysteries of the kingdom to us. Focus on Jesus, keep your eyes on Jesus, follow Jesus – become His disciple!

IMAGE

The Un-Jung Archetype

When I first began to write this book, I titled it "The Prototype" because Jesus came to us as the architect of a better way, but this did not seem like an accurate name to describe Jesus, so I went to Jesus in prayer and I asked Him: "Jesus, what name do you want me to call You?" And He replied with one word: "Jesus." So, I explained to Him that I am writing a special chapter about Him, so I would like to use a special name. He replied, "My name is Jesus." Then He gave me the understanding: "I like My name. I gave it to Myself. The angel Gabriel told Mary what name to give Me because this is the name I want to call Myself."

Well, I guess if you created the entire universe, then you can call yourself whatever you want.

Jesus is begotten of the Father, not made, preexisting, one in being with the Father, since "before the world ever was" (John 17:5). However, to help us understand the nature of man as a created being, who was made and created according to a pattern in the likeness of Jesus, in *His Own* image, the word Archetype was as good a character-descriptor as any... until I became aware of the teachings by Carl Yung who developed many archetypes to explain the psychology and metaphysical reality of God within the human psyche apart from the reality of God – or in other words – our spiritual reality without any relationship to Jesus as our Lord and Savior. Thus, the best name to describe Jesus was rendered incompatible by an antichrist teaching that celebrated the mental ascent of man's intellect above the knowledge of God. Bummer!

So, I returned to the first and best occurrence that describes Jesus as – "Image."

> [26] Then God said, *"Let Us make man in Our image, according to Our likeness; let them have dominion over the fish of the sea, over the birds of the air, and over the cattle, over all the earth and over every creeping thing that creeps on the earth."* [27] So God

*created man in **His own image**;* in the image of God He created him; male and female He created them. ²⁸ Then God blessed them, and God said to them, "Be fruitful and multiply; fill the earth and *subdue* (*kabash*) it; have dominion over the fish of the sea, over the birds of the air, and over every living thing that moves on the earth" (Gen. 1:26-28).

When I first tried to wrap my head around this phrase a year and a half ago, I focused on the prepositions. Did "in" mean 'in' as "in Our image in Our likeness" or "as His image according to His likeness?" I read multiple Bible translations to see how other versions translated it and even consulted Hebrew commentaries to find meaning and truth. Theologians have written books about how to translate and interpret the meaning of this one preposition: *EN*. However, it seems they missed the message.

The second words that I parsed were "made" and "created," as distinctly different from the word "formed" in verse 2:7. These ideas and concepts were adequate for the first book, Regenesis, but they were woefully inadequate for the "Image Bearers" series.

Let us take a step back and see what God is really saying here. We know that men were created upright and very good, a little lower than the angels, as mighty judges and magistrates, called '*elohim*' (gods) by God (*Elohim*; see John 10:34; Psa. 82:6; Ex. 4:16; 7:1) and crowned with glory and honor (Psa. 8:5), so it should not surprise us in the least if we see this phrase within the context of scripture to gain a larger, deeper meaning: "Let Us make man like **Him**."

This may sound heretical, but I can assure you that it is not. I received this word of truth by way of early morning prayer, worship, meditation – and confirmation in the Spirit. I did not create it; it came to me as an understanding from the Holy Spirit. I even asked the Lord to strike me dead if this word was inconsistent with His word or His truth. Yes, I would rather die than be guilty of Divine treason.

IMAGE

"Let Us make man as Our likeness according to His Own image." "Let Us make man like Him – as His Own image." Slice it and dice it a hundred different ways, but the truth is simply this: we were made and created to be like Him, little *elohims* in the likeness of *Elohim* (Psa. 8:6), in the likeness of our Lord God and Savior, Jesus Christ. The "Us" in this regard, is Jesus in Oneness with our heavenly Father *and* His Spirit.

We were made and created according to His likeness, which is why we all appear the same, in the manner of all mankind, inside and out. We appear exactly as we were made to appear, according to His likeness. Jesus came to earth in the form of a man, and He didn't look any different than the rest of us. If fact, the scriptures say that He appeared somewhat ordinary in appearance.

> "He had no stately form or majesty that might catch our attention, no special appearance that we should want to follow Him" (Isa. 53:2 NET; note – this was prophesied hundreds of years before the Messiah was manifest in the flesh).

Why would God come to earth as an ordinary human and appear ordinary? Because He is not interested in what the outside of the house looks like; it is what's "inside" that matters!

There have been national and stately leaders in times past and present who regarded themselves as godlike, even divine; there are some practitioners' of law, medicine and architecture who act as if they are gods, and there are titles given to people in authority, such as chief, lord, father, master and such that indicate a similar pattern. We know that all leaders in authority are to be prayed for, not because they are worthy, per se, but because they are in a place of position that operates under God's authority and utilizes His power over His dominion.

It is difficult to see God's big picture by starting at the beginning of scripture and try to discern truth in a linear fashion, nor can we incrementally look at the aggregate of many small biblical fragments of scripture in order to come to the correct conclusion (yes, it is possible, but this is precisely why we have so many denominational interpretations of scripture). That would be like trying to put a jigsaw puzzle together without benefit of knowing what the original image looked like – with some pieces missing. Do you see my point?

Jesus is the original "Image" and we were made and created – according to His likeness – by Him. Jesus is the "*image*" of God (2 Cor. 4:4), "He is the *image* of the invisible God, the firstborn over all creation" (Col. 1:15), "who being the brightness of *His* glory and the **express** *image* of His person, and upholding all things by the word of His power" (Heb. 1:3). Jesus manifested Himself as a Man and revealed to men who He is, who the Father is – *and who we are*. Now that we know "Who" we are supposed to imitate, let's consider how we are supposed to "live and move and have our being" (Acts 17:28).

So, what is the likeness of Jesus Christ that He manifested? In Summary:

- Jesus is the *express image* of God (Heb. 1:3)
- Jesus is the *image* of the invisible God (Col. 1:15)
- Jesus revealed the Father to us, who is Spirit revealed in substance
- Jesus came to show us "Who" we were created in the likeness of – and to show us how to live , so that we may live according to the pattern in which we were created, whereby we should return to the original pattern of walking with Jesus in the cool of the day – as in the Garden of Eden. He came to show us how to live and teach us what to do (Gen. 3:8; Ex. 4:15) – as spiritual beings having a human experience, but when we lost our way and became captive to the things of this world *and* the prince of darkness, whereby He came as "the Way" – to remind us, and teach us, and show us once again the manner in which we are supposed to live – as His image bearers

- Jesus came as Logos, the Word of Truth and the Word of Life
- Jesus is the life-giving Spirit who is "the Life" and gives Life
- Jesus came as liberator and redeemer to set us free from the penalty of sin (which is death) and sent the Holy Spirit so that we have the power to resist the temptation to sin (deliver us from evil)
- Jesus came as the Archetype –the Divine template and pattern that we are to imitate

Jesus is the image that we were created according to, as patterns of Himself, so that we may fill the earth – yes, even invade earth – with the atmosphere of heaven within us as the body of Christ! We are to fill this earth as His representatives in oneness as the physical, representational "body of Christ" in the face of His enemy!

Jesus continues to manifest Himself upon the earth through His Spirit within us, which we also know as the Spirit of Christ, and He continues to manifest His presence in the earth through His disciples as the Body of Christ – His church. The physical reality of Christ is still upon the earth – and the gates of Hades shall not prevail!

The enemy cannot ever get rid of Christ's physical presence upon the earth because "the earth is the Lord's, and the fullness thereof" and because those who profess Jesus Christ as Lord are hosting His presence and manifesting His works upon the earth. Your faith in Christ is a physical reminder to the enemies of Christ that they have been defeated, so, regardless of your status in this life… your positional importance as a disciple of Jesus Christ upon the earth is why demons tremble when you proclaim Jesus Christ is Lord. Your voice is being joined to a multitude of voices on earth, as in heaven, for the tearing down of strongholds of darkness upon the earth. As you walk in faith, just remember that Christ is in you and you are walking in His victory as an official representative of heaven upon the earth, and you are united in oneness with your spiritual brethren as the physical, representational Body of Christ, which is the Church. Jesus said He would never leave us or forsake us, and this truth is revealed in His body – and within your heart – through the residency of the Holy Spirit.

> "Now you are the body of Christ, and members individually" (1 Cor. 12:27).

If Christ is in you, then you have already passed from death into life eternal, and you are members of His body.

> "He who overcomes shall be clothed in white garments, and I will <u>not</u> *blot out* his name from the Book of Life; but I will confess his name before My Father and before His angels" (Rev. 3:5; *blot out 'exaleipho'* (1813) – to erase, to obliterate).

> "Examine yourselves as to whether you are in the faith. *Test yourselves*. Do you not know yourselves, that Jesus Christ is in you?—unless indeed you are disqualified" (2 Cor. 13:5).

Is Christ in you? Does the Spirit bear witness within you through Whom you were sealed for the day of redemption (Eph. 4:30)? This book is all about Jesus – *and* the Spirit of Christ *in you* is a highly significant part of Christ's eternal Presence upon the earth whereby He manifests Himself through sons of grace called "disciples." Jesus is Lord God, and the Spirit of God continues to guide all seekers of truth into a divine relationship with Jesus Christ, the Lord *your* God... as His workmanship to finish the Father's business upon the earth.

The Pattern Made Known

All the types and shadows of the Old Testament were a foretaste to show us three things: Who Jesus is, Who the Father is – and who we are, having been made in the likeness of Christ. Life is not about you. The story of the earth and the history of man as we sojourn with God is *His* story as it is being revealed in you, with you and through you – in unity with the Holy Spirit.

So much has been taught about who Jesus is and, yet, we seem to know so little because we try to wrap our human understanding around a Divine "X" that cannot be comprehended in the natural. We need to see Jesus from a spiritual perspective, as the fullness of God being fully expressed and manifested in human form, as Spirit essence manifesting Logos substance. The Jews knew the Messiah would come and be made manifest, but they misinterpreted His appearing as a conquering King, not as someone who emptied Himself to become a Suffering Servant – like us! This idea of emptying has been construed to mean Jesus left His Divinity and His glory in heaven, but this is just not the case. Jesus, abiding in human form, never emptied Himself of His Divinity or His glory OR His Father; Jesus is God, Jesus is Divine and always *is* Divine, even while living on the earth as the Son of Man.

> "And the glory which You gave Me I have given them, that they may be one just as We are one" (John 17:22).

Jesus came to earth in human flesh, just like you and me, to show us how to live as men according to the Spirit without any regard for the flesh. Jesus was not only the Archetype of the Way, He left nothing unfinished when He came as the Divine pattern and template to teach us the manner in which we are to live… wherein we have been called to imitate this pattern as we walk according to the Spirit, operating with glory, in oneness with the Godhead.

Jesus is the Divine Pattern for mankind who revealed to us "who and what" we really are so that we may imitate His example for us. Everything Jesus said and did was to teach us: this is how you are supposed to live. Just as the Father was in Christ Jesus, likewise – the Father is in you! Now, live according to this truth: the Father is in you! Live like Jesus lived "that you may be one with the Father" just as Jesus lived in oneness with the Father.

> "If you had known Me, you would have known My Father also; and from now on you know Him and have seen Him" (John 14:7).

"If you "had definitely come to know Me," "you would have known My Father also" (*oida*) "would have had perception of": "from henceforth, you have known Him" (*ginosko*), i.e. having unconsciously been coming to the Father, as the One who was in Him, they would now consciously be in the contact and progressive experience of "knowing" Him."[60]

Our quest on earth is to come into this intimate, personal and more progressive knowing of the Father who dwells in us… until we know Him perfectly (John 8:55)… as shown to us by Jesus.

> "Philip said to Him, "Lord, show us the Father, and it is sufficient for us." [9] Jesus said to him, "Have I been with you so long, and yet you have not known Me, Philip? He who has seen Me has seen the Father; so how can you say, 'Show us the Father'? [10] Do you not believe that I am in the Father, and ***the Father in Me***?" (John 14:8-10).

The Father is in us! The problem, it seems, is… we do not really believe the Father is in us… or else we would live radically different than we do! And likewise, the revelation of this truth: 'Christ dwells in us' should initiate a revolution in our mind… yet it seems has had little effect on us as well. Gain the substance of living… by knowing this and living accordingly: the Father dwells in you!!! "Let the word of Christ dwell in you richly" (Col. 3:16) and also, "The Spirit who dwells in us yearns jealously" (James 4:5).

In The Spirit, Jesus Lived

While Jesus resided in the flesh, He did everything as "soul with spirit" abiding in human flesh. The miracles Jesus performed were

---

[60] Strong's Concordance, word study on '*oida*-1492.'

not done in the power of His Divinity (*kratos* power) but through the empowering of the Holy Spirit partnered with the spirit within Him.

> And from that time, Jesus walked in the "power [*dunamis*] of the Spirit" (Luke 4:1, 14).

This is one of the most important points of this book: Jesus operated and performed all His miracles through His spirit (small 's') within Him to show us that we, also, can do the same things He did – and even more so. How can this be possible? Jesus came to show us "the way" to live as spiritual beings with the power of God flowing through us – as gateways and conduits for divine power flowing through our divine nature (spirit). This is who, what and why we were created, but we tripped over the threshold of sin and then we forgot about the image made manifest in us.

Jesus is God – always and eternally – and Jesus is One *with* His Spirit, so why did Jesus need to be baptized by the Holy Spirit? Bingo! He didn't!!! He did it to teach us and exemplify how we are supposed to live… with our spirit partnered with the Holy Spirit!!!

Jesus willingly submitted His will and yielded the operation of His glory to the Father; He laid His will – and the operation of His glory – aside for one season of eternity to be with us… and become like us. He always had Divine power and glory – He just never operated in them; and in all things, Jesus became subordinate to the Father as a Son to demonstrate to us the spiritual pattern that men must imitate – and become sons of God. In this, Jesus completely submitted His will to be the instrument of the Father's plan, as Way/Truth/Life – for our benefit! Jesus laid down and yielded His life as a servant and submitted Himself in this manner in order to teach us who we are and to show us how to live. Jesus came as "God incarnate" (in the flesh) *to teach us* to remember how we were intended to live and walk in our divine nature (spirit: as spiritual beings) in the humble humility and frailty of humanity... as servants yielding their lives in order to accomplish perfectly the Father's will.

> "For we do not have a High Priest who cannot sympathize with our weakness, but in all points tempted as we are, yet without sin" (Heb. 4:15), "who, in the days of His flesh... though He was a Son, yet He *learned* [*taught us*] obedience by the things which He suffered" (v. 7-8). "For to this you were called, because Christ also suffered for us, leaving us an example, that you should follow His steps" (1 Pet. 2:21).

Jesus suffered as a man, in every respect, just like you and me. But, you ask, if Jesus did not perform all the miracles, healings, signs and wonders as "God," then how on earth did He do them? This is precisely the right question to ask. Jesus did these miracles and mighty works by yielding to the operation of the Holy Spirit's working through His spirit. Jesus walked in yielded submission of His spirit, always listening to hear the Father's voice in an uninterrupted flow of Presence and Spirit, and this is the way in which Jesus came to teach us and show us how to live... and how to walk with the Lord in an uninterrupted flow of Spirit and Presence through our spirit (that God gave us) under the guidance of the Holy Spirit. We are spiritual beings... a soul with spirit.

This is the linchpin to completely understanding who we are as we intentionally live life on planet earth: walk by faith, live according to the Spirit of life in Christ Jesus, under the anointing of the Spirit, partnered with the Holy Spirit and empowered by the Spirit to say and do all that Jesus directs us to say and do – according to the Spirit.

We are spiritual beings having a human experience on earth for one season in eternity. From the basis of this one truism, we are now able to operate out of *and* fulfill all other mission mandates, including, most especially – having dominion.[61]

---

[61] "Dominion" is book #3 in the Image Bearer series.

Jesus came in the flesh and operated in the power and fullness of the Spirit to be what Jesus was sent to be, as the Way, and to "say and do" what He saw His Father "say and do." He did this as a spiritual being with a spirit-nature wrapped within human form. Likewise, we were given a spirit so that we can walk in the fullness of the Spirit, as spiritual beings in the similitude of Christ, yet because of free will, we have been given two choices: either we can follow the example of Christ (who walked in the power of the Spirit – but never sinned, even though He was tempted and put to trial just like every human being, and yet, lived a sinless and perfect life) – or – we can walk in disobedience to gratify the desires of our flesh.

But, you say, of course He was sinless and perfect because Jesus was God Incarnate. Yes, He was, and is, but as I already mentioned, Jesus did not operate out of His Divine nature; He operated out of His spirit-nature wrapped within human form. Unlike us (who have a dual nature), Jesus has a triune nature (spirit, human and Divine), but He only operated out of His spirit-nature, as a spiritual being who was clothed in humanity (a human covering) just like you and me. The true nature of "who" Jesus is – and this goes for all of us – is on the inside; we are soul with spirit. And it is for this reason that Jesus came: to teach us how to live according to the Spirit.

So, if what I am telling you is true, then what are the implications of this teaching? This means that we can operate "in the spirit" in the same manner, likeness and similitude of Jesus, who was fully human and yet operated out of His spirit-nature in the fullness of the Spirit, and therefore, we can do the same things Jesus did!

"As He is, so are we in this world" (1 John 4:17).

All the miracles, healings, signs and manifestations that Jesus performed were done so that glory may be revealed, not only the glory of the Father in Jesus, but also the glory residing within us. Everything that is accomplished on earth happens because of two things: glory and grace.

And the things of earth (physical reality) are merely a type and shadow of the heavenly reality (spiritual things; Heb. 8:5) that surround us even now. We were sent to inhabit and change earth by the empowering of the Spirit... with the truth of heaven dwelling within us.

Jesus is God, who revealed the Father to us and manifested His glory – as His Son; likewise, Jesus revealed the Holy Spirit to us so that we may manifest the glory that the Father placed within us. (Read that again!) The children of God are in the process of being awakened from a long slumber – and all those who are willing to submit their entire will to Jesus, in order to walk in the fullness of the Spirit, just as Jesus did, *will perform* even greater signs and wonders than Jesus did. And for this reason we are called image bearers. Through our own free will, we will lay down one life, the life of the flesh, **and exchange it** in order to walk in our spirit-nature with the indwelling Holy Spirit, in newness of life, according to the Spirit of life in Christ Jesus. We are literally trading the shadow of earthly things for the unsurpassing joy to walk in the substance of the divine nature (2 Pet. 1:4), as spirit-beings operating in the power of the divine nature (2 Pet. 1:3)... just like Jesus!

> Jesus said, "Greater works than these you will do" (John 14:12).

This is the gospel truth, yet somehow, I get the sense that words will never be enough to fully communicate the Logos Gravitas inherently present in this message. Jesus is Lord; the Spirit indwelling and the Spirit empowering us to imitate Christ – walking and living in the anointing of the Spirit – like Christ!

Do you mean to tell me that Jesus did not perform all those signs, wonders and miracles from His Divine nature? (Again) Yes, that is what I am telling you. Being fully God, yet "being in the form of God, did not consider it robbery to be equal with God" (Phil. 2:6). He did not count equality with God (i.e. reckon Himself as God during the time He was upon the earth) as something to be grasped (able to be attained by man or comprehended by the mind of man). He lived in the manner of all men, as soul with spirit in the flesh, yet He lived His life according to the Spirit in complete obedience to "the Father." And now, this is how we are to live – in complete obedience to Jesus Christ according to His example!

Jesus is our Archetype and our Divine example to imitate, and we need to see His life as a divine expression of living a completely consecrated life to God whereby He did not sin, not because He could not... but because He desired not. This is what He taught us – by example: His love for the Father was so great that He did not desire to enter into sin, and therefore, became our example for a future "new earth" time when we will have this same free will in eternity with Him... but will have _no_ desire to sin (much like the angels that are now in heaven). And thus, we will love Him so completely that our desire to sin will never overcome our love for Him. We will be able to sin, but we will not have the same desire that we have now in earthen vessels, which even Jesus was able to overcome on this earth "in the flesh" because of His great love for "the Father." People who continue to dwell in sin – do not know God or understand the love of God (1 John 3:9; 5:18) – nor will they experience this love in the hereafter.

Jesus and the Father are One and abide in Oneness, so why did Jesus need to submit His will into the Father's hands? He did not do this for Himself – (now pay careful attention here) He did it for our benefit, in order to show us how to live according to grace. His prayers were said out-loud not for His benefit, but for our benefit so that we might learn from Him; Jesus never prayed "to" His Father... He simply prayed "the Father." He did it (once again) as a Teacher to show us how we are supposed to live as spiritual people being guided and directed and filled with the Holy Spirit as men "in the flesh" who desire to live in union and divine relationship with our heavenly Father.

And yet, the Spirit-filled church has adopted an entire doctrine of imitating the Father. Huh? Jesus told us to imitate Him, not imitate Him imitating the Father... but that is how far off course the church has gotten, which does not even recognize Jesus as the Head of His Church anymore.

The church has been teaching us *what to believe* (doctrine) and then teaches us *how to think about* spiritual matters, and then it even tells us *how to feel* the closeness of God, but it cannot explain to us "why." WHY do we believe this or that? To tell us the salvation answer so we do not forfeit eternal life in heaven is the soft answer; to tell us it is because we are lost and separated from God because of our *sinful nature* is a false premise; God is everywhere and He is close to everyone, especially the brokenhearted, but the message we continually hear is that "we did something wrong" when in reality – the wrong was done to us by "the sin of the world," but the problem is… we partnered with it! The church has generated emotional appeals to placate our fears, thereby creating a Sunday service addiction and a pastoral intercessory dependency rather than helping people seek God themselves and talk directly with Him by hearing His voice… whereby the Divine relationship with the Father is restored within us.

It may seem as if I am coming down hard on the church, but this is done for good reason, in the spirit of admonition with encouragement, not condemnation – because the church is doing the same thing Judaism did. Religious leaders and teachers in that day had created so many doctrines and teachings of men which generated so much toxic theology that they could not comprehend God's mystery revealed in Christ, such that, even some of the apostles as they were standing next to Jesus in resurrection glory… still *doubted* (*distazo* , 1365 – to stand in two ways; Matt. 28:17). They saw Him standing there… and some still doubted!

Jesus is the way, and the truth and the life! No intercessors are needed. Jesus has a message that He wants to say to you and through you, but you must focus your attention on Him… and start listening to the sound of His voice!

Jesus showed us the way we are supposed to live as spirit-anointed men and women living spiritual lives as life-giving spirits to help

IMAGE

the lost and, in the process, are now able to return to God and abide in an uninterrupted divine relationship of unity in oneness that "the Lord God" originally intended for us to live – in Presence and Spirit – as in the Garden. Jesus came that we might have life abundantly – with His *'zoe'* life in Genesis again, with regeneration newness happening each and every new day that we walk *in faith* without doubt. Every day in the Lord is a new day, because **all** former things have passed away... and, in Christ, they are remembered no more!

Jesus came to us – and by the word of His testimony alone He asked us to believe in Him. The disciples, the religious leaders and the people had little more to go on than that. Yes, they said He was a good teacher, and by many miraculous signs some believed that He was sent by God... but not all believed that He was the Messiah. He did Godly works, but this evidence was insufficient proof that He was the Messiah. Godly wisdom, yes, Divine works, certainly, but the Son of God? Well, perhaps....maybe...

And the same is true today – otherwise, our lives would look much differently, and this world would have been converted into the kingdom of heaven ages ago. We were sent here to be world changers (not fixers), to have dominion over the earth, and to be sons of light to overcome (disperse) the darkness with the truth of God revealed in Christ Jesus – and to manifest His Presence with the Spirit of God in us.

Jesus submitted His life in subordinate obedience to the Father unto the cross so that we may live again in newness, as in the beginning; however, there is only one thing that Jesus yielded while He lived upon the earth: His spirit. Three gospels recorded this event at the moment of His death on the cross, and use three different words:

- Matt. 27:50 – *yielded* up the spirit; *aphiemi* (863) to send forth, send away, yield up
- Luke 23:46 – *commend* My spirit; *paratithemi* (3908) to commend, to commit, draw near

205

- John 19:30 – *paradidomi* (3860) to give up, give over, deliver, as when fruit is brought forth (ready for harvest), as in the sense of delivering something to be kept by another

This is an extremely important point. If Jesus operated out of His Divine nature, then how could He yield up His spirit if they are one and the same? Indeed, He could not because they are not. His Divine nature and His spirit nature are nearly identical in operation, but Jesus never abandoned or gave up or laid down His Divinity, His Deity or His glory. Ever! Because Jesus is God, He could yield up His spirit in this manner to the Father as all men must do at death. Jesus operated out of His spirit man, and this is the same manner of spirit that is given to all men, as having been given by the Father (Luke 9:55), whereby we "live and move and have our being" (Acts 17:28). Just like Jesus, the anointing of the Holy Spirit can rest upon us and fill us (Luke 4:1; 1 Pet. 4:14) and move mightily in us – in word and deed (Col. 1:29; 3:17).

Jesus is the God-man, true God and true Man, in His birth as well as His death whereby He reconciled within His body the family of man and the family of God. This is highly significant because Jesus satisfied the requirements of the Old Covenant *in His body* and then rendered it "obsolete" (Heb. 8:13) through His death upon the cross to institute a New Covenant.

But what this really means is … we killed God.

Regrettably, and brutally, yes we did! Selah.

Jesus had Divine authority all His life – He had full authority to lay down His life and He had the authority to pick it up again (John 10:17, 18). As a child, Jesus became strong in spirit (Luke 2:40), began His Galilean ministry in the power of the Spirit (v.4:14), rejoiced in the Spirit (v.10:21), sighed deeply in His spirit (Mark 8:12), was troubled in His spirit when one of the disciples was going to betray Him (John 13:21), and yielded up His spirit to the Father in His final moments on the cross (notice when Spirit is capitalized, referring to the Holy Spirit, and when it is not).

Jesus had Divine authority all His life (Matt. 11:25-27; Luke 10:21, 22; John 3:35; 5:27:17:2), and all authority had been delivered to Him by His Father, so why do you think He consulted the Father and submitted His entire will to the Father?

- Jesus is Holy God and without sin, and yet He was sanctified (John 10:36; 17:19) and then was sacrificed as a sin offering
- Jesus is the Son of/from God, and He is God Almighty, and yet He participated in ritual cleansing and ceremonial purification according to Jewish law
- Jesus is God, and yet He was baptized by John to fulfill all legalistic righteousness under the very law that He instituted (Matt. 3:15)

'Let me say that another way... Jesus is God – and Jesus and the Father have always been God in Oneness, so...why did Jesus live His life in total yielded submission to the Father? For only one reason: ***to teach us by example how to live life*** as mere men and women (in the flesh) operating out of (through) our spirit man, partnered with the Spirit in yielded obedience through faith... and to walk "in the way and example and pattern" of our Archetype according to the Spirit. There is no other reason. ***Jesus operated from His sprit – to teach us how to do it!!!***

'Jesus came as "the Way" to teach us the way – and to show us how to walk in the way – as a yielded servant operating out of our inner spirit-man, to live in supernatural (spirit normal) victory, in the fullness of the Holy Spirit.

- Apart from the Vine, you *are* nothing
- Apart from Christ, you can *do* nothing (John 15:5)
- Apart from the Spirit, we *can* know nothing
- Anything we do apart from the Spirit of Christ Jesus – counts for nothing!
- Partnered with the Spirit, we can do all things through Christ who strengthens us

Consider this: Jesus gave (spoke) the law to Moses, He came under the law as a man and then He fulfilled the law as the Holy One of Israel in the form of a man. Truly, Jesus came to liberate us from the law so that we might walk in spiritual freedom according to "the new law of the Spirit of life in Christ Jesus" (Rom. 8:2). So, what was the whole purpose of the law? I am glad you asked: to bring us to faith in Christ!

> "But before faith came, we were kept under guard by the law, kept for the faith which would afterward be revealed. [24] Therefore the law was our tutor *to bring us* to Christ, that we might be justified by faith. [25] But after faith has come, we are no longer under a tutor" (Gal. 3:23-25).

We are no longer under a tutor – ***we are under Grace***! We are no longer servants under the law; and if you are a Gentile, then you never were! We are now servants under the Headship of Christ! Focus your eyes upon Jesus and yield to the guidance of the Holy Spirit... "For you are all sons of God through faith in Christ Jesus" (v. 26). And furthermore, do not allow yourself under any circumstance to be put under the bondage of religious doctrines made by men. We need to stop listening to the opinion and secondhand truth of others rather than going to Jesus Himself for firsthand knowledge and truth. Jesus is the Lord your God – and – your Teacher. Hear His voice, follow Him and walk in His Way!

That which is Spirit spirit is...

Therefore, we can walk and say and do the same mighty works that Jesus did – when we walk by faith and live as a spirit man "being filled with the Holy Spirit" in the fullness and power of the Spirit just as Jesus did. Jesus came to teach us how to walk "in the way" as spiritual beings whose spirit is yielded to the Spirit of God – and this is how we originally walked with Him – in the Garden. Furthermore, this is how we can live again, since the dividing wall of hostility has been removed, the penalty for our sin has been paid in full, and the sin of the world that separates us has been taken away by the atoning work of Christ on the cross. Even the veil was torn in two, from top to bottom, so that heaven is now completely open for us! We have been living within an open *'dianoigo'* heaven for the past 2,000 years and there is nothing that is preventing us from walking with God right now and abiding in uninterrupted presence with Him – on earth as it is in heaven!

Jesus came in the anointing of the Spirit and taught us how to live as spirit-beings according to the Spirit – as *beings* directed by the working of the Holy Spirit dwelling within us. Jesus is a soul like us, He has a spirit like us and He *had* a human body like us. Jesus came in the flesh, in the same manner of all mankind, as soul with spirit, and He humbly submitted His will to the Father so as to live His life – being directed by the Father – through the Holy Spirit... as the example that He intended us to follow. He said and did what He saw His Father say and do. And this was His primary mission: to show us the way by being "the Way" – the Perfect Living Example to imitate and follow. And He also came as "the Truth" to testify against the darkness of lies and deceit upon the earth, and He came as "the Life" to overcome the penalty of sin, which is death, and to bring us into life eternal by abiding in His Presence and Spirit.

So, how do we die to the desires of the flesh in order to walk in the anointing and power of the Spirit? Well, there are two options, but only one will result in the ability to live according to the divine nature within you: 1) live as a self-willed man directed by the flesh and intellect... or 2) live as a spirit-yielded man directed by the Spirit with intelligent understanding. We must reckon ourselves completely dead by surrendering our ego and self-directed life and, thus, consider ourselves dead to the cares of this world (Gal. 2:20), then be born anew from above *according to the Spirit*, and then submit our will to the Sovereignty of the Lord's plan – and "enter in."

About a hundred years ago, ministers used to ask pre-saved saints if they were able to lay down their will. The traditional response was, "no," and then the minister would ask, "Are you willing to let the Lord lay it down for you," and most often, the answer was "yes." We must be willing to "let go and let God" so that He can have His way in us. This is grace – and nothing but grace!

Grace is the work of God that is done to us *and in us* by the Spirit of grace, so that we may become transformed into the likeness of Christ. Grace is: the allowance of God to prevail in any situation! Let God's grace have its way and prevail upon you!

"The spirit is willing but the flesh is weak," so let your spirit-man be disciplined by the Spirit, being guided by the Spirit of truth, who comes alongside us to help us. In this effort, we have the gift of the Holy Spirit who was sent by Jesus to strengthen us in our weakness so that we can be sanctified, renewed, strengthened, empowered, and yes, anointed by the Holy Spirit to live supernatural lives according to the Spirit-directed life. You cannot accomplish this divine working through will power or self determination or any human effort, superiority of intellect or any special subscription to religious teachings or doctrines (John 1:12, 13). You must be led by the Spirit, be obedient to the way of the Spirit and enter into the flow of the Spirit (Rom. 8:14; Gal. 5:25). This is not a mental exercise to get closer to what God intended us to be; this is the spiritual reality of living a life of spiritual discipline to deny the gravitation forces of the flesh that want to conform us into the pattern of this world of darkness (and destroy your soul). It is not you doing it; it is you allowing the Spirit of God to do a work of grace in you that we are all unable to do in the flesh. The manifestation of grace in us is the work of the Spirit through us – according to the Spirit – as He determines. It is the Spirit of Christ flowing through us like a stream of living water, a gentle breeze, perhaps a mighty river, or even a gust of wind or a whirlwind to accomplish the things of God in us and through us. To each one of us, we have been called, and to each one of us, a measure of faith is given, so that each of us may be the manifestation of Jesus that God predestined us to be – and to fill the earth with His light and glory in order to '*kabash*' the darkness of the worldly system that has ensnared and trapped us and our brethren in slavish servitude since the beginning.

There are two realities within you: the self I and the Christ I.[62] There is the life that "I" live in the flesh – and there is also the life that "I" live according to the Spirit of Christ in me (Gal. 2:20). You can live according to "the self of flesh" or you can live according to "the Spirit in truth" with the "Spirit of Christ" dwelling in you. Living life according to the flesh results in eternal death, but living life according to the Spirit of Christ in you is "the hope of glory" resulting in eternal life. Every individual person has a choice to make... therefore, you cannot keep standing in between two ways! (1 Kings 18:21; Joshua 25:15) So, the time has come for people to take a stand; if Jesus is your Lord, then imitate Jesus. It was for this primary reason that He revealed Himself as the Way, Truth and Life; He sent Himself as the Way, to show us the way, so that we might live according to His example – in spirit and in truth.

When we adopt this teaching into our life, then we are now faithful ones abiding in Christ; we are no longer lemmings of this world; we are living as followers and disciples of Jesus, as sheep who hear His voice and follow the Good Shepherd – may we live accordingly.

Manifested Spirit-Filled Life

There is so much more to life than living on the humanity treadmill that grinds all of us back into dust every day. We have been liberated and set free from the bondage of this world and the penalty of sin (death) to walk in glory as Spirit-directed men. And while we were already dead in our sin and trespasses (Col. 2:13), Jesus sent the Spirit to guide us into a "dead, very dead" state through faith in Christ, so that it is no longer you who live – it is Christ's life now manifest in you (Gal. 2:20).

If what I am telling you is true, then we should be able to do all the things that Jesus did when He lived upon the earth. Well, yes and no (yup, you knew there was a catch). Yes, we can do all the

---

[62] Naturally Supernatural, p.36, Mark Virkler.

things that Jesus did while He lived upon the earth, but there is one condition: you must be willing to do greater works than Jesus did. Huh?

> Jesus said, "Most assuredly, I say to you, he who believes in Me, *the works that I do he will do also*; **and greater works than these he will do**, because I go to My Father" (John 14:12), "now to Him who is able to do exceedingly abundantly above all that we *ask or think*, according to the power that works in us" (Eph. 3:20).
>
> "He who promised is faithful" (Heb. 10:23), and "He who calls you is faithful, who also will do it" (1 Thess. 5:24).

Jesus sent the Holy Spirit so that our spirit can partner with the Spirit to do all the exceedingly greater works that Jesus planned since before He created the world. Just as Jesus operated in His spirit under the anointing and power of the Spirit, so, also, we can do the "greater works" that Jesus told us we would do when we submit to the prompting, leading, direction, administration and anointing of the Holy Spirit. This is the working of the Spirit: to continue the manifestation of Christ upon the earth within the lives of humbly submitted followers and disciples of Jesus to become the physical, representational body of Christ on the earth. Not our will, but "Thy" will be done, on earth as it is meant to happen – just as is always happening in heaven. Anew again – just as it is in heaven. Think about it and meditate on this: you are ambassadors of heaven, having been sent in human form to "be" His likeness and His workmanship, and to "work" the Father's will… in the fullness of the power of the Spirit. We are not just sinful men saved by grace – we are the redeemed of the Lord and are image bearers of Christ upon the earth.

How else can you explain Peter walking on water? Peter was a man like every other man, but in the presence of Jesus, Peter was invited by Christ to operate from his spirit – in Presence and Spirit. Peter wasn't walking in his human power; he was walking in grace, which is a supernatural power that is much greater than the forces of nature. The gravitational forces (laws or powers) of nature were never rescinded, nor were the physical properties of water changed; an invisible spiritual '*dunamis*' power greater than all physical powers was released at that moment... and Peter walked on water. It's all grace – from beginning to end.

Peter was not doing; Peter was *being* "who" he was created *to be* – and, therefore, was able to accomplish what he was predestined to accomplish in His presence. If you have acknowledged Jesus as Lord of your life, then invite the Holy Spirit to reside within you by grace through faith. If the Spirit resides in you according to grace, then you are now able to be (not do, but "be") the workmanship of Christ Jesus upon the earth. There are some things that the Father's manifest will has predetermined you to accomplish, but you must be willing to surrender your plans of self-attained glory that seeks its own honor (John 7:18; 8:50, 54) in order to attain the glory that has been hidden in you by the Father who wills that His works be accomplished in you and through you – as the manifest image of His Son, Christ Jesus, upon the earth.

Consider the other spirit-manifested events that have occurred to other human beings who are just like yourself:

- Paul was taken up into the third heaven (2 Cor. 12:2)
- Isaiah saw the roundness of the earth 200 years before Plato theorized it (Isa. 40:22)
- Philip was physically translated to another location miles away (Acts 8:38-40)
- Elijah was often translated (transported) by the Spirit of the Lord (1 Kings 18:7, 12)
- Elisha was able to make an iron axe-head float in water (2 Kings 6:6)
- Ezekiel was lifted up between earth and heaven (Ezek. 8:3; also 3:14; 11:1)
- Peter (in the flesh) walked on water (Matt. 14:29)

- Peter's chains fell off of him in prison with the help of an angel (Acts 12:6, 7). When he knocked at the door afterward, they were in unbelief and said, "It is his angel" (v.15)
- John experienced heavenly visions (Revelation)

There are over 143 spiritual events in the Bible that are supernatural, plus thousands of documented extraordinary events since the early Christian era. Whether these events happened in the flesh or the spirit, the Apostle Paul said "I do not know" (2 Cor. 12:2, 3), but one thing I do know: they were experienced by the spirit-man that dwelled within them and they were recorded so that we may believe. I no longer refer to these occurrences as supernatural events because they are "spirit-normal" events that should happen to "any" of us when we live according to the Spirit – to those who have invited the Holy Spirit to partner with their spirit. The Holy Spirit is an invited guest who will not violate your free will; in this regard, the Spirit is always a gentleman; however, on the flip side, we must test the spirits because some have unwittingly invited 'other' spirits to govern their life. Any "spirit" that does not acknowledge Jesus as the Son of God, who came in the flesh, is not from the kingdom of heaven (1 John 4:3).

> "But you are not in the flesh but in the Spirit, if indeed the *Spirit of God* dwells in you. Now if anyone does not have the *Spirit of Christ*, he is not His" (Rom. 8:9).

In the past couple months, since I began to share and write about spirit-normal events, many people have told me some incredible first-hand accounts: people have been raised from the dead, ministers have been protected by angels, missionaries have walked on water (not once but twice), children are seeing large angels with swords, entire villages are being converted to Christ overnight by dreams, one man walked through his living-room wall into a bathroom (that was locked from the inside by his roommate who was in the shower). There are so many, that I plan to create a page on the Genesisagain.org website so that people can record these events to encourage others "do not doubt…believe."

However, this has not been my experience thus far, so don't come to me looking for proof. I asked the Lord if I could experience these manifestations, and He told me that I do not need to experience these manifest events... I am "His writer" and I am to tell others about the good news of Jesus and to share this truth because this age is coming to an end. I am to write so that others may manifest and experience the glory that was hidden within them long ago. Others will testify and be a witness and a sign of this truth. And in this, I have learned to be content in all things...

The Atmosphere of Heaven

When we walk in the knowledge of this truth, it is spiritually liberating. When we fully comprehend this mystery of life as we live in this world, though not partners with it, we know that we can be saved, we have been saved, we are being saved and we shall be saved because we have been rescued from the penalty of sin, which is death. Now that we know the reality of the kingdom, that when Christ is abiding in you through faith, then you are no longer dead but living *in* the "life paradigm" of faith. You have "*entered into*" '*zoe*' life in Christ. So, what will happen to you when you die? Indeed, if you are "in Christ," you will be in the kingdom of heaven. Isn't that wonderful? Yes; however, let me ask you this: are you going to heaven – or are you already in the kingdom of heaven?

You are already in the kingdom of heaven. Let me explain.

Just a couple seconds ago you read a paragraph that stated a fact: if Christ is abiding in you, then you are in the kingdom of heaven. Use this as a benchmark for your salvation; you are saved and you are a citizen of heaven – at this moment! How long will you live? Do you have fifty years? Do you have forty years? Five years? How about one minute? Yes, at some time in the future, your physical body will die and then you will be made alive again in the kingdom of heaven. Ok, now this is going to blow your mind – your minute is up. You can keep on reading or you can go back and re-read what you read. You can go backward and forward according to the faith paradigm because time does not exist in the eternal dimension. If you died one minute ago (yes, I understand that you would not be reading this, but there is a principle theory we need to embrace here)... if you died one minute ago, then you would be in the kingdom of heaven right now! Regardless of whether you have one second or one hundred years left to live, according to faith that is lived according to the Spirit of life in Christ Jesus, and if Christ abides in you, then you are living in eternity – right now! You are living in the kingdom of heaven – now! You were not sent here to accept the gospel truth of Christ and then tread water until you die and go to be with Jesus; you are already operating in the kingdom of heaven as His workmen, redeemers, ambassadors, captive-liberators and image bearers for one purpose: TO BE THE LIGHT OF CHRIST for others to see RIGHT NOW! We are workers, who abide in the truth, who are called to take the light of Christ and shine it all around us. So, take the atmosphere of heaven and breathe the anointed word of life upon every human being and tell them the truth: they are a spiritual being. You don't have to keep living in the manner of all men according to the flesh; you can live according to the manner of Christ Jesus *now* and live in the power of the resurrection according to the Spirit of Way, Truth and Life that abides in you *right now*! This is the Good News! This is the gospel that was preached by the Apostles. This is the message that John the Baptist preached – repent and be washed (sins forgiven). And this is the message that Jesus preached – do not doubt... believe... the kingdom of heaven is at hand! Once we have repented, our soul is washed clean whereby we are given a new heart and a new spirit (Ezek. 36:26, 27), and then our lives will become transformed by the renewing of our mind as a working of the Holy Spirit in us so that we can live this new regenerate life "in spirit" to fulfill our original mission, as spiritual beings invading earth with the atmosphere of heaven! You are already operating in eternity, by grace, through faith – right here and now... when Christ reigns upon the throne in your heart!

"He has put eternity in your heart" (Eccl. 3:11).

The glory is already in us – and for this reason the Holy Spirit was sent – to release the glory of God that is already within us and to empower us to be who we were sent here to be: as image bearers in the likeness of Jesus Christ. We are *elohims* imitating Elohim, sons of God imitating the Son of God, judges and magistrates imitating the Chief Judge and Magistrate of this world.

Now that you know who you are, perhaps you should reread the Sermon on the Mount and start living according to least understood – and least followed – sermon by Jesus. He was teaching us how to live in the manner consistent with our original calling – as earth redeemers, empowered with His love, invading the darkness and overcoming it with the light of truth.

Making the Father Known

Jesus came to reveal Himself as Lord God Almighty and was sent to reveal the Father to us. For many of us, the Father is still relatively unknown, but even if we cannot understand Him, we can know Him and be known by Him as He manifests His love in us on account of Christ.

> "No one has seen God [the Father] at any time. The only begotten Son, who is in the bosom of the Father, He has *declared* Him" (John 1:18)

The operative word is declare, '*exegeomai*' (G1834) meaning, to declare, to make known from (*ex*) out of; to unfold a teaching, to uncover, *to declare by making known revelation by one who commands authority*.[63] In other words, Jesus is able to declare and make known all truth through revelation because He has the authority to do so. Jesus is the Message *and* the Revelation of God! Exegesis, a similar word in English, means "to lead (out) interpretation of a word, passage, especially in the Bible." Truth is being uncovered, unfolded, and revealed – and Jesus is the Truth of God who revealed Himself as God Incarnate so that we may live in obedience to the truth and imitate Christ our Redeemer and Savior.

> "And the Father Himself, who sent Me, has testified of Me" (John 5:37).

Jesus, The Way

Jesus came as the Way to show us the way. Jesus wants us to seek His face and to hear His voice and to know Him – so that we '*oida*' understand and thoroughly comprehend what living this spiritual life is all about. Jesus wants to teach us the secrets and the mysteries of the kingdom, just like He did with the disciples (Matt. 13:11). Jesus does not want to withhold from us any good

---

[63] Definitions combined from Strong's and Vines.

thing, and He has even given us the keys of the kingdom (Matt: 16:19; Luke 12:32).

> "Then Moses said to the LORD, "See, You say to me, 'Bring up this people.' ***But*** You have not let me know whom You will send with me. Yet You have said, 'I know you by name, and you have also found grace in My sight.' [13] Now therefore, I pray, if I have found grace in Your sight, ***show me now Your way***, that I may know You and that I may find grace in Your sight. And consider that this nation is Your people" (Ex. 33:12, 13).

By now, if I ask you just who it is that Jesus will send with Moses, you know better than to say Joshua or Aaron… it is the Presence and Spirit of God. Jesus will send His Presence with His Spirit to go with him. And what is "the way" that Jesus wants Moses to walk in? I am so glad you asked!

Jesus said, "I am the Way" (John 14:6). There are many paths that portend to be pathways of truth and righteousness, but there is only One Way. Moses did not know who was going to be going with him to show him the way, but today, the followers of Jesus know the way – because we also know "Who" we are listening to and following. Jesus told Moses, "My Presence will go with you and ***I will give you rest***" (v.14).

One thousand five hundred years later – and even today, another two thousand years after that, Jesus is telling us the same message, if only we will hear Him – and trust:

> "Come to Me, all you who labor and are heavy laden, and ***I will give you rest***" (Matt. 11:28).

Who can give us rest? Who can deliver us from our enemies? Who can give us peace? Who can restore the balance and state of equilibrium in our lives so we may be healed from sickness and disease? There is only one person who can give us rest, deliverance and peace; His name is Jesus, Lord Jehovah, and

Jehovah Shalom – the Prince of Peace, and through faithfulness to His voice, we are being delivered so that "we can enter into His rest".

> "And to whom did He swear that they would not *enter His rest*, but to those who did not obey?" (Heb. 3:18)
>
> "Therefore, since a promise remains of *entering His rest*, let us fear lest any of you seem to have come short of it" (Heb. 4:1).
>
> "For he who has entered His rest *has himself also ceased from his works* as God *did* from His. Let us therefore be diligent to *enter that rest*, lest anyone fall according to the same example of disobedience." (Heb. 4:10, 11).

What example of disobedience was that? It was the invitation by Jesus to hear His voice and draw near to Him, abide with Him – and enter His *rest* (*shakan*-H7931) – on Mount Sinai, but they refused to listen and obey – and they are still in rebellion to this day. Moses talked to Jesus face to face, but he never saw His face. Some traditions teach that Moses was conversing with the Father, but, how then, can Moses be talking with the Father (Ex.33:11) who then places him in the cleft of the rock (v.20) so that God can "physically" pass by and be seen by Moses? Truly, this is a Theophany of Jesus. God the Father is invisible, His attributes are invisible (Rom. 1:20), and "no one has seen God at any time" (John 1:18). The physical manifestations of God in the Old Testament are Theophanies of Jesus, for "He is the image of the invisible God, the firstborn over all creation" (Col. 1:15), and "the express image" of God (Heb. 1:3). But it seems the church prefers to play the game of mystical chairs when it comes to knowing God in the person of Jesus Christ.

Moses talked face to face with Jesus– and Moses listened. Now, fast forward one thousand five hundred years as we listen to Jesus telling His disciples in the middle of His teaching about the Parable of the Sower:

> "But blessed *are* your eyes for they see, and your ears for they hear; [17] for assuredly, I say to you that many prophets and righteous men desired to see what you see, and did not see it, and to hear what you hear, and did not hear it" (Matt. 13:16, 17).

Moses desired to see His face – and priests, prophets and kings desired to see His face – but they never did. However, a rag-tag group of ordinary men were sitting in the presence of the One who put Moses in the cleft of the rock so that He could pass by – and these disciples were listening to Him and looking at Him – face to face; **they were abiding in His Presence**; they entered His rest! How awesome that must have been! They are seeing the Lord of Glory face to face and are being instructed by Him, as one speaks to a friend… and they did not die… and neither will you.

> "No longer do I call you servants, for a servant does not know what his master is doing; but I have called you friends, for all things that I heard from My Father I have made known to you" (John 15:15).

Let me tell you the truth: you do not need to wait until you enter the kingdom of heaven in order to see Jesus face to face. We are instructed in dozens of places that the Holy Spirit will give followers of Jesus various gifts, including dreams and visions. Moses said, "Oh, that all the Lord's people were prophets and that the Lord would put His Spirit upon them" (Num. 11:29). Yet, the Holy Spirit dwells in us through faith (Ezek. 36:27; John 14:17) and we are able to experience dreams, visions and, through Spirit-anointed imagination, we can even see Jesus face to face. And what did the prophet Joel say:

> "And it shall come to pass afterward that I will pour out My Spirit on all flesh; your sons and your daughters shall prophesy, your old men shall dream

dreams, your young men shall see visions" (Joel 2:28)

Do you desire more? Do you desire to see Jesus? Do you desire to hear His voice and are willing to walk in His Way according to the way that He has prepared for you? Do you desire to take the next step? Well, there is nothing stopping you on His end. There is only one thing preventing you from seeing Jesus as He truly is: doubt that results in unbelief and rebellion. This is the same type of doubt that comes from being hardhearted.

We must be willing to talk with Jesus, face to face, like Moses did, and to turn aside, like Moses did at the 'burning bush,' and turn the fullness of our hearts' attention and affection toward Him in order that we may do one thing – and only one thing: hear His voice and walk in His Way. We must *"cease from our works"* and then humbly walk in the way that He has already prepared for us. Yes, the Lord has prepared a way for each of us, but we cannot know which way is right unless we are walking "in the Way" that comes by hearing His voice.

"Hear Him!" The Lord told Moses that he had found grace (favor) in His sight because he was walking "in the way." So, therefore, Moses gave us a template to serve as an example in accordance with obedience that comes by hearing His voice: "Show me now your *way*, that I may know You and that I may find grace (favor) in your sight." This was the prayer of my heart for over a year – and *then*... I began to hear the voice of the Lord clearly.

When we turn our heart toward Jesus, we will be walking in grace, and when we walk with Jesus, we find favor in His sight. Jesus is Grace incarnate. Selah.

There is no other way in which I can explain this any simpler than this: Hear Him! Do whatever it takes, do whatever is necessary, do the impossible, think the unthinkable and believe the incredible if you must, but do not forfeit the grace that can be yours just because you think that you cannot hear. You can hear – and Jesus desires to speak to each and every one of us, face to face as a friend – without exception – but you must desire this more than anything.[64] Proclaim Him Lord, declare Him Sovereign over your life, ask for forgiveness, repent of your sins, forgive others their trespasses, and then – ask the Lord of love incarnate to remove your doubt-hardened heart of stone and give you a soft heart and a new spirit, and then fill you with the Holy Spirit so that your mind may be transformed for one purpose: to hear His voice and become the likeness of Christ! This was the plan from the beginning: "Let Us make man like *Him*." You are an image bearer and you were created for this purpose.

It is so simple. It is all about Jesus – and God gets the glory!

No Ordinary Man

We learned already that Jesus came in the manner of human flesh, in the physical form and appearance of a man, and was acquainted with trials and temptations and sufferings as is typical for all manner of men, but with one exception: He did not sin.

What seems remarkable is that Jesus did not look extraordinary, that we might delight in His appearance or comeliness, nor did Jesus look like some human kings that may be chosen based upon physical attributes or persuasive speaking abilities. Jesus looked ordinary and He preached a simple message. Why? Because if He can do it, then so can you. You do not need to become special in order to share the good news; you already are special – you just forgot who you are.

We were created ordinary in appearance on purpose, just as Jesus was. We were created as a common thing in order for the purposes of God to be manifested in us to become "uncommon" and holy. We were formed of the dust as earthen vessels, lacking any special jewels or precious metals; as a created thing, we are very ordinary,

---

[64] For this reason, the first book in the Image Bearer series is "Listen: How to Hear the Voice of God." Hearing His voice is rarely if ever audible to the hearing of the ear, so read what it means to hear "the spontaneous thought."

except for one element: we are His image. It is not about the outside, which is a common thing (Greek *'koinoo'* – ordinary thing; Acts 10:14, 15; 11:9), yet the Lord regards us as saints whom He calls – holy (*'hagios'* – not common). The outside of the vessel was made common and ordinary because God intended all along that what He put *inside* the vessel is what makes us uncommon, holy and significant. Once again, Jesus is the living example whereby we are to be conformed to His pattern of holiness, not according to the outward earthly pattern of worldliness or outward shows of religious piety, but according to "the way of Christ" operating within us.

This next point may blow your mind. You were created as a house in the likeness of a house. The scriptures tell us we are like tents, tabernacles, vessels and hollow objects to contain something of value. We are houses and abodes for the Divine, made in the likeness of Jesus to host His Divine Presence. Before we came to the knowledge of the truth – of Jesus as the Messiah, we were a common, ordinary house, created on purpose for a purpose, but without any understanding what that means. Now, through faith, we live according to grace and now we are a precious, holy, consecrated, saintly, sanctified vessel for divine service; and now we are an instrument of worship, not just an article for worship… we are an instrument "of" worship.

Where do holy, consecrated people worship? Do they worship in holy places, like temples and churches – or have they themselves become a consecrated temple to worship God from within? Now ask yourself this: "When you go temple, synagogue, church or assembly, do you expect God to be there or not? If not, then why not? Do you not know who is living within you? Do you know what it means to come into the presence of a jealous God?" Think about this before you ever step foot inside a holy place ever again. The Lord comes into the building *when you bring Him abiding within you.* Either His presence is in you – or it is not. Either you have entered into His presence and His Presence is already abiding with you, and you being changed from glory to Glory, or you aren't. So now, do you go to church to be entertained and fed – or do you go to be changed from glory to Glory?

Jesus was begotten of the Father, not created, yet He came in the form of a man through the power (overshadowing) of the Holy Spirit (Luke 1:35). Jesus became a house, just like us (or rather, we are a house, just like Him, according to His likeness).

One of the names for Jesus is Immanuel: God with us. The tabernacle in the old covenant was the place where the presence of the Lord resided; the tabernacle was a type and shadow of Jesus Christ, a foretaste of Him who *IS* the Tabernacle *AS* the Most High God (Gen. 14:18-20; 17:1). In the Old Covenant, the Tabernacle was an object residing in a place where God dwelt among His people as a physical abode for the Divine. The temple was created *as a house* for the Tabernacle and Holy of Holies, so that wherever the Lord resides, He is surrounded by a tabernacle. Since the Lord Jesus resides in our hearts through faith (Eph. 3:17), we should all perceive ourselves as new covenant tabernacles that house Jesus – through faith in Christ! We are New Covenant tabernacles who are being built up into one body, the church, whose head is Christ Jesus.

The design for the Jewish temple was one way in order for the Lord to teach us how He constructed our physical being to host His presence. We have an outer court that interfaces with this world, we have in inner court where our soul and spirit reside, and there is a most holy place where the Lord tabernacles within us. Now does the design of the temple make sense?

The temple described by Ezekiel had a very elaborate design with many rooms. Jesus said that He was going away to prepare a place for us – and in God's house there are many *abodes* (*mone*; John 14:2). We are the living stones that are being built together into a "house" of Divine worship. On earth, we are not just tents and houses for the Divine, we are living tabernacles for Jesus, who is the One True Tabernacle…and yet, there is one more tabernacle that remains yet unbuilt (Rev. 21:3).

IMAGE

Now, can you see why we were created in His image according to His likeness? It is not for just any reason that we have become a permanent abode for Jesus Christ. We were created to become consecrated holy vessels to host the presence of the Divine – Jesus Christ. We were created for His glory – and the glory of our Father in heaven!

What is the one thing about all houses that makes them abodes? The thing that makes a house a permanent abode is when someone is living inside; otherwise, it is just the shell of a building that was built on purpose for a purpose – but it is not being used for that purpose.

> "Heaven is My throne, And earth is My footstool.
> What house will you build for Me? says the Lord,
> Or what is the place of My rest?" (Acts 7:49).

The same is true with all people. We were all made and created on purpose for the purpose of hosting the presence of Jesus Christ; we were intended to be an abode for the Divine abiding within us. So, what happens to these human abodes if they are not utilized as a tabernacle for Jesus Christ? Well, what happens to common, ordinary sheds after they become dilapidated and obsolete? Are they not torn down and thrown into the fire?

You may say, banish the thought! God would not casually just throw people into the fire. We are human beings; we are special; we were wonderfully made; we were created a little lower than the angels and have been crowned with glory and honor. Why would God ever do such a thing? Indeed, He must, on account of His justice – but the choice is yours. The person that throws you into the fire, as an unfruitful branch, is yourself (John 15:6). Or do you think yourself better than Christ Himself? If you live your life the way you want according to your plan, and then go to church expecting that you have met the minimum obligation whereby you are saved from the unquenchable fire, then you have been sold a false gospel that is really no gospel at all. It is unbelief and doubt that keeps you from becoming the holy thing that God intended you to be.

To put it bluntly... unless the presence of the Lord abides within you, then give God just one reason why you are more worthy than a jackal to be granted eternal life? You were created as a common thing by Jesus; you came to earth and were given the breath of life by Jesus; you are living in the manner of all men, just like Jesus; and He has also offered to you this same Holy Spirit to dwell within you, through faith. You are no different than Jesus in your earthly manner, so why should God save any wretched, miserable, common vessel that refuses to serve Jesus in the beauty of His holiness when He Himself suffered in the flesh and died on the cross at the hands of corrupt, evil men – for your sake?

> "Yet it pleased the Lord to bruise Him; He has put Him to grief. When You make His soul an offering for sin" (Isa 53:10).

Read all of Isaiah 53 to get a greater sense about the life of Christ that was wounded for our transgressions and bruised for our iniquities. Jesus never *surrendered* anything; He was victorious in His birth, life, death and resurrection. And yet, Jesus *submitted* His life as a *yielded* servant unto the will of the Father, so that the chastisement for our peace would be upon Him. "We considered Him stricken, smitten by God and afflicted," and yet, we continue to hold Jesus lowly in this regard when we deny Him sovereignty over our earthen vessel.

The Father was willing to do this to the house of His own Son, so, why do you think you are more entitled, more special, more exceptional, more distinctive, more extraordinary and more worthy to continue living in your "tent" when Jesus desires to live as Lord in your house – but you reject His command to host His presence?

You were created as a common thing in order to become a holy thing having one thing in '*koinos*' common: Jesus Christ. You were created in the ordinary manner of men in order to be consecrated, set apart, sanctified and made holy for one purpose: to serve the Lord Jesus, host His presence and worship Him in Oneness with the Father in spirit and in truth. You were created in weakness and, by your own free will, you have entered into sin, yet God created a way of escape for you through faith in Jesus Christ, and you have been given every opportunity to turn away from this common existence by returning to God, but if you choose not to repent, convert and return, then there is no hope for your soul. If you do not accept His command to repent and believe, then it is by your choice that you have forfeited the grace that was made available through faith in Christ Jesus whereby you might be saved.

And one more thing: God wants His house back. Damnation to hell is done in the nakedness of your soul. Now can you see why the damned are wailing in their nakedness? Everything that belongs to God will return to Him, including your house and your spirit. He gave them to us to use for one season on earth, and then they will return to Him; even the ash and dust belongs to God. Your body was never yours to begin with; you were merely a steward and caretaker of it for one season upon the earth. You can do whatever you want with it while you are living in that human tent, but when His life is taken from you, as well as your spirit, the things which belong to God will return to God. Your soul belongs to you – and it will go to one of two places…either to the place created for unredeemed souls so you can worship yourself in your hellish commonness – or to live in the kingdom of heaven to worship the Lord in His holiness.

If we are so much like God, then why does He allow us to fail and risk eternal damnation? He has given every created thing an opportunity through choice and free will to make a declaration of the soul – either in obedience to Him in His kingdom – or self-determination in your kingdom.

You can pretend to look *and act* like God all day long in your kingdom, but not in His.

We were created as image bearers to bear His image and to operate as His likeness in the majesty of a soul – as a life-giving soul worshipping Him in the majesty of His holiness. The outer man, the human tent, does not matter; the only thing that matters is if you are functioning as a tabernacle to host the presence of the Divine. Either the presence of God is in you or He isn't; either the Holy Spirit is in you or He isn't. There is no standing between or a middle ground concerning faith. ***Either you are all in or you are all out***, and the faith you believe is the manner of faith you live according to. Therefore, the choice is yours and yours alone.

God chose Israel as one nation among many nations, as a people, so He could reveal His nature to them and through them, but this mission was circumvented by their refusal to listen to His voice… followed by religious legalism. Then God sent His only Son to show us the Way. Now, therefore, we are to reveal Jesus to others through this living and true way because He has called us to be a people in which He speaks to us and reveals Himself as Immanuel – God with us, in us and through us, as living tabernacles with Christ in us – our hope of glory. Jesus revealed the Father to us, and likewise, we are to reveal Jesus to other people and make disciples by living like His disciples in the manner in which we were created: as image bearing disciples of Jesus Christ... as life-giving tabernacles.

God does not dwell in temples or churches made by hands; He dwells in temples that have hands.

Christ Is The Mystery

"Now to Him who is able to establish you according to my gospel (Paul's) and the preaching of Jesus Christ, according to the revelation of the mystery kept secret since the world began" (Rom. 16:25), "having made known to us the mystery of His will, according to His good pleasure which He purposed in Himself" (Eph. 1:9) "by which, when you read, you may understand my knowledge in the mystery of Christ" (v.3:4) "and to make all see what is the fellowship of the mystery, which from the beginning of the ages has been hidden in God who created all things through

Jesus Christ" (v.9), "the mystery which has been hidden from ages and from generations, but now has been revealed to His saints, to them God willed to make known what are the riches of the glory of this mystery among the Gentiles: which is Christ in you, the hope of glory" (Col. 1:26, 27).

This is the mystery of man: Christ in you, the hope of glory!

> "And He [Jesus] said to them, "To you it has been given to know the mystery of the kingdom of God; but to those who are outside, all things come in parables" (Mark 4:11).
>
> "And without controversy great is the mystery of godliness: God was manifested in the flesh, Justified in the Spirit, Seen by angels, Preached among the Gentiles, Believed on in the world, Received up in glory" (1 Tim. 3:16), "but has now been revealed by the appearing of our Savior Jesus Christ, who has abolished death and brought life and immortality to light through the gospel" (2 Tim. 1:10), "that their hearts may be encouraged, being knit together in love, and attaining to all riches of the full assurance of understanding, to the knowledge of the mystery of God, both of the Father and of Christ" (Col. 2:2), "meanwhile praying also for us, that God would open to us a door for the word, to speak the mystery of Christ" (v.4:3)

And this, also, is the mystery of man: sanctification.

This is the Christ I preach, Creator of all things, Lord God, Immanuel – God with us, and Jehovah Makoddishkem – The Lord Who Sanctifies.

Who Has Known Him

"For who has known the mind of the Lord? Or who has become His counselor?" (Rom. 11:34). "For "who has known the mind of the Lord that he may instruct Him?" (1 Cor. 2:16a).

"But we have the mind of Christ" (1 Cor. 2:16b). "Now by this we know that we know Him, if we keep His commandments" (1 John 2:3). "Therefore, from now on, we regard no one according to the flesh. Even though we have known Christ according to the flesh, yet now we know Him thus no longer" (2 Cor. 5:16).

Let us regard Christ according to His glory, being seated in Glory at the right hand of the Father.

More Than Just A Man

Jesus was more than just a sin-bearer. It may shock you that this was not His primary mission because we have been taught theology by faith-merchants and sin-merchants selling the doctrine of sin. Jesus came as Truth-bearer, Light-bearer and Dominion-bearer, but before He could fulfill His Dominion-bearer mission and re-commission us, He had to conquer sin and death as Cross-bearer, the Messiah. In this, Christ became Glory-bearer, Grace-bearer, Justice-bearer, Kingdom-bearer, so that He could establish His righteousness upon the earth and bring us hope and peace, and therefore, restore His kingdom. In all this, He was Love-bearer, God Himself. And He became Logos-bearer that we may believe in Him as Lord God, the Holy One, as the Living Word, as both Messenger and the Message to trust for our salvation – who is the fullness of God Himself – *that we might attain to "the fullness of God in us through Christ Jesus*." He became for us "the Life," not just to embody the essence of the Divine nature, but to reveal the Substance of God Himself so that we could touch Him and behold His glory.

If everything was written about the life of Jesus regarding what He said and did, these books would not just fill libraries, they would fill universities. "But these *words* were written so that you would believe" (John 6:29; 19:35). Just do one thing: BELIEVE! The only reason for the written word is this: BELIEVE! And teach others to believe. Luke said the same thing, "So that you may know" (Luke 5:24). And Paul took it all the way, "So that you may understand [and thoroughly comprehend] how great His love is for you" (Eph. 2:4; 3:4; Col. 2:2).

> "These things I have written to you who believe in the name of the Son of God, that you may know that you have eternal life, and that you may continue to believe in the name of the Son of God" (1 John 5:13).

Do you believe? If you do, then hear His voice and follow Him (become His disciple). If you do not believe, then read the written word and pray, so that you may begin to believe – and then listen to hear the *rhema* truth with a softened heart so that you may hear His voice – and live!

I'll Show You How To Live

You are a spirit-being having a human experience, so let's get going. We need to walk according to the Spirit in the anointing of the Spirit to accomplish all that Jesus prepared for us to do. Jesus taught the disciples "the Way," how to live and move, and the Lord's disciples taught their disciples "the way;" so, now it is time to teach all men "the way" and to walk according to the Way of Christ according to the Spirit. The time is right for harvest, but will we hear and obey?

Now You Do it

The miracle of the feeding of the 5,000 men, not including women and children, represents a fresh starting point in the Lord's teaching to the disciples, as well as us, concerning how we are to live. Jesus seems to be saying all along, "I've done it, now you do it." That is what good teachers do; they teach, then demonstrate by example, and then they give tasks to perform.

Jesus selected the Twelve (Mark 3:13; Luke 6:17) and continued to perform miraculous signs, wonders and healings in their midst for the better part of a year – then He sent them out on their own, without Him, *yet under His authority* (Mark 6:7-13), and they cast out demons and healed the sick (these miracles were done in the spirit before the Holy Spirit was sent at Pentecost; John 7:39). When the Twelve returned, Jesus withdrew with them "to a deserted place to rest for a while" (v.31), but the multitudes followed them. Now, here is where the ministry of Jesus seems to experience a change in atmospheric pressure, and power is about to be released through the disciples in an extraordinary way. Jesus was their teacher and a worker of miracles, but now He has transitioned from teacher to being their mentor who is now going to instruct them to be workers of miracles.

When the disciples told Jesus the multitudes were hungry, He simply said, "You feed them" (Mark 6:37), but the disciples questioned among themselves how this was possible? "Jesus asked Philip, "Where shall we buy bread that these may eat? But this He said to test him'" (John 6:5, 6). They were nowhere near Chick-fila, Subway, TGI Friday's or Country Kitchen; they were in the middle of nowhere, and yet, that is exactly where we need to begin, sometimes, in the midst of nowhere – with no immediate assistance or support – and with nothing but trust and obedient dependence upon God alone… with eyes lifted up to heaven in prayer. Jesus was not throwing them into the deep end; they were already in the deep end with Him – and now Jesus was teaching them how to swim in '*exousia*' delegated authority and power. Jesus is about to teach them that the authority and power being given to them is a result of being "in His Presence," and the miracle is already "at hand" and now the miracle needs to flow through them.

Jesus was waiting on the disciples for one thing: for them to figure it out. They had witnessed and experienced miracle after miracle by Jesus with the same result: lift your eyes up to heaven, pray, believe – then do what the Lord tells you to do. It does not appear the disciples knew what to do, so Jesus told them, "Make the people sit down" (v.10).

Jesus had already demonstrated that miracles occur when you trust God – and believe – and do what He tells you. The miracles were flowing through Jesus; they were flowing through His hands, His words, His clothes, His spit, and now, they were going to flow through His disciples. Through His abiding and intimate trust relationship with His Father, Jesus taught us to believe – that you can do all things and you can accomplish all things… but do not doubt. You must be thoroughly persuaded and convinced – you must have faith… and believe!

Jesus had already fed the multitudes once before and now it was the disciples turn. But wait, you say, there is no mention of feeding any multitudes before this point in time by Jesus. Yes there was, so turn in your Bible to Exodus chapter 16 to see a familiar story portrayed with Israel, Moses – and Jesus.

- Moses brought Israel up from the Red Sea *into the wilderness* (Ex. 14)
- Then they came to Elim and when the multitudes became hungry, they complained to Moses – and "the Lord" rained down bread (manna) from heaven, which He did to feed them, *but also* "to test their obedience" (Ex. 16:4)

Sound similar? Jesus told us that He *is* the true bread (manna) that came down from heaven (John 6:30-33), and then Jesus told us He *is* the Bread of Life (v.35), yet the Jews complained because He told them "*I am* the bread that came down from heaven" (v.41). Jesus provided the bread to feed multitudes of Israelites in the desert, and verily, He fed them out of Himself; and now it was the disciples turn to feed the multitudes "out of His Presence" among them.

And this is precisely where we find ourselves, today, in the midst with Jesus only, who wants the same miracles to flow through us just like what happened with the disciples – but we must host His presence and be a habitation for the Divine with the indwelling

Spirit in order for this to happen. There are many teachings about how and when the loaves were multiplied, but it seems fairly obvious now, doesn't it? Jesus told them to feed the multitudes – and He never rescinded this command; He commissioned the disciples to disperse the bread after He blessed it and broke it, whereby the multiplication happened when the disciples broke it and shared it with the multitudes. The people were set down in groups of fifty (the size of a company lead by a Captain) and the bread miraculously multiplied as it was shared 'from hand to hand' by the disciples. They kept breaking, the bread kept materializing, and the storehouse of heaven was being poured out – through the disciples.

When God tells you to do something, then He will give you the power, the authority and the provision to do everything He has commanded you. The disciples were learning to believe!

Today, we are also at a pivotal time in history when the release of God's power is about to be poured out and manifested through a multitude of signs, wonders, miracles, and healings the likes of which prophets cannot even predict. Many will seek after signs and wonders; however, the Lord wants us to "seek Him first." Seek the giver of the gifts – not just the gifts. It is not a manner of "if" but "when." It *will* happen, so trust "the Lord" and give thanks to the Father. We were created for just such a time as this, when the world seems to have become unglued at the seams and has seemingly gone berserk. We are all like sheep without a Shepherd, but the events about to take place in the near future will be utterly astonishing. Those saints who host the presence of Jesus will perform even greater works! "See, I have told you beforehand."

The church has spent much time teaching about Christ and His wonderful benefits, but now the time has come for the church to make disciples, who imitate Christ and submit their will into the Lord's hands to be an extension of His hands and feet and glory. Jesus called men to Himself to be His disciples, not just followers who shout Hallelujah and give glory to God – as a type of shadow that follows behind the encounter; Jesus called the disciples to be imitators of His way who go "ahead of" the encounter and "be gateways of a new expression" so the encounter may become manifest, thus creating ripples of "workings" everywhere they go. Just as Jesus told the disciples to cast out demons, heal the sick and "feed them yourself," likewise Jesus is telling us today, "Go ye therefore and do likewise." These disciples did not have the "gift" of healings or miracles or demonic deliverance; they were simply disciples who were living out of (through) His Presence according to the Way of Christ abiding among them. And this is the same Spirit that is in each of us through faith, to believe in the One who called us to walk according to His way, not just to believe through faith, but to live according to true faith, according to the Spirit of life in Christ Jesus, and to continue the ministry of Jesus Christ for one reason: to set captives free and build His church. And so, we are to build, not with human intellect or with bricks and mortar, per se, but with Spirit-anointed reasoning... with eyes lifted up in faithful expectancy.

For this reason we were created, as image bearers, to do the will of the Father, by imitating the works of Jesus "in the spirit" through the *'exousia'* delegated authority of Jesus under the anointing and *'dunamis'* power of the Holy Spirit.

For this reason, Jesus sent the Holy Spirit to us, to partner with our spirit, so that we may be His image bearers, to walk as His likeness, to abide in His truth, and to live according to His example and similitude whereby signs and wonders follow us as we imitate Jesus and focus on Him.

Since you are an image bearer, get ready, because we are in the last days... and there is much work to be accomplished. Walk in grace, go in peace, focus on Jesus, love one another, believe – and have dominion – for the praise of His glory!

What Would You Do?

How shall I describe the attitude of this present church...

If you were the head of a major corporation and you wanted to teach your senior vice-presidents, by personal example, how to conduct the affairs of the company... how would you demonstrate it? Would you invite them to attend a power-point presentation, or would you get down to their level and show them experientially how to think and act like "your" vice presidents' should? You would teach them everything about the corporation from the top down and how to conduct the affairs of the corporation from your vast leadership perspective, but soon... you realize they are more interested in doing it their way, they pick and choose which rules and policies they will implement, they begin making their own rules, and they resent your presence in their affairs. What would you say or do to these subordinates?

Let me put it to you another way...

If you were the head of a major corporation and you put your son in charge of everything because you were going away for a while, then what would you do if people kept coming to you to conduct business only with you? For whatever reason, they will not recognize your son's position or respect his legal authority except when it comes to putting his name and signature on paperwork. Even though all power and authority has been delegated to him, they will not acknowledge him as the head of the corporation and continue to reject his leadership and counsel by continuing to go back to "the head." What would you do if you were this leader?

Let me put it to you another way...

How shall I describe the attitude of the current church in its relationship to Jesus?

It is like a young man who meets a young woman and begins telling her all about his life, including his hopes, dreams and future plans, whereby he invites her by formal proposal to enter "*into*" his life within a covenant relationship and to live under his name to fulfill these plans, with the two becoming one in relationship with one another to partner and co-labor together with common purpose. However, soon after the two have entered into oneness, the bride disregards her covenantal promises and begins to live deceitfully, and then modifies her husband's covenant to meet her expectations. She doesn't respect the groom, so she tries modifying his behavior to match her personal criteria and, because she also rejects his leadership, she adopts a spirit of control and inserts herself as head of the house. She rejects and disregards his rules, and then speaks deceitfully with only partial regard to the whole truth. This husband is seemingly trapped in a relationship based upon false representation and forfeiture of marital covenant, but this is of no concern to this wayward bride because she has his name, his property, his posterity and will continue to claim all of his things as hers. She doesn't want him... she just wants his things to make herself happy.

What do you think God would do if you acted like this wayward bride and rejected His covenant, and then disregarded His plan with subsequent acts of defiance and disrespect that creates a schism between Him and His children? Do you think God is under any obligation to honor the covenant He made with the church than the covenant He made with Israel which He rendered obsolete because they disregarded it? (Read Hosea 2:2; Isaiah 50:1; Jer. 3:1, 6-10). How dare we test the Lord's indignation! How dare we construe Jesus to be a weak patsy Head without any regard to His Lordship in His kingdom, as if we are still entitled to all the rights and privileges of His kingdom by showing utter contempt and disregard toward Him! Any man who has lived in a house with a contentious bride will eventually leave the very house he labored to build with his very own two hands – and such is the current state of the Church... because this is exactly where we see Christ standing – knocking outside of the door of *His* church (Rev. 3:20).

And again, Jesus says, "What house will you build for me?" (Acts 7:49). The church model has been broken for centuries, but we create more programs with hype and showmanship to create a false demonstration of the Lord's presence. We do things in the church today that would appall Him, such that even His adversaries are appalled, and we rarely acknowledge Him except in footnoted fashion at the end of prayers.

Most recently, at the funeral Mass for my mother, the name of Jesus was rarely mentioned... except as the person who takes away the sins of the world and takes us to heaven. Do not misunderstand me, for I rarely use the name of any religion because we are all guilty of Christ's indignation when we disregard Him by failing to see His presence in all 5,775 years of history, to focus on just 3+ years of His life, then leave God's butchered body hanging upon the cross we murdered Him on, and then place it above an altar that continues to offer sacrifices that He Himself satisfied completely and rendered obsolete, once and for all, by His death – which rendered all future sacrifices and any obligation to a sacrificial system completely obsolete, but then professes to be the one true church when it is only a tepid halfway hybrid of what Christ truly desires for His church. Is this what Jesus had in mind! And yet, we feel quite smug and self-righteous when we devote 50 minutes on Sunday to maintain weekly membership at "the local church" and claim unflinching obedience to Papal authority presumably established by Peter that systematically disregards the teachings of Jesus Christ. Anathema!

God hates divorce, indeed, so He will do for His church what He did for Israel: fulfill His covenant obligations and then nullify the covenant (Jer. 3:6-8). If the church does not come to her senses and start acting like the Bride of Christ and reverence Him as Head of His church, rather than Father God or Holy Mary, then what, pray tell, is preventing Him from entering into another covenant with a people that will reverently keep His kingdom covenant and do all His will? Do you think the Groom is coming back to live with this immature, self-centered, and narcissistic bride for a millennia without doing a major course correction? I think not – and how dare we continue to see Jesus as a wimpy weak and frail King who will tolerate anyone that disregards what He commands.

The church talks a good talk, but can it answer this: has she honored her covenant agreement?

The House of God

On Sunday mornings, we often attend church by going to "the house of the Lord." We rightly say that the Lord dwells in that house because the Lord dwells in houses, right? Well, yes – and no. The Lord does dwell in houses all right, but He does not dwell in houses *made* by human hands; He dwells in houses that *have* human hands. The Lord enters the building when you bring "Christ in you" into the room.

Men Are Houses

If you were to construct a house, what would it look like? In our minds' eye, we can see it, envision it and embrace the concept. We know exactly what it should look like because the pattern already exists *in our mind*. We call this the conceptual or preliminary phase of building a house. Next, you determine how large it will be, one story or multi-level, how many bedrooms and bathrooms, the layout and orientation of private rooms and public spaces, including the most important room of the house. This one room is where your heart resides to become the central, focal feature around which the entire house is conceptually designed.

Next comes the design development phase where the conceptual plans, having been conceived (made), are then given to a design technician or Architect in order to put all the elements together so that the house can be built (created) according to the pattern of the concept. This is where the word of God is truly amazing regarding the creation of man.

> "So God created man in His *own* image; in the image of God He created him; male and female He created them" (Gen. 1:27).

Jesus is God our Creator, so re-read this verse to see man's creation from the Lord's perspective.

God established a pattern for all of creation and He is continuing it here – anew. After He created the birds and the fish, He blessed them and told them to "be fruitful and multiply." Likewise, man was created, in oneness of male and female, and He blessed *them*, as His image bearers, to "be fruitful and multiply." The divine pattern of God's creation has always been to create life and bless it so that it can re-create life. All creation exists for one purpose: to create and sustain "life." Plants replicate according to this pattern as well. Everything that God created and blessed is intended to be fruitful and multiply for a reason: to fill the earth with the fullness of His glory and life (in a world of darkness that was lifeless, chaotic and disorderly).

If you think this is just conjecture and that God would never demean himself or His Divinity to create man like Himself, then ask yourself, "why not?" If you could (and nowadays, this is possible) to create a human being according to your likeness with all your wonderful attributes, would you? All creation is coded with an internal drive to re-create and populate, but only man has the ability to selectively choose a mate based upon personal criteria. Other species perform mating rituals to select their mate according to natural instincts, but man's regeneration to begin again is based upon free will, individuation and personal choice. For what reason, you might ask? Is it not two-fold: the perpetuity of a good name and personal pleasure? Yet we are no different than God in that manner. Is it not for God's good pleasure that we live and are fruitful in order to manifest His name and manifest His presence *and glory* upon the earth? Was this not the intent behind "have dominion" since the beginning?

Men are like houses, having been designed and created by Jesus our Archetype, to operate according to His purpose according to the will and intent of "the Father." Form follows function. "We are His workmanship, created in Christ for good works" (Eph. 2:10). "You are God's fellow workers, you are God's field, *you are God's building*" (1 Cor. 3:9). The majesty of Christ is being revealed in men, as houses, who open the central room of their house to make an abode for Him. In doing so, Jesus invites us to dwell with Him as He abides in us. In His House are many rooms

– and His House is a gate and a door (Gen. 28:16, 17; John 10:7) which connects heaven to earth. I heard someone explain it this way; the gate to heaven is a house... and the house is Christ. When Christ is in you, then the gate to heaven is also in you – and you are now a gateway for heavenly things to pass through you. Men are like houses – and when our home becomes a room for the Father to abode (*mone*), God's kingdom is being built within us as an open gateway for heavenly things to pass through. Men are gateways for the kingdom of God.

"As a man thinks in his heart, so is he" (Prov. 23:7).

I have heard this used many times in numerous applications, so let me tell you what the literal meaning of this scripture says:

"As a man *thinks* (*shaar* – to act as a gatekeeper for an open gateway) in his *heart* (*nephesh* – living soul Gen. 2:7), so is he (so he becomes)."

Man is an open gateway – and, as the gatekeeper of this gateway; whatever he allows to pass through his soul... he becomes (either for good or for evil). When we open our hearts to Jesus, we will become like Him as an open gateway for His presence to abide in us, not just for Jesus to enter in but for the kingdom of heaven to pass through us. How incredibly awesome is this! We become world-changers with heavenly things flowing through us. This concept will be explained further within the sixth book in the Image Bearer series called: Gateways.

A Little Lower than Angels

There was a time at the beginning of my search to know Jesus in the manner of His glory and greatness that I ran into a scripture that was difficult for me to reconcile. It seems the writer of Hebrews had a very different interpretation who "a little lower than angels" referred to that seemed to contradict the Psalmist. The writer of Hebrews (2:7-9) indicated it referred to Jesus, but the text in Psalm (8:5) refers to men. If one of these interpretations was incorrect, then which one, but if the scriptures are indeed infallible, then how can both of these two interpretations be correct?

> "You have made him a little lower than the angels;
> You have crowned him with glory and honor, And
> set him over the works of Your hands" (Heb. 2:7).

I cannot take any credit for the wisdom which was given to me, so without any elaboration, this is the interpretation that was given to me by the Spirit in order to reconcile both interpretations, because this scripture applies to both men *and* Jesus:

The Hebrew word for God, 'Elohim,' can also be translated 'angels' in the Septuagint, but this does not help us reconcile this matter. How can Jesus be lower than the angels when He created them? Impossible!

Jesus is God our Creator, who created angels and is greater than angels, then became lower than the angels that He created, by coming to earth as the Son of God in the form of a man, in order to remind us how to live like "sons of God." Jesus created us to become like Him – and then He became like us – coming to earth as a Man (by being subordinate to the Father as a Son) so that, according to His example, we could become like Jesus, according to His likeness. Thus, two perspectives become one unified thought of truth.

Jesus created everything – and then came unto His creation as a man – to show us the way.

And such it is in the kingdom of God. There are always going to be two perspectives, so which one are you going to follow? Which one are you going to trust in: the earthly perspective seen through the lens of man – or the spiritual perspective seen through the lens of Jesus?

But – have you ever wondered what angels think of these things?

"We are told that angels desire to look into the things of salvation (1 Pet. 1:12). Surely some of these things which transpired during the earthly life of our Lord must have filled them with joy and pride. They marveled at His birth. They were inspired by His sermons and thrilled by His miracles. But how did those holy heavenly creatures react when they watched their beloved celestial Creator being systematically slaughtered by brutal mortal sinners? We cannot tell, but surely astonishment and outrage must have flooded their beings." [65]

"How constant their attendance on the Incarnate Saviour during His mysterious life amongst men! At His birth, they were heralds, and with songs exultant announce the glad tidings to mankind. In His temptation, they minister to Him; in His agonies they succor Him; on His resurrection they are the first to proclaim His triumph; on His ascension they come to escort him to the mediatorial throne; in His glorified state they render His supreme homage as their Lord; and when He returns to judge the world they will form His retinue! What sublime thoughts would be suggested, what emotions of wonder and joy would be excited, by the scenes witnessed on earth and still witness in heaven, in reference to Christ, His two-fold nature, and His great redeeming work. God Incarnate! This was new to them. They had seen the Son in His deity; but never till now enshrined in humanity. What amazing condescension! Obeying His own law as if He were a mere creature, and in the attitude of a servant! This was new. They had seen Him as the governor of the universe; but never till now as a subject! Encountering Satan in conflict and prolonged temptation! This was new. They had seen Him frown the arch-rebel from His presence and hurl him to perdition; but never till now submitting to be tempted by him whose subtlety and power had seduced myriads to eternal ruin. Suffering the scorn and reproach of sinful men! This was new. They had seen myriads of happy spirits worship, adore, and love Him, but never till now had they seen Him personally insulted, reproached and maltreated by His creatures. Groaning in Gethsemane, and crucified between two thieves, and

---

[65] Willmington's, p. 623, XIV.A.3.

dying as a sacrificial victim! This was new. They had seen Him supremely happy and glorious; but to see Him agonize, to hear that dying wail, and to behold Him a bloody corpse, and all this to save the world which had revolted from Him! What mysterious love! To see Him, after all this, enthroned and glorified in human nature. This was a new fact in the moral history of the universe. The whole scenes were full of interest, wonder, and mystery; a gradation of wonders rising in succession, until they culminated in the permanent presence of the God-man, resplendent with a glory that fills the heaven of heavens. Here were chapters of instruction for angelic minds to ponder; here were developments of hidden truths; here were discoveries of Divine perfections, never known before, and still unfolding in brighter effulgence as ages roll on."[66]

Perhaps this is why angels look down on us with dread in their eyes (Rev. 12:12). Not only because Satan has come down to us, but that man, having been crowned with glory and honor, having been made a sanctuary for the Divine, having been made in the image of God, could butcher God with utter contempt. Truly, "we know not what we do."

He lived in the manner as all men, to teach us and show us how to live as sons of God, as we live and prosper in the light of His glorious love, in order to manifest His glory in the earth, and by showing love to one another, that we might do the will of our gracious, loving and merciful Father and then return home!

He did it all for love! Pure, precious, gracious, unmitigated, agape love!

"God, who made the world and everything in it, since He is Lord of heaven and earth, does not dwell in temples made with hands" (Acts 17:24); however, Jesus is Lord of heaven and earth, and He desires to dwell in temples that have human hands – which are to used for love.

---

[66] IBID, p. 781. Dr. Lewis Sperry Chafer quotes Dr. Cooke (Systematic Theology, Vol. II, p.22)

We are the Lord's hands and feet. We are His witnesses with mouthpieces to proclaim Jesus is Lord of all. And we are His gateways through which heaven is being established upon the earth – one yielded soul at a time. Now, go ye therefore, declare the glory of the Lord Jesus – and have dominion.

      It's all about Jesus – and God gets the glory!

Jesus is Lord Almighty. "All things have been given to Me by My Father."

Jesus is the Message and the Messenger. "Hear Him!"

Jesus is our mediator of all covenants and agreements. "Do what He tells you."

Jesus is our only mediator between God and man, and He sent the Holy Spirit to intercede on our behalf to reveal all truth to us so that we may get back to being about our Father's business.

The time for Father God, Spirit God and Mother God has come to an end. "Use My real name… and then you will know who I am."

"Stop coming to Me with many words and with special speech. Talk normal to Me as you would any other friend – face to face. Superfluous and boiling words are not from Me. Rantings are not from Me. Stop flailing around to get My attention. Either I am there or I am not. And if I am there, then I will perform according to My word."

"You are My gateways. Now act like My children – and not the children next door."

      It's all about Jesus – and God gets the glory!

"Yours, O Lord, is the greatness, The power and the glory, The victory and the majesty; For all that is in heaven and in earth is Yours; Yours is the kingdom, O Lord, And You are exalted as head over all (1 Chron. 29:11).

Brethren and Friends of Jesus

"For whom He foreknew, He also predestined to be conformed to the image of His Son, that He might be the firstborn among many brethren" (Rom. 8:29).

When we declare Jesus as Lord, Redeemer, Master and Savior, we have been adopted into the family of God whereby we are given these wonderful promises and assurances of faith.

We are the brethren of Jesus (Psa. 22:22)
- When we do the Father's will (Matt. 12:48)
- When we profess Jesus as Teacher and Christ (Matt. 23:8)
- When we do what Jesus tells us to do (Matt. 28:10)

We are the friends of Jesus (John 15:14)
- When we know the Father's business and do it (John 15:15)
- When we love one another in sacrificial service (John 15:13; 1 John 3:16)
- When we do what Jesus commands (John 15:14; Matt. 28:20)

We are beloved of Jesus (Rom. 1:7; Eph. 1:6)
- When we are steadfast and immovable (1 Cor. 15:58; Phil. 4:1)
- When we are always abiding in the work of the Lord (1 Cor. 15:58; Col. 3:12)
- When we know that our labor is not in vain (1 Cor. 15:58; 2 Pet. 3:8)

- When we do not avenge ourselves (Rom. 12:19) but edify others (2 Cor. 12:19)

We are the beloved brethren of Jesus (1 Thess. 1:4; 1 Cor. 15:58)
- When we give thanks to God always (2 Thess. 2:13)
- When we are not deceived (James 1:16)
- When we are swift to hear, slow to speak and slow to wrath (James 1:19)

We are children of God (Rom. 8:16, 17)
- When the Spirit Himself bears witness with our spirit (Rom. 8:16)
- When we receive Christ and believe in His name (John 1:12)
- When you become blameless and harmless in the midst of a crooked and perverse generation (Phil. 2:15)
- When we are imitators of God in the similitude of Christ (Eph. 5:1)
- When the love of the Father has been bestowed on us (1 John 3:1)
- When you practice righteousness and love your brother (1 John 3:10)
- When we love God and keep His commandments (1 John 5:2)
- And if children, then heirs—heirs of God and joint heirs with Christ, if indeed we suffer with Him, that we may also be glorified together (Rom. 8:17)

We are sons of God and heirs according to hope
- When we are led (guided) by the Spirit of God (Rom. 8:14)
- When we profess faith in Christ Jesus (Gal. 3:26)
- When the earnest expectation of the creation eagerly waits for your revealing (Rom. 8:19)
- When you are counted worthy to attain that age, and the resurrection from the dead (Luke 20:35)
- When you walk in obedience according to manner of your calling (Deut. 14:1, 2)

- When you call God "My Father" (Jer. 3:19)
- When you shout for joy (Job 38:7)
- When you do justice to the afflicted, and deliver the poor and needy (Psa. 82:6)
- Then, you are equal to the angels and are sons of God, being sons of the resurrection (Luke 20:36)

Now, therefore, we are children of the Most High God and members of a royal family!
- Jesus is the Son (τοῦ, *tou*) *of /from* the Most High God (Mark 5:7)
- Melchizedek is a priest of the Most High God (Gen. 14:18-20)
- We are children of the Most High God (Psa. 82:6)
- We are servants of the Most High God when we proclaim Jesus is the way of salvation (Acts 16:17)
- And, "we are the saints of the **Most High** and we shall receive the kingdom, and possess the kingdom forever, even forever and ever." (Dan. 7:18)

Truly, when we live according to the Spirit of life in Christ Jesus, we are more than conquerors – we are the mighty ones of God Most High who do His bidding according to His good pleasure.

The Father has given us the kingdom (Luke 12:32), Jesus has given us the keys of the kingdom (Matt. 16:19) and He has given us the authority to forgive sin (Matt. 6:14; Luke 24:47; John 20:23). All authority was delivered to Jesus (Matt. 11:27) and Jesus has delivered all authority back to us (Matt. 28:18); and to top it off, the glory that the Father gave Jesus (John 17:24) Jesus Himself has given to us (John 17:22) and He is glorified in us (John 17:10).

Can it get any better than this?

> "And now, O Father, glorify Me together with Yourself" (John 17:5) "that they may be one as We are" (John 17:11).

We have been invited to enter into oneness with the Supreme Highest Commander of all things in heaven and on earth. And for what reason? Is it not to establish heaven in the midst of His enemies! The Lord removed Satan and His rebellious angels who made war in heaven (Rev. 12), He cast them down to earth, and now He has sent the host of men to earth to make war with Satan and overcome his dominion, clothed in mere human weakness, with nothing more than the truth, the power of their testimony, the fullness of the indwelling Holy Spirit – and the grace of God. And in this, the Lord will make known those who belong to Him according to the hearing of His voice and follow Him as His disciples, or those who live in rebellion by refusing to hear, believe and obey.

As the famous dictum puts it, "When the literal sense makes good sense, seek no other sense lest the result be nonsense." Let's follow this dictum throughout the remainder of the series.

In conclusion: in order to understand the big picture regarding why man is on the earth, we need to comprehend Jesus and the reason why He came to us: to show us how to live as sons of God.

The Father expressed Himself through Jesus as His manifest expression within humanity, and Jesus expresses Himself through man as His manifested expression within His creation. And Jesus has given us His Spirit, the Holy Spirit, sent by Jesus to help us in our earthly mandate to have dominion in His Name. The Spirit of God is given to us by Jesus; it is His Spirit... and the Lord is the Spirit! Do not refuse Him who speaks to you.

> **"Now the Lord is the Spirit; and where the Spirit of the Lord is, there is liberty"** (2 Cor. 3:17).

Jesus manifested the Father – and we are to manifest Jesus – as sons of God. This is God's plan for all mankind. It begins with a profession of faith in order to become His disciple whereby we are transformed into His manifested ones to become saints of the Most High God, Jesus Christ. Believe in Jesus, become His disciple, and be transformed to become a saint through sanctification. This is the mystery of man upon the earth – to manifest Christ who dwells within us. His Presence and His Spirit are with us and in us, already, and now we must manifest Jesus – to the glory of the Father.

    It's all about Jesus – and God gets the glory!

    Amen.

Who is Jesus? (In summary)

It is imperative for us to understand who Jesus is – now – more than any other time in history. Why? Because man was created in His image and we get our identity from Him! If our understanding of Christ is incomplete, then our identity will also be incomplete.

Jesus is the Head of His Church, yet I have heard statements that imply Jesus was not God while He was on the earth, or He was unable to accomplish the work of God in us, so He sent the Holy Spirit. These statements may be taught in seminaries and schools of theology, but they are inaccurate and represent *incomplete understandings* by the church regarding who Jesus truly is.

> Jesus said: "I am the Alpha and the Omega, the Beginning and the End," says the Lord, "who is and who was and who is to come, the Almighty" (Rev. 1:8).

Who is the Lord? Jesus
Who is the Almighty? Jesus
Who is the Living God? Jesus
Who is Lord God? Jesus
Who is Lord God Almighty? Jesus
Who is Almighty God? Jesus
Who is God Most High? Jesus
Who is *YHWH* (Yahweh/ Jehovah)? Jesus
Who is Immanuel – God with us? Jesus
Who is the One who is and who was and who is to come? Jesus
Who is the First and the Last? Jesus
Who is the Beginning and the End? Jesus
Who is the Lion of Judah? Jesus
Who is the Lamb of God? Jesus
Who is the Lion and the Lamb? Jesus
Who is the Lord of Hosts? Jesus
Who is the Commander of the Army of the Lord? Jesus
Who is the Root and the Offspring of David? Jesus
Who is the Bright and Morning Star? Jesus

Who is the Light of the world? Jesus
Who is the Way, and the Truth, and the Life? Jesus
Who is the Resurrection and the Life? Jesus

Whose Life abides in us? Jesus
Through Whom – were all things created? Jesus
For Whom are all things – and in Whom do all things consist? Jesus

Who is Lord of all? Jesus
Who is King of kings and Lord of lords? Jesus
Whose is the name above all other names? It's Jesus (not Father)
How many names for the Spirit are there in the New Testament? Seven
How many times is the Spirit attributed to the Father? Only once!
How many times is the Spirit attributed to Jesus? All the others!
How many times does the term "Father God" appear in the scriptures? None!
Who is the Son of/from God? Jesus

Who is Jesus? He physically manifested Himself as least 30 times before His *parousia* (Theophanies) and at least 15 times to over 500 people after His resurrection. He manifested Himself in Revelation seven different ways, and there are 111 names and titles attributed to Jesus in the scriptures, including 45 names in Revelation alone. **Jesus is the Manifested One**, and He manifests Himself to whomever He wants – whenever He wants – and however He wants!

Jesus is not limited by our perception of Him… yet we are limited in our misperception of Him… because we get our identity from Christ Jesus.

Who is the Messiah (the Deliverer of Israel)? Jesus
Who is the Christ (the Anointed One)? Jesus

These terms Messiah and Christ are often used synonymously, and Jesus is identified as being both Messiah and Christ (John 4:25), but they represent different reasons why Jesus came to earth; the

IMAGE

Messiah (*mashiyak*-H4899/*mashiach*-G3323) the Promised One, is the Deliverer of Israel, yet Christ (*Christos*-G5547) the Anointed One, is "the Savior of the world" (John 4:42)... to whoever (Jew, Gentile, Muslim, anyone) calls upon Jesus as Lord – will be saved!

Faith in Jesus – as Lord God, as *YHWH* – is the only Way anyone, including Jews, can be saved.

Who is Jesus? When Christ appeared, He accomplished multiple missions in one visitation that are impossible for one man to accomplish! Indeed – God fulfilled it – in Himself!!! He fulfilled "the Law of Moses and the Prophets and the Psalms" (Luke 24:44); He manifested Himself as Messiah to the Jews, as Savior to the world, as a testimony to the truth, as the Way and the Truth, as covenant keeper to fulfill the Old Covenant and render it obsolete by His living sacrifice as the Lamb of God, as the Witness against Israel for unbelief, as the covenant Maker of a new and better Covenant with better promises as the Resurrection and the Life, as the Victor over sin and death, as the Light and Deliverer leading men out of out of darkness, as Redeemer and King who restores the authority of the kingdom to His ecclesia, as the Promise of many promises for a much better hope, and as the Son of God to teach us how to be like and act like sons and daughters of God.

Jesus is more than "the firstborn over creation" (Col. 1:15) and the firstfruits of the resurrection; Jesus is "the Image" and "Preeminence" and '*charakter*-5481' of the invisible God! And no other earthly examples of '*charakter*' exist! *Christ purposed in Himself, regarding the purposes of God, which He purposed in us, in order that the purpose may result... in bringing forth fruit* (Eph. 1:9-11; 3:9-12). Jesus Christ, the firstfruits of His creatures... is the firstborn of many brethren... that we may be conformed to "His image" and imitate His example as "sons of God."

- "For whom He foreknew, He also predestined to be conformed to the image of His Son, that He might be the firstborn among many brethren" (Rom. 8:29)

- "Of His own will He brought us forth by the word of truth, that we might be a kind of firstfruits of His creatures" (James 1:18)
- "But now Christ is risen from the dead, and has become the firstfruits of those who have fallen asleep" (1 Cor. 15:20)

Jesus is God! God is everywhere! And since God is "above all, and through all, and in you all" (Eph. 4:6) – then Jesus is dwelling in your father, your mother, your brother, your sister, grandparents, children, friends, acquaintances, neighbors and strangers. When Jesus said "Love one another" this was not a suggestion; it is a command... even toward our enemies. Jesus was being quite literal when He said: "Inasmuch as you did it to one of the least of these My brethren, you did it to Me" (Matt. 25:40). Whatever you do to another person, whether good or evil... you are doing it to Jesus... who is all in all.

Before Jesus began His earthly ministry, there was an 18 year period of time in which nothing is known about the God-man, Christ Jesus, as He dwelled in the wilderness. And yet, much like Jesus Himself, we have all gone through a wilderness experience of one sort or another and the Spirit brings us out of that place that we may begin anew – in newness – in oneness with the Spirit, to do the work of God on earth for which we were created, predestined and purposed to perform. What you were before is irrelevant because now – in born again newness – your Lord is sovereign over you and your new life in Him is significant, relevant, revelatory and life-giving.

Who is the Holy Spirit subordinate to – the Father or Jesus? The scriptures indicate Jesus!

- The Holy Spirit has names that are attributed only to Jesus: "the Spirit of Christ" (Rom. 8:9); "the Spirit of Jesus Christ" (Phil. 1:19); "the Spirit of Jesus" (Acts 16:6); and "the Spirit of His Son" (Gal. 4:6) because it is the Spirit of Christ who reveals Christ to us.

- In Romans 8:9, there is an interesting correlation between the Holy Spirit and Jesus: "But you are not in the flesh but in the Spirit, *if* indeed the Spirit of God dwells in you. Now *if* anyone does not have the Spirit of Christ, he is not His"
- The Spirit is often referred to as "the Spirit of God" and, since we also know Jesus is God, it is not surprising to see these next couple terms used in context with Jesus: "the Spirit of Jehovah" (Isa. 11:2); "the Spirit of the Lord Jehovah" (Isa. 61:1)
- Jesus is Lord, and the "Spirit of the Lord" is mentioned 28 times
- Jesus is the One, true living God (Jer. 10:10), and "The Spirit of the Living God" (2 Cor. 3:3) helps mankind realize the truth regarding who Jesus is… as the Manifested One
- And finally, Jesus is the only mediator between God and man, yet Jesus *and* the Holy Spirit are referred to as our "intercessor" (Rom. 8:26, 27, 34; Heb. 7:25)

More specifically, pay attention to what Jesus tells us about the Holy Spirit:

- "However, when He, the Spirit of truth, has come, He will guide you into all truth; for ***He will not speak on His own authority***, but whatever He hears He will speak; and He will tell you things to come. ¹⁴ He will glorify Me, for ***He will take of what is Mine*** and declare it to you. ¹⁵ ***All things that the Father has are Mine***. Therefore I said that He will take of Mine and declare it to you" (John 16:12-15)
- "But when the Helper comes, *whom **I shall send** to you from the Father*, the Spirit of truth who proceeds from the Father, He will testify of Me" (John 15:26; both Jesus and the Holy Spirit proceeded from the Father and speak under His authority – John 8:42)
- "But the Helper, the Holy Spirit, whom *the Father will send **in My name***, He will teach you all things, and bring to

your remembrance all things that I said to you" (John 14:26)
- "Nevertheless I tell you the truth. It is to your advantage that I go away; for if I do not go away, the Helper will not come to you; but if I depart, *I will send Him to you*" (John 16:7)
- "*For He whom God has sent speaks the words of God*, for God does not give the Spirit by measure" (John 3:34)
- "But you shall receive power when the Holy Spirit has come upon you; and you shall be *witnesses to **Me*** in Jerusalem, and in all Judea and Samaria, and to the end of the earth" (Acts 1:8).

Jesus, in Oneness with the Father, told us, "the Father will send (the Holy Spirit) **in My name**" (John 14:26), "*whom I shall send to you from the Father*" (John 15:26), and again, "*I will send Him to you*" (John 16:7). Jesus is telling us, in addition to the inner witness we have by the "Spirit of your Father" that Jesus will send an outpouring of the Spirit to us after He is reunited with His Father in heaven; therefore, the Holy Spirit speaks on behalf of Jesus – and the Holy Spirit will manifest Christ *in us* to continue His work upon the earth.

Jesus is the Message and Messenger, who came to reveal the Father and declare His word to us (John 1:18; 17:26); and then sent the Holy Spirit to reveal Christ to us and declare His word:

- "He will glorify Me, for He will take of what is Mine and declare it to you" (John 16:14)
- "All things that the Father has are Mine. ***Therefore*** I said that He [Holy Spirit] will take of Mine and declare it to you" (John 16:15)

And yet, the institutional church has no clue who the Spirit is, who He is subordinate to, or Whose words He speaks. The Spirit is best known as the Spirit of God because He comes of/from God, and also as the Spirit of the Lord because He comes of/from Jesus, yet we see in the above verses that Jesus is the One who sends the

Holy Spirit while on the throne "in Oneness" with the Father, so that He (i.e. the Holy Spirit) is given without measure and continues to do the work of Christ Jesus upon the earth. "Christ in you – the hope of glory."

Jesus expresses Himself as "the voice" in the Old Testament and then manifests Himself as "the Word of God" in the New Testament. Jesus is "the voice" we hear, which is why He said this about the Father, verily, "You have neither heard His voice <u>at any time</u>, nor seen His form."

The institutional church has been teaching us to focus our attention on the Father plus many other things rather than on Jesus, but now – the time has come to focus the fullness of our attention and affections upon Christ Jesus, the Manifested One.

"Jesus is God. And "God created man in <u>His own</u> image." Once again, who is the Creator? Jesus. Who created man? Jesus. Who formed man? Jesus. In Whose own image was man created in? Jesus. Who has all dominion? Jesus. Who gave man His own dominion? Jesus. Who gave man His Own glory? Jesus. If the epiphany has not happened yet, then consider this: who said that He is the light of the world? Jesus. And who told men that they are the light of the world? Jesus (Matt. 5:14). I could fill another fifteen pages of similar questions and answers to illuminate the same truth to you so that everyone can confidently proclaim:

Who you are (your identity) is because of Who Jesus is!

Jesus only!"[67]

Jesus manifested Himself as a Son to teach us how to be sons and daughters, and to teach us about the Father – as He abides in Oneness with the Father – as God in Oneness of expression and Oneness in manifestation, but the church has changed the Churches' cornerstone of faith to focus on the Father instead of the

---

[67] Excerpt copied from "Dominion" section titled "New Earth Dominion" p.65.

Son… and now a course correction is needed. "You shall call Me, "My Father," and not turn away from Me" (Jer. 3:19) was said by Jesus because He knew we would create institutions that would turn His sheep away from Him, just like Israel did… and now it's time to return to the Lord – and worship Jesus!

And this same Jesus "Will baptize you with the Holy Spirit… and fire" (Matt. 3:11).

> "And He [Jesus] is before all things, and in Him all things consist" (Col. 1:17).

> ***It's all about Jesus – and God gets the glory!***

> ***Jesus is Lord!***

> ***"The Lord our God, the Lord is one!" (Deut. 6:4).***

> ***"I and My Father are one" (John 10:30).***

> ***"He who has seen Me has seen the Father" (John 14:9).***

Therefore: there are not two kings in Heaven. There is only one: King Jesus is Lord of Heaven and Earth! And now, the revelation of God's mystery revealed in Christ:

Jesus is the Image of the Father who sent Himself as a *Son*…

… to teach us how to live as spiritual sons and daughters of our Father – the one in Heaven!

> *God so loved the world… that He graced us with His presence!*

> *Amen!*

The Final Word

> "In the beginning was the Word, and the Word was with God, and the Word was God" (John 1:1).

Perhaps the hardest point of view to overcome regarding the identity of Jesus is when He speaks of God as: My Father. Jesus is God, so why would He refer to Himself as Father? It seems odd, yet there is a very good reason why. So, if I say Jesus never said "Our Father" – the Lord's Prayer should immediately come to mind and call into question that statement. How can I say this? In order to understand the depth and breadth of Jesus and comprehend who Jesus is, you need to see this from the perspective of Jesus… as the Son sent from the Father… who abides in oneness with the Father. So get ready… more of this awesome mystery is about to be revealed.

The literal Greek for the Lord's prayer is: Πάτερ (Father) ἡμῶν (of us) ὁ (the one) ἐν (in) τοῖς (the) οὐρανοῖς (heavens). God is – the Father of us. This slight yet enormously vast distinction on the identity of Jesus is able to put clarifying light between – Jesus who is God – and God who is the Father of us all… who sent all of us here as Our Father in heaven. Jesus is God, who sent Himself as a Son, to teach us how to live in relationship with the Father of us – so that by faith in the Son we are adopted as spiritual sons and daughters into the spiritual kingdom of our Father – the one in the heavens. If you are having a hard time comprehending this, then jump back and re-read "Undercover Boss." God sent "the Son" here… and God sent us here as well.

Now do you see why I made the statement: Jesus never said "Our Father"? Jesus is God, yet He was identifying Himself with the family of man, so He called God: the "Father of us." It's a step back from claiming a paternal connection. Likewise, a similar distinction can be made when Jesus says "My Father" as being "the Father of Me." When Jesus talked about the Father, He knows He is God Incarnate, yet He had to teach us using terms that would remain long after His ascension to "the right hand of God" (indicating His proper position in terms of authority and power, not as a place along one side of God). Jesus also knew His word and His identity would become shrouded in mysticism for a season by men unwilling to listen to the Voice of the Spirit.

Subtle distinctions are important. For example, a church pew seats six, yet sometimes we say there are six seats available… which describes the number of open places where believers can sit, not the number of chairs in the row.

God (***the Expression***) made every one of us, including the Man called Jesus, which is why Jesus referred to God as "the Father of Me" and as "being sent from the Father" indicating He came from the Father just like you and me; however, the Nicene Creed describes Jesus in this manner: "begotten, not made, being of one substance with the Father." So I ask: how can God make Jesus and be "His Father" yet not make Him? This is a very deep mystery that may take years to fully grasp; it took over two years for this truth to be revealed to me … and while this mystery can be comprehended… it is marvelously brilliant yet infinitely unsearchable at the same time. God is able to do anything. All things are possible… for the God of Oneness!

Thus far, we have explored the marvelous identity of Jesus in the bible as Lord, as Lord God Almighty, as the God with 111 names and 30 Theophanies – who revealed Himself to John seven different ways in Revelation alone – and also as God who manifested Himself (***the Manifestation***) many times and in many ways to teach us, guide us and save us.

The bible is clear: God is invisible. Yet Jesus is God and He was visibly seen. How can this be reconciled? God our Father (the Expression) is invisible, yet God manifests Himself in two ways to make His ways known to man: in Presence and in Spirit. Jesus is the physical Presence of God (substance) and the Spirit is the spiritual Presence (essence) of the Father of us. Thus, God is one Expression with two Manifestations – Jesus and the Spirit – our Divine intercessors.

How many ways can the Presence of God be manifested? Infinite!

> "For unto us **a Child is born**,
> Unto us **a Son is given**;
> And the government will be upon His shoulder.
> **And His name will be called**
> Wonderful, Counselor, Mighty God,
> **Everlasting Father**, Prince of Peace" (Isa. 9:6)

The main reason we've struggled to comprehend the true identity of Jesus in the bible is because we continue to perceive Jesus in a mono-type manner – as Jesus of Nazareth who died on a cross – instead of also seeing Him as the Friend of Abraham, as a Priest in the order of Melchizedek, as the Commander of the Army of the Lord, as the Son of/from God, as the Lamb of God, as '*Charakter*' – the express Image of God, and as the Manifested One of/from Heaven who is not limited in His infinite ability to express and manifest Himself however and whenever He wants.

Jesus is the Image of the Father... who sent Himself as a Son... and God gets the glory!

Perhaps, now, we can understand why Jesus knew the Father so perfectly. This is why Jesus was able to say regarding the Father: "You have neither heard His voice at any time, nor seen His form" (John 5:37). This is why Jesus is the only person who has seen the Father in glory (John 6:46). He knows... because He is. And this is why the Father sends the Holy Spirit, as does Jesus... because Jesus is the Messenger and the Message and the Express Image of the Father.

God is One... with His Spirit.

God create man in His Image, which means.... so are we!!!

I began this book by hearing a message from Jesus: "No one has seen the Father or heard His voice at any time (related to John 5:37) – not once but twice. So I asked Jesus if He made the Father up, and He said, "No." Then I asked Him to explain the Father to me... and so He did. This book is what I learned by listening to the Voice of the Spirit... layer by layer which I was not even aware of until I got to the end two years later. Jesus explained the Father to me – and it circled back to Jesus. God is invisible, the Father is invisible, but we can see Jesus, so let's focus on Jesus. When we look to the Father, we will see Jesus. When we pray to our Father, Jesus hears us. Focus on Jesus only! He is the best Friend you will ever have!

Tell this world about Jesus, the Living God, and teach them to seek the One we are able to see and hear and touch. Hooked on Jesus is what our Christian faith is all about. Seek the Lord – and love Jesus with all your heart, soul, understanding and might.

God so loved the world... that He sent Himself as a Son – to show us He loves us like a Father! Words cannot describe a love as great as this!

Theologians have struggled to understand the Father – whose identity is only made known to us by words from Jesus. Both Jesus and the Holy Spirit are manifestations of the Godhead, but "who" is the Father? It seems we've been asking the wrong question. Discovering "what" the Father is – is our quest to comprehend. The Father is the Mind of the Godhead. The reason we cannot see His form is because the "thought of His intellect" has no form.

> "Let this mind [5426] be in you which was also in Christ Jesus" (Phil. 2:5).

> "Now He who searches the hearts knows what the mind [5427] of the Spirit is, because He makes intercession for the saints according to the will of God" (Rom. 8:27; *phroneo* [5426] means: to be minded a certain way; to think a certain way).

Jesus is the Father (in glory) – and the Father is the Son (in grace). They are One. Jesus is the Manifested One who manifests the multifaceted, manifold expressions of God for this reason: to help us understand who God is. And this is why Jesus said: "No one comes to the Father except through Me." The Father and Son are One! No one can come to the Father except through faith in the IMAGE known as the Son of/from God – Jesus Christ! This Divine mystery is absolutely brilliant! And here is another one: Jesus is Lord, and the Lord is the Spirit...

> **"Now _the Lord is the Spirit_; and where the Spirit of the Lord is, there is liberty" (2 Cor. 3:17).**

> END.

What's Next...

> "Beloved, now we are children of God; and it has not yet been revealed what we shall be, but we know that when He is revealed, *we shall be like Him*, for we shall see Him as He is" (1 John 3:2).

> "But we all, with unveiled face, *beholding as in a mirror the glory of the Lord*, are being transformed into the same image from glory to glory, just as by the Spirit of the Lord" (2 Cor. 3:18).

Now we know in part, yet we shall see Jesus as He is, as beholding His image in a mirror (1 Cor. 13:12), yet another important question we should be asking ourselves is this: if Jesus created us in His image according to His Own likeness, then "what" exactly... is man? And "what" is man that God should be mindful of him? (Psa. 8:4; 144:3). These questions will be answered in "Gateways" which is the second half of "Image."

Grace and peace be yours in abundance!

It's all about Jesus – and God gets the glory!

Amen and Amen!

[page left blank for notes]

Read the entire Image Bearer series!

Grace and peace be yours in abundance, paul.

Made in the USA
Middletown, DE
12 November 2018